Learning Through Work

Drawing on three decades of practical investigations, this book establishes new understandings about the importance of learning through work, outlining its purposes, contributions, conceptions and the curriculum, pedagogical and personal practices that shape its effectiveness.

Against views proposing it as being informal and leading to concrete outcomes, this volume presents learning through work as being central to human development, informing individual choices and developing one's capacity for working life and occupational competence. In Part I, Billett makes a case for the value of learning through work and why it should be considered and engaged with as a legitimate mode of learning and model of education. Part II sets out the foundations for the processes of learning through work that have underpinned its utility across human history. Part III sets out bases by which this educational model and mode of learning can be understood through the concepts of practice curriculum, practice pedagogies and personal practices. These are presented based on the kinds of knowledge that they generate and how they can be realised in and through day-to-day work activities in practice settings, including the development of innovations in work settings.

A much-needed resource from a leading expert in the field, this book will be of interest to educators, workplace trainers in a variety of settings, policy-makers and students in professional education courses.

Stephen Billett is Professor of Adult and Vocational Education at Griffith University, Australia, a fellow of Social Science Academy of Australia, National Teaching fellow, Australian Research Council Future fellow and Fulbright scholar and was awarded honorary doctorates from the universities of Jyväskylä (Finland), Geneva (Switzerland) and West (Sweden). He has worked in manufacturing as a vocational educator, teacher educator, professional developer, teacher and researcher at Griffith University, and held policy roles in vocational education.

"In this book, Professor Billett provides an exceptionally rich account on the diverse value of workplaces as sites for learning. In our fast-changing world, this book is extremely timely and must-read for all who wish to develop deep understanding of how learning takes place, how it can be facilitated and how it can lead to innovations."

Päivi Tynjälä, *Professor, University of Jyväskylä, Finland*

"Billett draws on evidence-based knowledge and a well-articulated theory of workplace learning to trace the continuities and adaptive responses of occupational knowledge over time. He shows how societies often privilege declarative knowing over professional or vocational knowing. Rejecting that stance, Billett reconceives occupational knowledge and its effective learning strategies as ... complex, sensory-inclusive, adaptive and based on an interdependent mix of procedural ('knowing how'), conceptual ('knowing what') and dispositional ('knowing for') capacities. Organisational leaders will appreciate chapters offering pathways for developing sequenced occupational capacities through work; practice pedagogies; and examples for how to catalyse both learning and innovation by transforming work practices."

Victoria Marsick, Professor, *Adult Learning & Leadership, Columbia University, Teachers College, New York*

"This book makes strong theoretical, epistemological and conceptual contributions to the topic of workplace learning and offers empirically grounded and explicit pedagogical resources for sustaining learning through practice. It advances an explicit conceptual frame for understanding and sustaining learning through practice and is a must-read for students, researchers and practitioners. The author is one of most cited and renowned authors in the field of adult education and learning through work."

Laurent Filliettaz, *Professor of Adult Education, Language and Work, University of Geneva, Switzerland*

Learning Through Work
Practices, Purposes and Outcomes

Stephen Billett

LONDON AND NEW YORK

Designed cover image: Getty Images

First published 2026
by Routledge
4 Park Square, Milton Park, Abingdon, Oxon OX14 4RN

and by Routledge
605 Third Avenue, New York, NY 10158

Routledge is an imprint of the Taylor & Francis Group, an informa business

© 2026 Stephen Billett

The right of Stephen Billett to be identified as author of this work has been asserted in accordance with sections 77 and 78 of the Copyright, Designs and Patents Act 1988.

All rights reserved. No part of this book may be reprinted or reproduced or utilised in any form or by any electronic, mechanical, or other means, now known or hereafter invented, including photocopying and recording, or in any information storage or retrieval system, without permission in writing from the publishers.

Trademark notice: Product or corporate names may be trademarks or registered trademarks, and are used only for identification and explanation without intent to infringe.

British Library Cataloguing-in-Publication Data
A catalogue record for this book is available from the British Library

ISBN: 9781032856865 (hbk)
ISBN: 9781032856858 (pbk)
ISBN: 9781003519416 (ebk)

DOI: 10.4324/9781003519416

Typeset in Optima
by codeMantra

Contents

Preface vii
Acknowledgements xiii

PART I
Learning through work 1

1 Learning through work 3
2 Occupations, occupational knowledge and its learning: origins and legacies 24

PART II
Foundations of learning through work 41

3 Learning through work: personal processes and social contributions 43
4 Occupations, situations and knowledge required for work 61
5 Being innovative: aligning learning and workplace innovations 79

PART III
Practice-based learning and educative experiences 99

6 Practice curriculum 101
7 Practice pedagogies 119
8 Personal (epistemological) practices at work 138

9	Prospects for learning through work	157
	Index	*175*

Preface

There has been a strong and growing interest in learning for working life and occupational capacities in places and circumstances where that work is undertaken – that is, in workplaces. This process is often referred to as 'workplace learning' with that term now becoming orthodox. This current interest is also a return to the past, acknowledging the contributions of experiences in these settings. That is, before the relatively recent advent of educational institutions and programmes for developing occupational capacities, most of these capacities were learnt through engaging in work settings as the most natural ways to do so. Indeed, for most occupations, these work settings were often the only circumstances in which those capacities could be learnt at that time before the advent of educational institutions and provisions for a range of occupations. However, the contributions of work settings in developing those capacities have become less acknowledged since the advent of 'schooled societies' – those in which education provisions are compulsory and tertiary education provisions are almost mandatory. In many countries, particularly those with industrialised economies, progressively over the last century and more, there has been the development of programmes in educational institutions whose aim is to develop occupational capacities. These institutions comprise hybrid environments and offer experiences that are shaped by their exigencies, rather than those reflecting the circumstances in which the knowledge to be learnt will be applied (i.e., work settings).

However, now there is a broadening interest in learning through experiences in work settings and how they can contribute to individuals' learning. Such interest includes that from individuals who want to learn how to perform effectively upon graduation from their educational programmes, or from those in the workforce seeking to maintain their employability and secure advancement. Also, both public and private sector enterprises want skilled employees able to perform work tasks and respond to emerging challenges through what they can learn in those work settings. Tertiary education institutions also want to provide, embrace and, in some cases, augment experiences in work settings so their students can be ready to practise what they have learnt in work settings after graduation.

The focus on and requirements for learning through work are now far more broad, complex and potentially demanding than in the time before schooled societies. More than being primarily concerned with initial and ongoing development of occupational capacities and innovating, the potential contributions of experiences in work settings have expanded. They now include assisting people in identifying what occupations they are suited to and whether it should be either directly after schooling or later in life. Moreover, the integration of experiences in work settings with those provided within educational institutions and programmes when preparing people for occupations has come to the fore. This is, in part, because of the realisation of the distinct contributions arising from engagement in activities and interactions in both kinds of settings. Also, the realisation that the constant requirements for ongoing development of occupational capacities and workplace competence can be provided through participation in work settings has become an important priority in light of the requirements for individuals to maintain their employability and to contribute to workplace viability. Furthermore, there is growing acknowledgement of the potential alignments between the developmental learning opportunities in workplaces and the generation and enactment of innovations in and for those settings.

The key point here is that the interest in learning experiences in work settings is now far broader than that associated with the development of occupational capacities in young people. It is this wide range of purposes that are elaborated in the first chapter in this volume, followed by those explaining how experiences (i.e., activities and interactions) in work settings can be organised to engage and support individuals in their initial and ongoing learning for occupations, making decisions about the kinds of occupations they want to pursue and how they can engage in contributing through innovations to the viability of the enterprises that employ them. It is an elaboration of these issues that is the focus of this book that summarises and consolidates my research and theorising since the previous book published in 2001 – *Learning in the Workplace: Strategies for Effective Practice*. This volume builds upon that earlier work and adds in further empirical studies and concepts advanced since that time. It seeks to offer a more comprehensive explanatory basis for the purposes and processes of learning through work and the ways in which workplace experiences can be organised, augmented and supported to achieve a range of outcomes for individuals, their enterprises, communities and nation states. That is the aim for this volume.

Structure and organisation of text

In making its case, the opening section comprises two chapters that set out bases for understanding the current and growing importance of learning in and through work in contemporary societies and the cultural, social and historical genesis of learning in and through work settings.

The first chapter – *Chapter 1 – Learning through work* – explains that the importance of learning in and through work resides in contributions that those settings can afford individuals in terms of occupational choice and preparation, workplaces that employ and provide the goods and services that communities want and need, tertiary education provisions that focus on employability and the ongoing development of capacities across working life. Throughout, it is individuals' participation in goal-directed activities and interactions with others that provides access to and engages individuals with the kinds of knowledge that they need to construct to effectively perform work tasks. More than meeting the goals of those activities and interactions, their legacies extend to the learning that arises in the form of what individuals know, can do and value (i.e., their conceptual, procedural and dispositional knowledge) – that is, their learning and development.

The second chapter – *Chapter 2 – Occupations, occupational knowledge and its learning: origins and legacies* – sets out the historical and cultural context for the pivotal role that learning through work has played across human history and that has been central to the progress of humanity. This includes the generation of innovations that have responded to new technologies, requirements and imperatives of others. Consequently, understanding and accounting for the origins and legacies of learning through practice lay a foundation for understanding its importance to contemporary societies and offer distinct views about how those capacities might best be developed. Part of the case made in this chapter is to suggest that despite most individuals learning their occupational practice through workplace experiences across human history, the salience of workplace experiences has been downplayed and marginalised in what might be described as the era of schooled societies. That is, the development of education systems, including those that specifically focus on the development of occupational knowledge and largely through the provision of experiences in hybrid institutions (i.e., schools, colleges and universities), has tended to marginalise and downplay the qualities of learning in and through work settings that have served human society well over many millennia. What has become viewed as orthodoxies in educational practices within contemporary societies works against acknowledging the contributions of workplaces as learning environments, providing instead a popular and scientific discourse that prevents those circumstances of learning, the processes they incite and the outcomes that they achieve to be fully acknowledged and utilised.

Yet, having established these premises, it is also acknowledged that there are aspects of knowledge that cannot easily be learnt in practice settings alone and that require specific pedagogic interventions to assist their development. Indeed, in making the case for learning through work settings, it is not intended to ignore, deny, downplay or denigrate the many contributions to learning and development that arise through participation in intentional educational programmes, assisted by educators and within the confines of educational institutions. The project here is to acknowledge and optimise the contributions of experiences in work settings.

The second section comprises three chapters that set out key foundational bases for understanding learning through work and the generation of workplace innovations. Such foundations are helpful to distinguish processes of learning through work from those adopted and enacted in educational settings. More importantly, they offer bases by which learning through work and the initiation and enactment of workplace innovation can be understood, guided and supported.

The first chapter in this second section – *Chapter 3 – Learning through work: personal processes and social contributions* – elaborates the processes of learning through work and the kinds of goals that learning needs to be directed for the purposes of employability, occupational competence and workplace performance. *Chapter 4 – Occupations, situations and knowledge required for work* – discusses what constitutes the knowledge required for workplace performance, standing as the goals to which learning through and for work might be directed. So, understanding what constitutes those performance requirements and the kinds of knowledge enabling it is a necessary starting point. Following this, *Chapter 5 – Being innovative: aligning learning and workplace innovations* – elaborates the reciprocal process of workplace innovations and workers' ongoing learning. In different ways, these chapters draw upon empirical findings and explanations found within the cognitive, sociocultural, cultural psychology and anthropological literatures.

The third section discusses how learning through work might be organised, augmented and guided to optimise the opportunities that afford engagement in everyday work activities and interactions, informed by reviews of literature and empirical work. These efforts are directed to assisting individuals' learning, development and employability and to building workplace capacities, including innovations. Efforts directed towards such an optimisation are informed by foundational premises of learning theories, curriculum, pedagogic practices and the personal epistemologies and practices of working-age adults. Beyond efforts to intentionally organise (i.e., practice curriculum) and enrich learning experiences (i.e., pedagogic practices), personal practices are central to how individuals ultimately elect to engage with these processes of learning.

The first chapter in this section – *Chapter 6 – Practice curriculum* – defines, describes and elaborates the concept of practice curriculum, that is, the intentions behind, organisation of, and enactment of the pathway of activities in working life that individuals can progress along in structured ways to allow sequenced experiences providing incremental exposure to and development of the kinds of capacities required for effective practice at work. Drawing on foundational concepts of curriculum theory and practice, bases for understanding and identifying pathways of workplace experiences likely to be generative of learning of occupational competence and workplace requirements are set out.

The second chapter in this section – *Chapter 7 – Practice pedagogies* – describes and discusses a range of pedagogic practices that can augment the learning potential of what is experienced through everyday activities and interactions in work settings. It draws upon understandings premised in anthropological studies of how learning through work has been guided and supported across a range of cultures and perspectives. This leads to advancing a list of pedagogic practices derived from and shaped by the requirements of work settings and the kind of goals to be achieved by them. These pedagogic practices are often quite distinct from those developed for and enacted in educational settings. Instead, they comprise practices that are inherently engaged in the enactment of sharing and learning cultural practices called occupations.

The third chapter in this section – *Chapter 8 – Personal (epistemological) practices at work* – describes and discusses the central role that what individuals know, can do and value (i.e., their personal epistemologies) plays in processes of their learning, further development and being innovative in and through their work activities and interactions. Fundamental here is the process of mimetic learning – observation, imitation and rehearsal – that has been central to processes of learning and development across human history and is ever present, and the potent way of learning through and for work activities. Thus, beyond what is afforded by work settings in terms of invitations to engage in activities (i.e., practice curriculum) and supportive interactions (i.e., pedagogic practices) and interventions will always be how individuals elect to engage with those affordances and the degree by which they exercise their agency and intentionality in those engagements. The basis of these practices is likely to be person-dependent as they arise from the earlier or premediate experiences that individuals had that shape what they know, can do and value.

Finally, *Chapter 9 – Prospects for learning through work* – looks to the near future and offers some observations about the broadening purposes of workplace learning experiences in terms of their contributions to assisting people identify to which occupations they are suited and in which they have interest, integration of experiences in workplaces with those in tertiary education programmes and finding ways of continuing education and training of working age adults through workplace experiences, thereby offering alternatives to course-based and taught programmes of study. Moreover, this final chapter identifies emerging issues for working life and learning, including the transformation of some kind of work and ways of working, the requirements for conception and symbolic knowledge associated with the digitalisation of many aspects of work and occupations. Finally, it considers how working as part of teams has become more prevalent and how, as a consequence, working and learning is moving from being an individual to a collective process.

Stephen Billett, Brisbane, March 2025

Acknowledgements

I would like to acknowledge the funding provided through the Australian Research Council's Future Fellows scheme that supported much of the work that is presented in this volume, as well as other forms of support provided by Griffith University and the Griffith Institute for Educational Research (GIER) in funding the copy editing of the text.

I would also like to acknowledge and praise the assistance in producing this volume provided by Dr Leah Le, a research fellow within GIER. Her work and contributions were invaluable in ensuring that this volume could be prepared and submitted within an allotted timeframe. Also, I would like to acknowledge the copy-editing work by Elizabeth Stevens from Griffith University.

Part I
Learning through work

1 Learning through work

Learning through work

The importance of learning in, through and for workplaces has gained prominence in the last few decades.[1-4] There has been a shift from viewing learning experiences in workplaces as being limited to how trade skills are learnt, or learnings from tertiary education programmes refining and honing what students learnt in either university or technical college.[5] These experiences are now seen as central to some aspects of senior secondary education to inform about post-school pathways, initial occupational preparation, remaining employable across working life and being able to innovate and improve workplace practices in ways that can contribute to sustaining the viability of the public and private sector enterprises that employ workers. Then, collectively, the learning derived from these experiences is seen as being able to assist with the capacities and adaptabilities of entire national workforces.[6,7] It is acknowledged that before the advent of educational institutions and programmes for developing occupational capacities, most occupations were learnt about primarily and solely through work settings. Indeed, the sites of work were often the only circumstances in which those kinds of experiences could be accessed and engaged with and occupations' capacities be learnt. They were the most natural, the most accepted and orthodox means by which occupations were prepared.[8] However, with the advent and ubiquity of educational institutions within what can be referred to as 'schooled societies' – those in which education provisions are compulsory and tertiary education provisions are almost mandatory for occupational preparation – the role of workplace experiences has been downplayed and even portrayed as being limited in effectiveness and presumed to generate only narrow learning outcomes that were not adaptable to circumstances beyond those in which they were learnt.[9] This led to descriptions of these experiences being 'informal'[3,10] and 'non-formal'[11] from which concrete (i.e., non-transferable) learning outcomes would arise.[12]

Now, beyond work experiences being seen as mainly developing trade skills with their allegedly manual components, these experiences are valued more widely. They can be helpful in secondary education to assist young people to understand the world of work beyond education[13] and, importantly, inform their choices of preferred occupations[14] that they will be prepared for through their tertiary (i.e., vocational and higher) education programmes. With growing expectations that tertiary education programmes focusing on initial occupational preparation will realise 'job-ready' graduates has come the realisation that workplace experiences are essential for building the capacities required to practise graduates' preferred occupations.[15,16] Hence, more than merely providing 'work experiences' during students' tertiary education, there is a growing acceptance that these experiences make specific contributions to students' learning and these need to be provided and then intentionally augmented and integrated within tertiary students' preparatory programmes.[17] Moreover, when considering their learning across working life, adults often report workplace experiences as the most efficacious means by which they can continue to develop their occupational practices.[18] These experiences are also seen as being central to sustaining that employability across working life, including where individuals engage in and transition to occupations that are entirely new to them. Here, engagement in tertiary education programmes will also be necessary, but these programmes alone will be insufficient for career transitions without experiences in practising new occupations in work settings.

Moreover, as enterprises seek to sustain their viability through responding to changing requirements of work, new technologies and novel ways of working and producing the goods and services, this is often dependent upon learning arising through their employees' development that is often best secured through their work experiences and in those enterprises.[19-22] Perhaps less understood and not fully utilised is the learning that arises through workers being encouraged and permitted to be innovative in response to emerging challenges. This quality is likely to become an increasingly important facet of work competence as the requirements for work and occupational competence continually evolve.[7] However, there is reciprocity here because the process of engagement in workplace innovations is also aligned with employees' ongoing development, because it is through the process of innovation, practising, honing and evaluating new practices that learning arises,[23] as elaborated in Chapter 5 – *Being innovative: Learning and workplace innovations*. This is a reminder that such learning and development, as well as innovations, are not solely directed towards increasing the profitability of private sector enterprises. Instead, they address social concerns and goals, such as occurred in healthcare facilities to combat the Covid-19 pandemic. So, there is the potential of learning experiences in workplace settings to enhance the efficacy and effectiveness of public sector enterprises to meet the needs of communities and the individuals who reside within them.

In summary, learning in, through and for workplaces is now being recognised as increasingly important for individuals to

  i make appropriate choices about post-school destinations,
 ii develop the capacities to practise those occupations,

iii further develop those through work experiences and
iv engage in and realise workplace innovations.

Equally, private and public sector enterprises need the kinds of learning that arise through their employees' work experiences to sustain their viability. Moreover, the communities whose needs for goods and services are largely furnished by the capacities of competent workers stand to be important potential beneficiaries of learning experiences in work settings. Furthermore, and collectively, nation states are needing skilful and adaptable workforces to maintain and improve their social provisions and economic capacities, including building capacities for self-sufficiency and self-reliance. In this way, they are, collectively, the beneficiaries of effective learning experiences in work settings for the reasons stated above.

By way of introduction, this opening chapter sets out the key elements of the case made in this volume, that is, the importance of learning through work to develop applicable, robust and worthwhile knowledge associated with occupations and workplace performance requirements. Indeed, given their interests, those who teach (i.e., educators) and administer educational institutions may well be reluctant to acknowledge the contributions of learning experiences in work settings. My three decades of working in an education faculty have provided many instances to suggest this is the case. Yet, throughout human history, the settings in which work has been conducted have been and remain central to the experiences of younger and not-so-young adults, as well as those who are working-age adults, and the learning derived through these settings has served humanity well and continues to do so. Even now, with the emerging and wider sets of interest in it, learning through work remains a process that is often viewed as being subordinate to what is learnt through educational institutions, and with little or no justification. However, there is no shortage of justifications, not the least being that these settings offer access to and engagement in authentic work activities that are directly aligned with the idea of 'activities structure cognition.'[24] That is, the kinds of activities individuals engage in can have direct legacies associated with the kinds of knowledge that is intended to be learnt.

Consequently, there is a need to illuminate and elaborate these processes to be able to legitimise, authoritatively conceptualise and provide evidence of the efficacy of learning through work and how it can be augmented to achieve the kinds of goals that individuals, workplaces, communities and national governments hope to be realised. This requires fresh consideration of curriculum, pedagogies and individuals' personal learning practices to be those that are aligned well and are helpful in explaining the processes, orthodoxies and outcomes. The concerns here are about how the affordances of activities and interactions and structuring pathways of experiences can be used to assist individuals to identify their preferred occupations, develop the capacities to practise those occupations and then continue to learn and develop further across their working lives, which includes the ability to innovate in and through their work. As an indication of the contributions that these learning experiences can make, it is worthwhile initially considering the interests that different parties have in learning in and through work.

Purposes, processes and outcomes of learning through work

Central to why workplaces are becoming increasingly viewed as productive, legitimate and essential learning environments is that they potentially have a range of educational, social and personal purposes. That is, they can make contributions to individuals' learning and development that would be otherwise unavailable. That is, they provide unique kinds of educative experiences. The parties interested in such learning and development process comprise: (i) individuals, (ii) workplaces, (iii) tertiary educational institutions, (iv) communities and (v) national governments and supranational agencies. Each of these five parties has specific focus on access to, the qualities of engagements in and learning outcomes arising from workplace activities and interactions. These are provided in overview in Table 1.1 that lists the interested parties in the left-hand column and previews the particular focus of interest in the column to its right.

In the sections below, and in turn, elaborations of these parties and interests are provided.

Individuals

Individuals have a range of interest in workplace learning experiences that can be helpful across their adolescent, young adult and adult working lives. That helpfulness is potentially assisting them to (i) identify the occupations to which they are suited, (ii) be prepared for practising that occupation, (iii) continue to be competent and employable within it and (iv) sustain those qualities across lengthening working lives, including making occupational translations. Even before these, perhaps an early contribution can arise from experiences in work that assist individuals to understand what constitutes the world of work (i.e., the requirements for participating in paid employment). More than a general introduction to the world of work, these experiences can be and perhaps should be used to assist young and not-so-young people to identify the occupations for which they are suited. Both are important educational goals, often attended to in the last years of compulsory education. In earlier times, most young people had little choice about the occupations in which they engaged because of the practice and expectation of contributing to the family's activities, and the work roles were divided based on what young children could do and, by gender. Moreover, they would have inherently learnt about working life from within their family and the kinds of roles and responsibilities associated with performing work tasks. Whilst modernity, enlightenment and industrial revolutions have done much to liberate young people from being pressed into having no

Table 1.1 Interested parties and interest

Parties	Interest
Individuals	Experiences introducing and orienting them to the 'world of work,' for identifying preferred occupations, being prepared for them, further development of occupational capacities, transitioning to new work roles, workplaces, and/or occupations.
Workplaces	Having skilled and currently competent workers who can achieve the workplace's goals, including meeting clients/customers etc. needs, responding to changing occupational and work requirements and being innovative to sustain the viability and advancement of private and public sector enterprises that employ individuals and provide opportunities for advancements.
Tertiary education institutions	Provision of work experiences and placements that are required to develop students' occupational and work life capacities and being able to integrate those experiences in students' study programmes can assist their employability and readiness for smooth transition to performance at work beyond graduation. Also, these experiences can assist the provision of efficacy of continuing education programmes.
Communities	For workplaces, being able to provide the goods and services that communities need and sustaining the viability of local enterprises and the employability of locals, are all dependent on the initial and further development of skills, much of which arises through workplaces, and can also contribute to the viability of and extending communities' activities.
National governments and supranational agencies	Workplaces' contributions to the current competency and adaptability of working-age adults are central to their employability and, therefore, their contributions to the nation state. Also, the viability of enterprises and their capacities to be both import competing and export oriented can contribute to the growing need for national self-sufficiency and reliance, which is becoming an increasingly important goal for nation states.

choice about occupational pathways and, second, the destruction of much of family businesses broke a system whereby family-run businesses were the norm, being pressed to work within family still occurs in some societies.[25] Yet, such circumstances are a rarity in societies with modern economies in contemporary times, except perhaps within farming communities and some small and family businesses.

Informing about the world of work and making occupational choices

There is a clear potential in workplace experiences to assist young people be informed about the world of work and to assist them in making informed occupational choices. Whilst rarely being seen as an educative experience, young persons' paid part-time work, whilst at school or in tertiary education, offers an opportunity to understand the requirements of working life.[13] That is, through engaging in that work, they are pressed to consider and practise a range of requirements that can be broadly applicable across the world of paid work. For instance, it can assist them to learn about the importance of being punctual, presenting themselves appropriately, working in teams, resolving problems and also fulfilling obligations such as paying tax, being a member of the union and fulfilling employers' expectations.[13] So, these work experiences, although not intended as such, can be useful for young people to understand the 'world of work' beyond schooling and how they need to engage in it and with others. Whilst not necessarily occurring in their preferred occupations, it can necessarily generate important learning outcomes associated with working life that will ease their transition into it.

Moreover, there is another role that workplaces can play in assisting young people to move into adult life and employment: that is, providing experiences that allow them to understand which occupation suits their interests and capacities. As mentioned, before industrialisation, many and perhaps most young people would have little choice about the occupations in which they would engage. This was because they would be restricted to what occurred within family or nearby work situations. However, in most countries, since industrialisation and as a product of enlightenment and modernity, young people now have more freedom to identify, choose and pursue the occupations in which they are interested, which they prefer and to which they are suited,[26] subject to them being able to engage in courses or apprenticeships from which they will be able to engage in and learn about those occupations. The more informed that young people can be about the kinds of occupations to which they are suited and can engage, the better. Attrition rates during apprenticeships in many countries indicate that young people are making choices that are not fully informed.[27-31] Also, high attrition rates in people leaving occupations such as the trades, nursing and hairdressing, once they have been prepared for them, indicate the importance of understanding what constitutes those occupations and their practice. There is considerable loss of personal and institutional investment, from education and workplace contributions, when unacceptably high levels of apprentices or graduates leave the occupation for which they have been prepared.

So, there is a key role here for workplace experiences to inform young people about what that occupation comprises in practice. This is realised through exposing them to and engaging them in the activities and interactions in the kinds of occupations to which they are attracted; that is, to see if attraction and the realities of practice are aligned. Assisting young people in finding the occupations to which they are suited was one of Dewey's[26] two purposes of education for occupations. He emphasises the importance of young people identifying with the kinds of occupations to which they are suited, rather than falling into occupations that are uncongenial for them: that is, not aligned with their attributes or able to meet their needs and aspirations. Early exposure to occupations being practised in work settings, particularly at the beginning of tertiary education programmes, seems to be an important means of informing young people about whether their preferred occupations are those in which they are interested and which are aligned with their capacities. Perhaps only through workplace experiences can young people come to experience (i.e., observe and/or participate in) those occupations in practice and in work settings. These kinds of experiences can assist them to make informed choices about the kind of occupations for which they want to invest their time and resources. Without that experience, they may make uninformed choices such as those that apparently are leading to low completion rates in programmes such as apprenticeships, which often have high levels of attrition as the realities of the occupational practice diverge from what young people expected, were attracted to and believed to comprise that work. As foreshadowed, there are often high attrition rates in many apprenticeship programmes, seemingly because young people – often males – decide that the trade they were being prepared for does not meet their perceptions of those occupations or fulfil their needs. Similarly, occupations dominated by young women (e.g., hairdressing, nursing, teaching) often have high attrition rates when what is experienced does not align with expectations about work and working life. Thus, these are two important educational purposes for young people to be realised through their engagement in work activities and interactions prior to engaging in working life. This allows them to understand the kinds of tasks in which they will engage and those with whom they will engage and with whom they need to collaborate, and within the requirements of the work settings in which they are having these experiences. Such experiences then can make these individuals more ready for initial occupational preparation.

Initial and ongoing occupational development

Beyond informing decision-making about the world of work and preferred occupations, workplaces can provide experiences that are essential for learning the capacities required to practise those occupations, that is, assistance in developing the skilfulness required to practise the occupation effectively. Forms of occupational preparation such as apprenticeships, partnerships, cadetships and those associated with medical, nursing and teacher education have included significant interludes of workplace experiences. These experiences are often now mandated by professional bodies and licensing agencies as essential for developing the capacities required to practise their occupations and to be certified to do so. The authenticity of the activities and interactions in which novices partake when engaging in work tasks has been shown to be helpful in supporting learning that is applicable.[32–34] This outcome arises because the engagement in these goal-directed activities and interactions has legacies that go beyond the completion of those tasks. That is, they contribute to changing what those who engage in them know, can do and value, sometimes transformationally, but often incrementally.[35] For instance, when individuals do something new (i.e., something they have not done before) or develop further understanding or have insights about value-related aspects of those activities, this experience can be generative of new knowledge (i.e., learning).

The evidence suggests that goal-directed activities and interactions occurring in work settings are highly informative in terms of generating the kinds of knowledge required to practise those occupations.[36] This is because they are authentic in terms of the kinds of activities and interactions that are needed to perform those tasks in those settings.[32] That is, rather than engaging in substitute activities in a different social and physical setting, these activities and the legacies arising from them are shaped by the goals to be achieved, as well as how they been achieved and are judged to be effective.[37,38] By degree, these experiences are more or less accessible to students, as are the kinds of support and guidance available for, and provided to, individuals participating in those workplaces.[39] So, there is a range of situationally authentic and potentially potent contributions that are afforded individuals through their engagement in these work activities. Affordances here refer to the invitational qualities – the opportunities, guidance and accessibility – that individuals might be offered to participate in and learn.[34]

Beyond the opportunities that are afforded when engaging in work settings is how individuals elect to engage with the activities and interactions that they encounter.[34] Whilst it is always the case that individuals take responsibilities for their learning, this is perhaps even more so and necessary when learning in the absence of teachers and educational programmes. In the absence of teachers, although often assisted by more experienced workers, much of the learning that arises in work settings is mediated not only by the opportunities provided or by the close guidance of more experienced workers, but also through the engagement with what they are experiencing and is being suggested to them in those work activities and interactions.[40–42] Therefore, kinds, qualities and intensity of that engagement are important, as learning is a constructive process arising from individuals' processes of 'experiencing': that is, how they come to engage, construe and construct with what they experience.[43] The centrality of engagement in workplace experiences is also evident in apprentices who spend much of their indenture in work settings, as is the case for many medical students' engagement in clinical experiences in hospitals and other healthcare settings. In those circumstances, the kinds and extents of learning that arise are often premised on the support and guidance from more experienced healthcare workers, that is, the degree by which they are afforded support by co-workers. So, it is not a question of merely having work experiences per se, but rather that the particular kinds of experiences in work settings have the potential to develop the kinds of knowledge that are required to practise the occupation.

However, that learning is not a process of socialisation, that is to say, the uncritical acceptance of what is experienced. Instead, the evidence suggests that individuals actively mediate what they experience and moderate their engagement in learning arising from those experiences. For instance, Wertsch[44] proposes that how individuals engage with these experiences can often be categorised as either mastery or appropriation. Mastery refers to a superficial acceptance of what is being suggested to them; however, they may well remain uncommitted and unconvinced, yet may have to indicate acceptance of what is being suggested for pragmatic purposes, such as to pass the test or meet the expectations of supervisors. On the other hand, appropriation is the uncritical acceptance of what is being proposed because it aligns well with individuals' beliefs, prior experiences, and so forth. Thus, what is suggested to individuals by social sources and suggestions will be subject to their construction, construal and appraisal of their worth.

Moreover, this arises perhaps most often through their everyday work activities and interactions, rather than through engaging in intentional developmental or educational activities. However, when individuals want to learn new occupational or workplace tasks or change their occupations, this often cannot be wholly undertaken through workplace experiences alone, and their participation in tertiary education programmes is likely to be essential. For instance, in his book on learning to produce fine wood crafting, Marchand[45] refers to experiences at a botanical garden where the trainees learnt about woodgrain and different kinds of wood and about their growth cycles and qualities. These kinds of educative experiences may not be available in work settings. It is the kinds and combination of experiences required to provide access to and engagement with the knowledge to be learnt that is crucial. These may need to be sourced in different kinds of settings that can provide contributions of the kinds mentioned above.

In sum, individuals have a range of needs that can be provided through work experiences that assist them in preparing for working life, selecting occupations to which they are interested and suited, the initial development of their occupational capacities, and then maintaining their ongoing development and opportunities for advancement that occur across lengthening working lives. Added here is the prospect that workplaces afford individuals through opportunities to innovate. Engaging in innovations can lead to the dual outcomes of their learning and contributing to the continuity and advancement of the enterprises in which they are employed.[46] So, more than promoting individuals' employability is the potential for making contributions to their workplaces' viability and continuity. Moreover, as noted, to optimise these opportunities and contributions, there are occasions when their everyday learning experiences need to be augmented through the provision of guidance and direct support for developing the kinds of knowledge that might not be realised through their own discovery efforts alone. Hence, when individuals are learning new procedures (e.g., ways of working and technologies), deepening understanding (e.g., their conceptual development associated with work activities) and dispositions (i.e., values such as safety, checking, qualities of care), such support and guidance is likely to be required. This then leads to a consideration of how work roles are organised in ways that can be used to initially develop occupational capacities and workplace competence that includes the sequencing of experiences and then, perhaps, providing guidance and support by more experienced workers. Thus, more than the provision of workplace experiences, individuals will be concerned about how their learning and development can be supported in and through work activities.

Workplaces

Workplace learning experiences are essential not only for individuals' employability, but also for the viability and continuity of the public and private sector enterprises in which they are employed. The viability of these enterprises is partially premised on employees' ability to provide the goods and services they generate and to respond to changes in those requirements. This ability is often premised on employees' skilfulness and current competence. So, having workers who are effectively prepared for their occupations and workplace requirements and then sustaining that employability (i.e., remaining workplace competent) and able to be responsive to new and emerging challenges are also essential for the viability and continuity of those enterprises. As noted above, much of this learning is derived in and through work activities, both in the preparatory and ongoing development phases.[1,18,47] As foreshadowed, this is not to deny the important contributions arising from experiences in educational settings. Instead, it emphasises the specific contributions that arise from participating in work activities; often these can only be accessed and experienced within work settings. This is because sometimes these activities are workplace specific. But, more generally, the authenticity of experiences that provide access to and engagement with the concepts, procedures and dispositions to be learnt seem paramount.[38] Therefore, it is often only through activities and interactions in those work settings that these requirements can be accessed, understood, developed and exercised effectively.

For instance, the roles that healthcare workers such as nurses perform across different kinds of healthcare settings differ. Those roles needed for specialist wards (e.g., oncology, surgery, intensive care) within large tertiary hospitals in metropolitan centres can be quite distinct from nursing roles undertaken in regional and small community hospitals. These roles differ again from those in industry, military and even roles within general medical practice. Yet, much of the nurses' preparation often occurs within tertiary education and large tertiary hospital settings. In those instances, the experiences in those hospitals are essential for developing their capacities to practise nursing effectively. Yet, the concern is that those capacities may not be easily transferred to other kinds of healthcare settings that have distinct activities and interactions, and, therefore, performance requirements. It is simply not possible, therefore, to 'parachute' workers into workplaces with which they are unfamiliar and expect them to be able to perform their occupation effectively. This suggests that, to meet the needs of those workplaces, support in the form of structured experiences may be required to orientate, assist and support healthcare workers in those transitions. This is often undertaken within the healthcare sector by individuals who are preceptors for nurses, and those with clinical responsibilities assisting medical students and first-year doctors. Yet, these practices are not only highly situated (i.e., have specific requirements), but they are also likely to be subject to changes in those requirements as circumstances (e.g., activities and interactions) and work performance requirements change as teams operate differently and as patient profiles and health challenges evolve.

One of the emerging requirements for contemporary work is for learning to occur for and through digital means (i.e., electronically). Increasingly, workplace artefacts, tools and processes are shaped by electronic processes, often referred to as 'being digital,' and the process of work being transformed through digitalisation (i.e., electronic tools and processes). These artefacts can often play a role in mediating the knowledge that needs to be learnt and how workers can access it.[48,49] On the one hand, work tasks and workplace performances are increasingly premised upon digitalised work processes; on the other, often the means for learning this knowledge is through what is provided through these digitalised artefacts.[50] These emerging requirements suggest consideration be given to forms of knowledge that are required to be learnt for these forms of work, and how these often symbolic and conceptual forms of knowledge can be learnt. A key consideration here is how to make this kind of knowledge accessible so that it can be experienced and constructed by individuals. Again, this emphasises the need for specific approaches for the kinds of knowledge required for contemporary workplace performance to be learnt. It seems that, in many but not all instances, because the applications of those forms of knowledge are related to work practices, their learning is most effectively realised through workplace activities.[51]

All these considerations emphasise that not only are workplace experiences essential for learning occupational practice, per se, but that they are also central to public and private sector enterprises' viability and continuity as they inevitably face new requirements for the provision of the goods and services. Having a currently competent and adaptable workforce is an essential requirement for that continuity and further development. Current understandings suggest that grounded experiences are essential for developing occupational capacities, and the ability to adapt them to other circumstances requires exposure to and understandings of the circumstances to which they have to adapt.[52–54] For many individuals, the first instance of this is when they transition from educational programmes to work settings and seek to apply what they learnt in them upon being employed. The point here is that both the requirements for workplace performance and occupational competence are associated with having experiences in the circumstances of practice (i.e., the work settings in which occupational performance occurs).

Being innovative and generative of solutions to emerging challenges is now also a requirement of effective occupational practice. Yet, there is a potential for workplace experiences to support workers' innovations and ability to bring about changes through the cooccurrence of their engagement in identifying, initiating and implementing workplace innovations.[55] Engaging in these activities can lead to extending what they know, can do and value. Given the kinds and extent of changes that are arising through changes in technology, ways of working, compositions of workforces and occupational requirements, the ongoing ability for workers to learn and be able to innovate in their work settings is essential for both forms of continuity (i.e., individuals; employability and workplace viability). However, workplaces are not alone in their interest in learning through work, as this is increasingly shared by tertiary education institutions.

Tertiary education institutions

Beyond the sites of work where individuals practise their occupations, tertiary education institutions are also increasingly interested in their students' accessing workplace experiences.[15] There have been longstanding traditions in some occupations, including medicine, nursing, engineering, teaching and social work, for periods of practical experience in work settings to be part of tertiary education programmes. However, that need is now becoming widely considered and adopted through providing experiences in work settings, in all occupations, not just those of the kinds mentioned in the previous sentence. These are variously described as work placements, practicums, clinical experiences and work experiences. Here, the term 'work placements' is used in referring to these experiences.

Work placements

There is now a widespread demand for students in all kinds of tertiary education programmes to have workplace experiences. This applies to disciplines that traditionally were almost averse to such experiences, such as the humanities.[56–59] The purposes of tertiary education now being exercised are to prepare students for employment upon graduation.[60] The term that is increasingly being used is making students 'job ready' when they graduate from tertiary education programmes. Much of the increasing interest in these placements has been driven by agendas emphasising the importance of graduates having capacities to move smoothly into employment, and that this is most likely to be realised by having had work experiences.[60] Prior to the 'job readiness' agenda, the emphasis in many countries was that graduates should be occupationally or industry ready.[61] That is, graduates should possess the canonical knowledge of the occupation (i.e., that knowledge which anybody practising it would need to know), which is a more general outcome than being prepared for a specific job (i.e., job readiness). Such an outcome is quite different from being job ready, which is now the imperative. It places greater emphasis on graduates being employable in work settings, rather than being broadly prepared for occupational practice. Regardless of views about this proposition, it has fuelled a growing interest in and requirement for students to have work experiences, and in all kinds of tertiary education programmes. So, workplaces where those occupations are being practised are seen as sites in which tertiary students can engage in the kinds of activities and interactions required for effective practice. This need for work placements is creating problems for the demand for these placements, and concerns about the quality of students' work experiences arising from this increase in demand. One of the reasons for the latter concern is that many workplaces are unfamiliar with and unprepared for providing student placements and are unable to provide the kind of experiences and support found in workplaces, such as hospitals, schools and social welfare agencies.[5] Certainly, having workplace experiences is now becoming a requirement of many tertiary education programmes and so workplaces, potentially, are playing increasingly greater roles in tertiary education provisions. Hence, tertiary education institutions are concerned to be able to provide those experiences.

In addition, increasingly, occupational registration or certification that is necessary for graduates to practise occupations has a mandated number of work experience days or hours to fulfil the registration requirements. That is, students and graduates must complete the allocated number of hours of workplace experiences before they can be registered to be employed in their preferred occupations. Because of these two kinds of contributions, workplaces as learning environments are being taken seriously by tertiary education institutions, perhaps now more than ever. However, on their own, whilst helpful, the greatest potential is when workplace experiences can be effectively integrated into students' overall programme.[15,61]

Intentional integration of workplace experiences

More than providing workplace experiences, tertiary education provisions are also seeking to actively integrate the experiences that students have in work settings into their programmes.[62-66] So, these experiences are now valued not only in their own terms, but also in terms of how they might be augmenting what occurs in educational settings.[61] Part of that augmentation is to align the kinds of experiences students have in those work settings with the aims of the educational programmes and the processes. It has been found that to most effectively integrate the two sets of experiences prior to students engaging in work settings, they are made ready to be able to participate and contribute effectively, supported during those placements and then on completion.[5] The interventions that can comprise these forms of support provide opportunities to intentionally align their experiences with their course objectives. So, there are considerations in tertiary education about how best to integrate the two sets of experiences from educational, teaching and evaluation perspectives.[5]

The other area of potential engagement of workplace learning experiences by tertiary educational institutions is the provision of continuing education and training (CET). These programmes are increasingly necessary for working-age adults to maintain their employability (i.e., being currently competent). Drawing upon and utilising workplace experiences can be a key element of CET programmes offered through tertiary education institutions. The evidence suggests that much of the ongoing learning of workers can be realised through workplace settings, except when they are transferring to a new occupation or an area of their existing occupation that is wholly new to them.[18] For CET programmes offered through tertiary education institutions, utilising students' experiences within their workplace stands to provide opportunities for learning that is grounded in practice, has relevance to their engagement and is pertinent in terms of outcomes.[67] Hence, with the developing interest in continuing the learning across working life (what is often referred to as 'lifelong education') being directed towards maintaining employability, engagement by tertiary education institutions with work settings to secure contributions to their students' learning is becoming increasingly imperative. Hence, models of CET able to accommodate and utilise experiences within students' working lives offer a means of providing effective and pertinent means of sustaining that employability.

Communities

Although they may not be able to directly influence much of what occurs in work settings, communities require that the provision of goods and services by public and private enterprises is premised upon the currency and competence of workers in those enterprises. That is, regardless of whether it is a service provision such as healthcare, aged care or social counselling, for access to workers able to produce foodstuffs or build and maintain accommodation, the competence of those workers is salient for local communities. In this way, these communities can be dependent upon that competence. In particular, for communities that are remote from large metropolitan or regional centres, the role of local workplaces in developing the skills of their employees becomes crucial. For instance, provisions of aged care and healthcare in rural, remote and regional communities are often premised upon a workforce that is recruited and prepared locally.[68] Often, the means of developing the capacities of these workforces will be conducted within local workplaces and through the guidance and support of experienced workers. There is sometimes also more strategic focus within community concerns about the development of capacities; that is, the ability of these enterprises to support the development of the growth and to extend the economic and social activities of those communities to sustain and grow them in ways which make them more viable.[69] As considerations of distance and remoteness play out in some communities, the ability to be more self-reliant becomes a key focus, and generating new sources of economic and employment activity is also prevalent here. So, these communities have an interest in local workplaces' ability to develop the kind of capacities required to meet their needs, which is represented at a national level in terms of workforce capacities.

National governments and supranational agencies

National governments are understandably concerned about the competence and currency of the national workforce, because high levels of employment and employability mean fewer working-age adults drawing upon social welfare benefits.[70] However, governments also have broader and more strategic interests associated with an ability to innovate. These include being able to be import competitive and export oriented in an increasingly globalised economy, heightening their ability to remain viable and sustain local employment opportunities and to contribute to the national skilled workforce. In this way, workplaces in all kinds and sizes of communities can play important roles in supporting and sustaining the skilfulness of the national workforce. This is becoming increasingly important in an era where self-sufficiency is becoming a national priority.

Those priorities include addressing key strategic interests that governments are seeking to secure. There are also concerns for enterprises to have the kinds and quantum of occupational competence to assist national efforts at being export oriented and import competing. As a consequence, national governments as well as supranational agencies are concerned with the level of skilfulness within countries.[70] This includes their ability to be effective in providing the goods and services needed within nation states and much of this is premised upon effective initial occupational preparation and then continuing to learn across the work lifespan. Moreover, governments might be concerned about the cost of education occurring within hybrid institutions, such as universities and colleges. They may well, and like enterprises themselves, prefer that much of the ongoing skill development is occurring within the work setting and utilising workers' occupational capacities.

An emerging focus on having a competent and competitive workforce is that many nation states are seeking to be more self-reliant and self-sufficient in an era of geopolitical tensions that include a rollback from globalisation. That is, the risks to national sovereignty when the goods and services required by the nation state are largely developed elsewhere and the access to and quality of those goods will be subject to other nation states' interests and priorities. Likely, this will mean a broader agenda associated with skill development and maintaining occupational competence, and across lengthening working lives.

In sum, what is indicated here is that the growing interest in learning through work is premised upon a growing set of needs from individuals as students, novices and experienced workers, requirements to support the viability and continuity of the enterprises in which individuals work and the production of the goods and services provided to their local communities. There is also the need for tertiary education students to secure experiences to make them ready for their selected occupations and the workplaces that employ them. Collectively, at a national level, the development of a workforce that is currently competent, able to respond to new occupational and workplace challenges and to assist nation states to become more self-sufficient and self-reliant, is of growing importance. Consequently, it is important to now consider the kinds of learning outcomes that need to be secured through workplace experiences.

Workplace curriculum, pedagogic and personal practices

It follows from the above, and to foreshadow what will be discussed in Chapter 6 – *Practice curriculum*, Chapter 7 – *Practice pedagogies* and Chapter 8 – *Personal practices*, that how learning through work can be enhanced is through those three sets of considerations. As noted, whilst it is accepted that much learning in work settings occurs as part of everyday work activities without necessarily requiring structured experiences, there is the need to consider how best to organise experiences so that individuals can engage in activities and interactions in ways that are sequenced and develop further their understandings, practices and dispositions.

Workplace practice curriculum is defined as the sequence of workplace activities and interactions that provides experiences for effectively learning the requirements for occupational practice.[71] Each work setting is likely to have a distinct curriculum, given that the particular requirements of the workplace and the sequencing of engagement in tasks will in some ways be specific to each enterprise. Identifying and establishing a workplace curriculum as a pathway of experiences can be helpful for providing a sequence of experiences that will permit individuals to develop the kinds of capacities that are required for that particular work setting, but in doing so also develop the kinds of canonical occupational knowledge in ways distinct from an approach structure that might occur within an educational setting. That is, it goes from the particular to the more general, whereas the opposite is usually the focus for what occurs within educational programmes. Later in this text, a thorough consideration is given to the organisational development of a workplace curriculum (see Chapter 6).

Pedagogic practices are defined as activities or interactions that can augment or enrich these learning experiences, often enacted by more experienced workers but including particular work activities and artefacts. These pedagogic practices are often quite different from those found within educational institutions because they are not necessarily led by teachers or even involve the direct and close engagement with a more experienced individual. Half-completed jobs, workplace activities and interactions that provide access to practitioners' knowledge, engaging in discussions about cases, problems or plans, the use of aid to memories (mnemonics), tricks of the trade or heuristics that are demonstrated, as well as direct engagement by more experienced or expert practitioners are all forms of practice pedagogies that are quite distinct from those used in classroom settings. It is these kinds of practices that are discussed and elaborated in Chapter 7.

Personal practices are defined as how individuals engage in work activities and interactions and how they come to construe and construct knowledge (i.e., learn based on what they know, can do and value). These practices are referred to as personal epistemologies[9] and shape how individuals think and act and how they are developing further through those processes of thinking and acting. Often, it is individuals' intentionality and agency[72] that make these epistemologies powerful and essential in learning through and for work. This is particularly the case when that learning requires effortful engagement. So, regardless of whether it is engagement to develop effective procedural capacities or understanding the range of variables that might impact occupational performance, these are the object of personal practices. Examples here are differential diagnosis undertaken by medical practitioners[73] or nurses, or active critical engagement associated with enhancing dispositions about patient care and safety.[74] A consideration of these practices and their development is discussed in Chapter 8.

Learning in and through work

This introductory chapter has sought to set out the range of interests associated with learning in and through work and why these have become more prominent in recent times; that is, its purposes, processes and outcomes. It has been proposed that more than representing a return to earlier approaches to learning through practice out of necessity, with all its strengths and weaknesses, and that has nevertheless been so helpful for humanity, there is now a broader set of purposes of providing and engaging in workplace experiences. These purposes are reflected in the interests of individuals' employability, the viability of public and private sector enterprises, meeting the needs of communities and, collectively, the needs of nation states to be able to respond to and address their social and economic challenges. Moreover, this chapter has foreshadowed issues that are discussed within this text, references made to the kinds of knowledge that is required for both occupational competence and workplace performance, captured as the canonical knowledge of the occupation (i.e., that every practitioner needs to know, do and value) and situational manifestations of that knowledge that underpin workplace performance. Then, it briefly introduced three other important bases for utilising and enhancing workplace experiences in the form of workplace curriculum, practice pedagogies and personal epistemologies. The subsequent chapters deal with these issues in greater depth and provide examples and instances, rationales and bases for progression.

References

1. Billett S. *Learning in the workplace: Strategies for effective practice*. Sydney: Allen and Unwin; 2001.
2. Billett S. Mimesis: Learning through everyday activities and interactions at work. *Human Resource Development Review*. 2014;13(4):462–482.
3. Marsick VJ, Watkins K. *Informal and incidental learning in the workplace*. London: Routledge; 1990.
4. Tynjala P. Perspectives into learning in the workplace. *Education Research Review*. 2008;3(2):130–154.
5. Billett S. *Integrating practice-based experiences into higher education*. Dordrecht: Springer; 2015.
6. Organisation for Economic Co-operation and Development. *Live longer, work longer*. Paris: OECD; 2006.
7. Billett S. *Work, Change and workers*. Dordrecht: Springer; 2006.
8. Billett S. The practices of learning through occupations. In: S.Billett, ed. *Learning through practice: Models, traditions, orientations and approaches*. Vol 1. Dodrecht: Springer; 2010: 59–81.
9. Billett S. Personal epistemologies, work and learning. *Educational Research Review*. 2009;4(3):210–219.
10. Eraut M. Informal learning in the workplace. *Studies in Continuing Education*. 2004;26(2):247–273.
11. Smith L, Clayton B. *Recognising non-formal and informal learning: Participant insights and perspectives*. Adelaide: National Centre for Vocational Education Research; 2009.
12. Lave J. The culture of acquisition and the practice of understanding. In: Stigler JW, Shweder RA, Herdt G, eds. *Cultural psychology*. Cambridge: Cambridge University Press; 1990: 259–286.
13. Billett S, Ovens C. Learning about work, working life and post school options: Guiding students' reflecting on paid part-time work. *Journal of Education and Work*. 2007;20(2):75–90.
14. Billett S, Choy S, Hodge S. Enhancing the standing of vocational education and the occupations it serves: Australia. *Journal of Vocational Education and Training*. 2020;72(2):270–296.
15. Cooper L, Orrel J, Bowden M. *Work integrated learning: A guide to effective practice*. London: Routledge; 2010.
16. Jackson D, Fleming J, Rowe A. Enabling the transfer of skills and knowledge across classroom and work contexts. *Vocations and Learning*. 2019;12(3):459–478.
17. Billett S. Promoting graduate employability: Key goals, and curriculum and pedagogic practices for higher education. In: Ng B, ed. *Graduate employability and workplace-based learning development: Insights from sociocultural perspectives*. Singapore: Springer Nature Singapore; 2022: 11–29.
18. Billett S, Dymock D, Choy S, eds. *Supporting learning across working life*. Dordrecht: Springer; 2016.
19. Gimpel J. *The Cathedral builders*. New York: Grove Press; 1961.
20. Turnbull D. The ad hoc collective work of building Gothic cathedrals with templates, string, and geometry. *Science, Technology, & Human Values*. 1993;18:315–340.
21. Epstein SR. *Transferring technical knowledge and innovating in Europe 1200–1800*. London: London School of Economics; 2005.

22. Hoyrup S, Bonnafous-Boucher M, Hasse C, Lotz M, Molller K, eds. *Employee-driven innovation: A new approach*. Basingstoke: Palgrave-McMillan; 2012.
23. Billett S. Explaining innovation at work: A socio-personal account. In: Pederson SH, ed. Employee-driven innovation: A new approach. London: Palgrave-MacMillan; 2012: 92–107.
24. Rogoff B, Lave J, eds. *Everyday cognition: Its development in social context*. Cambridge, MA: Harvard University Press; 1984.
25. International Labour Organisation. *Policy brief: Main findings from a pilot on upgrading informal apprenticeships in Jordan: A bottom-up approach*. Beirut: International Labour organisation; 2015.
26. Dewey J. *Democracy and education*. New York: The Free Press; 1916.
27. Jorgensen CH. The role and meaning of vocations in the transition from education to work. *International Journal of Training and Research*. 2013;11(2):166–183.
28. Deissinger T. Apprenticeship systems in England and Germany: Decline and survival. Paper presented at: Towards a history of Vocational Education and Training (VET) in Europe in a comparative perspective, 2002; Florence.
29. Powers TE. Motivated apprentices: The value of workplace and trade school. *Journal of Education and Work*. 2020;33(1):81–97.
30. Powers TE, Watt HM. Understanding why apprentices consider dropping out: Longitudinal prediction of apprentices' workplace interest and anxiety. *Empirical Research in Vocational Education and Training*. 2021;13(1):1–23.
31. Deissinger T. The standing of dual apprenticeships in Germany: Institutional stability and current challenges. *The standing of vocational education and the occupations it serves: Current concerns and strategies for enhancing that standing*. Dordrecht: Springer; 2022: 83–101.
32. Anvik C, Vedeler JS, Wegener C, Slettebø Å, Ødegård A. Practice-based learning and innovation in nursing homes. *Journal of Workplace Learning*. 2020;32(2):122–134.
33. Billett S. Recasting transfer as a socio-personal process of adaptable learning. *Educational Research Review*. 2013;8:5–13.
34. Billett S. Learning through work: Workplace affordances and individual engagement. *Journal of Workplace Learning*. 2001;13(5):209–214.
35. Billett S. Authenticity and a culture of workpractice. *Australian and New Zealand Journal of Vocational Education Research*. 1993;2(1):1–29.
36. Scribner S. Mind in action: A functional approach to thinking. *The Quarterly Newsletter of the Laboratory of Comparative Human Cognition*. 1992;14(4):103–110 (Reprint of 1983 lecture).
37. Billett S. Authenticity in workplace learning settings. In: Stevenson J, ed. *Cognition at work: The development of vocational expertise*. Adelaide: National Centre for Vocational Education Research; 1994: 36–75.
38. Billett S. *Mimetic learning at work: Learning in the circumstances of practice*. Dordrecht: Springer; 2014.
39. Billett S. Workplace learning: Its potential and limitations. *Education and Training*. 1995;37(5):20–27.
40. Edwards A. Relational agency: Learning to be a resourceful practitioner. *International Journal of Educational Research*. 2005;43:168–182.
41. Goller M. *Human agency at work: An active approach towards expertise development*. Wiesbaden, Germany: Springer Fachmedien 2017.
42. Eteläpelto A, Vähäsantanen K, Hökkä P, Paloniemi S. What is agency? Conceptualizing professional agency at work. *Educational Research Review*. 2013;10:45–65.

43. Billett S. Learning across working life: Educative experiences. In: Billett S, Salling Olesen H, Filliettaz L, eds. *Sustaining employability through work-life learning: Practices and policies*. Singapore: Springer Nature Singapore; 2023: 191–208.
44. Wertsch JV. *Mind as action*. New York: Oxford University Press; 1998.
45. Marchand TH. *The pursuit of pleasurable work: Craftwork in twenty-first century England*. London: Berghahn Books; 2022.
46. Billett S, Yang S, Chia A, Tai JF, Lee M, Alhadad S. Remaking and transforming cultural practices: Exploring the co-occurrence of work, learning and innovation. In: Collin K, Glaveanu V, Lemmetty S, Forsman P, eds. *Creativity and learning: Contexts, processes and impact*. London: Palgrave McMillan; 2021: 219–244.
47. Organisation for Economic Co-operational and Development. *OECD skills outlook 2013: first results from the survey of adult skills*. Paris: OECD; 2013.
48. Harteis C. Machines, change, work: An educational view on the digitalization of work. In: Harteis C, ed. *The impact of digitalization in the workplace: An educational view*. Cham: Springer; 2018: 1–10.
49. Hamalainen R, Lanz M, Koskinen KT. Collaborative systems and environments for future working life: Towards the integration of workers, systems and manufacturing environments. In: Harteis C, ed. *The impact of digitalisation in the workplace: An educational view*. Vol 21. Dordrecht: Springer; 2018: 25–38.
50. Harteis C, ed. *The impact of digitalization in the workplace*. Vol 21. Dordrecht: Springer; 2018.
51. Billett S. Mediating worklife learning and the digitalization of work. *British Journal of Educational Technology*. 2021;52:1580–1593.
52. Lobato J. Alternative perspectives on the transfer of learning: History, issues, and challenges for future research. *The Journal of the Learning Sciences*. 2006;15(4):431–449.
53. Lobato J. The actor-oriented transfer perspective and its contributions to educational research and practice. *Educational Psychologist*. 2012;47(3):232–247.
54. Beach K. Chapter 4: Consequential transitions: A sociocultural expedition beyond transfer in education. *Review of Research in Education*. 1999;24(1):101–139.
55. Billett S. The co-occurrence of work, learning and innovation: Advancing workers' learning and work practices. In: Malloch M, Cairns L, O'Connor B, Evans K, eds. *Sage handbook of learning and work*. London: Sage; 2020: 34–48.
56. Pretto G. Work integrated learning and the humanities: Possibilities and future directions. Paper presented at: THE INTERNATIONAL, 2012.
57. Tumarkin M, Paddle S, Radbourne J. Work-related and experiential learning in arts and humanities. Project report. Geelong, Victoria: Deakin University; 2008.
58. Stibbe A. Work-based learning in the humanities: A welcome stranger? *Practice and Evidence of the Scholarship of Teaching and Learning in Higher Education*. 2013;8(3):241–255.
59. Gansmo HJ. Humanities in practice–is placement/internship programs a solution to the crisis in the humanities? Paper presented at: EDULEARN18 Proceedings, 2018.
60. Bennett D, Richardson S, MacKinnon P. *Enacting strategies for graduate employability: How universities can best support students to develop generic skills*. Sydney: Australian Government Office for Learning and Teaching; 2016.
61. Billett S. Realising the educational worth of integrating work experiences in higher education. *Studies in Higher Education*. 2009;34(7):827–843.
62. Cardell E, Bialocerkowski A. Bouncing forward: A post-practicum workshop to promote professional identity, self-efficacy, and resilience in Master of Speech

Pathology students. In: Billett S, Newton JM, Rogers GD, Noble C, eds. Augmenting health and social care students' clinical learning experiences: Outcomes and processes. Dordrecht: Springer; 2019: 211–234.
63. Noble C, Armit L, Collier L, Sly C, Hilder J, Molloy E. Enhancing feedback literacy in the workplace: A learner-centred approach. In: Billett S, Newton JM, Rogers GD, Noble C, eds. *Augmenting health and social care students' clinical learning experiences: Outcomes and processes.* Dordrecht: Springer; 2019: 283–308.
64. Harrison J, Molloy E, Bearman M, Ting CY, Leech M. Clinician Peer Exchange Groups (C-PEGs): Augmenting medical students' learning on clinical placement. In: Billett S, Newton JM, Rogers GD, Noble C, eds. *Augmenting health and social care students' clinical learning experiences: Outcomes and processes.* Dordrecht: Springer; 2019: 95–120.
65. Steketee C, Keane N, Gardiner K. Consolidating clinical learning through post-rotation small group activities. In: Billett S, Newton JM, Rogers GD, Noble C, eds. *Augmenting health and social care students' clinical learning experiences: Outcomes and processes.* Dordrecht: Springer; 2019: 185–207.
66. Jackson D, Trede F. The role of reflection after placement experiences to develop self-authorship among higher education students. In: S. Billett, J. Orrell, D. Jackson, Valencia-Forrester F, eds. *Enriching higher education students' learning through post-work placement interventions.* Dordrecht: Springer; 2020.
67. Billett S, Choy S, Tyler M, Smith R, Henderson A, Tyler M, Kelly A. *Refining models and approaches in continuing education and training.* Adelaide: National Centre for Vocational Education Research; 2014.
68. Billett S, Le AH. Engaging young people in occupations served by vocational education: Case study from healthcare. *International Journal for Research in Vocational Education and Training (IJRVET).* 2024;11(2):200–222.
69. Billett S. Building VET systems to advance communities: Beyond responsiveness. Ammattikasvatuksen aikakauskirja. 2024;26(1):98–104.
70. Organisation for Economic Co-operation and Development. Jobs for all: Initial report. Paris: OECD; 2009.
71. Billett S. Constituting the workplace curriculum. *Journal of Curriculum Studies.* 2006;38(1):31–48.
72. Malle BF, Moses LJ, Baldwin DA. Introduction: The significance of intentionality. In: Malle BF, Moses LJ, Baldwin DA, eds. *Intentions and intentionality: Foundations of social cognition.* Cambridge, MA: The MIT Press; 2001: 1–26.
73. Richards J, Sweet L, Billett S. Preparing medical students as agentic learners through enhancing student engagement in clinical education. *Asia-Pacific Journal of Cooperative Education.* 2013;14(4):251–263.
74. Teodorczuk A, Mukaetova-Ladinska E, Corbett S, Welfare M. Deconstructing hospital dementia practice: Using social activity theory to inform education approaches. *Advances in Healthcare Sciences Education.* 2015;20(3):745–764.

2 Occupations, occupational knowledge and its learning
Origins and legacies

Historical origins and contemporary imperatives of learning through work

Across human history, most of the learning associated with the exercise and development of occupational capacities has arisen through practice.[1,2] That process of learning has supported, sustained and advanced communities across time, cultures, communities and continents. This includes the learning that arises through the innovations that have sustained and transformed occupational practice in response to new demands, technologies and requirements of those who use the goods and services provided by those occupations.[3] In an era of schooled societies,[4] with its powerful discourse privileging learning within hybrid institutions such as early childhood centres, schools, colleges and universities, and largely through the act of teaching, it is necessary to highlight the important contributions that learning through work has made and continues to make. Of course, educational institutions and acts of teaching are important for modern societies and for individuals' development, contributing to the development of occupational capacities. There is often no practical alternative for much of the focussed instruction that occurs within these institutions. This includes the kinds of structured educational experiences that cannot be provided elsewhere, or in the scale and kinds of ways needed for contemporary societies. Yet, it all too easy to deny, ignore or downplay the contributions of learning through the circumstances of practice. The interest in, and engagement with, workplaces as environments for learning differs across communities and cultures. For instance, whereas learning through work is an essential feature of most vocational education programmes in Germany and Switzerland, in France, work is often seen as being something that needs to be separated from education as a legacy of French republicanism.[5,6]

Yet, even in countries that include workplace experiences as part of tertiary education, the privileging of educational institutions often persists. Their compulsory and mandated attendance, commitment of societal resources, the physical and social entities they comprise and their intentional strategies for promoting learning and certification of occupational knowledge all promote their

DOI: 10.4324/9781003519416-3

legitimisation. Unsurprisingly, given the societal investment in these institutions, they are privileged within the public, governmental and scientific discourses. One consequence is to discount learning that arises through educative experiences outside of this institution. These experiences are often labelled negatively (i.e., informal, non-formal learning) because they occur outside of the physical and social circumstance of educational institutions or as a product of the experiences afforded students. More than mere labelling, this has led to claims and assumptions that such learning is being limited to the immediate circumstance of its occurrence (e.g., concrete, fixed, not-transferrable).[7] Such an assumption suggests that entire working populations would cease to learn adaptable knowledge beyond their participation in educational programmes in and across their working lives, which has been shown to be incorrect.[8] The evidence from specific studies of learning through work indicates that amongst the learning outcomes through practice is the development of adaptable knowledge.[8] And, despite claims that experiences within those institutions and from teaching are generative of adaptable knowledge, perhaps the most common problem those institutions face is a lack of transferability of what has been learnt to other circumstances.[9] This problem is particularly experienced by graduates, such as those who have studied medicine, as they move from educational programmes into the actual practice of their occupations.[10] So, there is a need for a more open discussion about how best occupational capacities can be developed and the role that experiences in work settings can play: They need to occur without being constrained by contemporary sentiments within schooled societies.[4]

Discussed here are the origins of the need for specific occupations, the occupational knowledge to be learnt and how the processes of their learning have evolved across continents. More than presenting a historical treatise, the aim is to redress the orthodoxy in schooled societies of domination and privileging of learning arising through hybrid institutions (i.e., schools, colleges, universities) and teaching. It aims to offer a more informed, legitimating and worthy role for learning through work within the public, policy, and scientific discourses. Part of addressing those challenges is redressing assumptions about the standing of those occupations. Whilst valued and important, across human history, many occupations learnt through practice have not enjoyed high societal esteem, even when they are central to realising the needs of those societies. More than providing a mere historical backdrop to a consideration of learning through work, which would be worthwhile on its own terms, it is important to acknowledge, understand and elaborate the role that learning through practice has played across human history and which continues to this day, which is often not adequately reflected in the public, governmental and scientific discourses.

In making this case, the next section discusses the key roles that learning in and through work has played to support and sustain humanity (i.e., individuals, communities and nation states). Next, the processes through which that learning has arisen are seen as comprising what is afforded by the circumstances of production and provision of services, on the one hand, and on the other, the active engagement by learners.

The historicity of learning through work

It is helpful now to consider the historicism of learning in and through the circumstances of practice (i.e., paid work) to elaborate the phenomenon of learning in the circumstances of occupational practice that has played such an important role across human history in supporting and sustaining communities. As foreshadowed, the exercise of occupational practice and its learning have been inseparable across most of human history, and out of necessity in those physical and social settings where that work was conducted.[1] That necessity was borne out of the need for developing the skills required for that work intergenerationally, perhaps most often in small and family businesses and through responding to local and situational requirements and needs, access to materials, and opportunities.[11] Often, the processes and outcomes of that learning were quite specific to particular work settings or communities, partially out of its own peculiarities, but also to maintain difference and advantage from other workplaces. For instance, in European mediaeval cities, each enterprise would protect the product it generated through secrecy and by binding apprentices to possessing specific knowledge. This knowledge would not be shared with the guild whose role was to authorise and regulate the craft, to avoid jeopardising competitive advantage. It is often assumed that mediaeval guilds played a key role in the organisation and development of skills; however, this appears to be far from the case, as they were primarily involved in authorisation and regulation of who could practice, not the preparation and advancement of workers. Guilds did, however, administer regulations about the conditions and treatments of apprentices, including certifying them to be 'journeymen'[i] and then committing them to practise as trades workers. The key point here is that whenever work is being conducted, learning is also occurring and often through processes that engage novices to become the next generation of skilled workers. As Lave stated, it is difficult to identify instances of practice that exclude learning.

Early and impressive accounts of skill development through work are those provided through what occurred within Early Imperial China. The context is important here. The need to meet societal needs and the ability to mass produce artefacts for human use arose far earlier in China than in Europe and Scandinavia. This was to meet the needs of a very large population. This included those living in cities who enjoyed amenities such as running water and sewerage disposal and an entire range of products that were produced by artisans and were organised and regulated far earlier than in the West. There were also organised forms of central and provincial governments, all of whose needs for goods and services had to be met for the continuity of this longstanding empire. That required considerable numbers of skilful practitioners able to respond to the needs of this advanced society.[12,13] For instance, a census in 1085 recorded that the Chinese Empire had a population of over 100 million people, whereas in 1086, the Doomsday Book recorded that the British population was between 1.75 million and 2 million people.

The difference in population and level of societal sophistication generated particular needs for skilled workers and their learning. Yet, long before this time, the evidence is of the intentional development of skills required for these kinds of tasks and the mass production of artefacts required to build houses, cover their roofs and produce metal tools and weapons, and the capacity for their production seems to arise through practice.[14] Large and highly decorative copper vats manufactured in the Shang dynasty (1600 BC) required skilful work including the bringing together of different sets of skills to produce and construct these vats. Stone moulds were manufactured and used to mass produce knife blades in the Zhou dynasty (1050–250 BC). Intricate bronze trigger mechanisms for crossbows, comprising three separate parts that had to be precisely cast to function effectively, were mass manufactured in the Qui dynasty (221–206 BC).[12]

Also, because of the scale of the societal demand for artefacts and materials for the construction of buildings, a modular approach was adopted for the manufacture of artefacts and these building materials and in ways that enabled the mass construction of buildings.[14] As mentioned, a noteworthy point here is that because of the scale of the population, skilled work focused on the mass production of artefacts rather than a skilled worker being able to make an entire house, for instance. Hence, what constituted a skilled worker in China at that time was shaped by these societal and cultural circumstances and in ways which are quite different from those that were to occur much later in Europe. That is, in European communities where the population of communities was far smaller, craft workers might be required to make an entire item, which was largely the norm before industrialisation.[15] Moreover, at this time in China, coins, drainage pipes, arrow heads, tiles, etc. were all mass produced. There is even evidence of the highly adaptive use of skilful work at that time. For instance, during the Qing dynasty, the so-called terracotta army was manufactured to accompany and protect the first Emperor into the 'after-life.' The clay that was used to make these warriors exhibits a very high level of consistency, indicating that it was deliberately manufactured to meet the specific requirements of this work.[16] Of those that have been uncovered, it has been found that each warrior is unique in some way and great differences are evident across the entire cohort of warriors. Yet, potentially, only eight different moulds were used to make them, albeit in a multitude of different configurations to realise the uniqueness of each warrior.[12] Each warrior was manufactured by a team of workers whose activities were overseen by a supervisor whose initials were marked on each completed warrior. To demonstrate the adaptiveness of these workers, it seems that they were potters whose work had primarily been associated with producing pipes for the reticulation of water in the nearby imperial capital of Xian.[14] They adapted their pottery skills to produce the cohorts of warriors. Beyond skills associated with the use of the moulds to produce the warriors were those of glazing and painting them in unique ways which were exercised through the production of this significant warrior cohort.[16]

The production of highly intricate porcelain items, many of which feature complex shapes and many layers of glazes,[13] became renowned within the Tang dynasty (618–906 AD). Then, to meet the needs of currency for financial activities in the Song dynasty, the Imperial mint is estimated to have produced over 6 billion coins a year.[12] The production of these coins required stone moulds into which molten metal was poured, followed by their cleaning, honing and preparation for use as a currency. This production required high levels of organisation for the production and use of the moulds, subsequent production activities, the securing of metal ore and fuel to melt the metal and a distribution system to transport the finished coins across the Empire. Doubtless, also there was quality control and associated mechanisms to protect the currency of the coins.

A later account of this kind of work is available from the Jingdezhen kilns in the Ming dynasty (1368–1644). This city is famous for its white porcelain which was used for the massive sets of porcelain for the Imperial Palace.[17] For instance, the order for the Imperial Palace in 1577 comprised over 170,000 items that had to be uniform in design and appearance and to have a high standard of finish.[12] An account is provided by a French missionary of how these porcelain pieces were produced from his visit to the kilns much later in the 18th century: he reported watching a cup pass through more than a dozen hands, one worker giving it an initial shaping on the wheel in a matter of seconds, another setting it on a base, another pressing it into a mould to make sure its size was uniform, another polishing it with a chisel and so on.[12] The missionary reported that up to 70 people were involved in the production of a single item. In 1743, division of labour employed in the decoration of a large set of dishes such as those referred to above was described in the following way:

> If the painted decoration on each piece is not exactly alike, the set will be spoiled. For this reason, the man who sketched the line will learn sketching, but not painting; those who painted, study only painting, no sketching; by this means the hands acquire skills in their own speciality and their minds are not distracted. In order to secure a certain uniformity in their work, the sketches and painters, although kept distinct occupy the same house.[12](p.217)

These examples from early imperial and later in China indicate that, more than the mass production of artefacts, there is also the development of artefacts requiring high levels of skill and also processes that require understandings and practices dependent upon significant knowledge and the coordination of a range of skilled artisans. All this skilful knowledge was learnt through practice. Similar examples are likely available from a range of other countries, particularly in Europe, Britain and Scandinavia, where the developments of artefacts and production of goods also became a key feature of evolving societies; what was valued and needed across points in their national development changed over time and in different ways according to their specific circumstances.

The overall point being made here is that the kinds of artefacts and goods required to meet the needs of these communities arose in different ways and at different times and are manifested in diverse ways, but the common thread is that these capacities were learnt through practice and the uses of these capacities were not restricted to the initial circumstances of their development. As indicated in the examples above, workers developed the capacities to innovate and adapt and this, indeed, was a necessity to respond to changing circumstances, needs and the vagaries of the demands placed upon them.

A shift from learning through practice to being taught in educational institutions

Despite being utilised effectively for over a millennium and preparing skilled workers across a range of European and Asian countries, the traditions of learning through practice were largely displaced by industrialisation.[18] At different points of time and in different ways across countries that were industrialised, the small and family businesses that provided these goods and services were incrementally and sometimes rapidly replaced by factories, and specialised facilities for services such as healthcare becoming sites of production and service. One of the features of this change was that, rather than engaging in entire occupational tasks, like in China beforehand, the reorganisation of work often divided occupational practices into small units of work.[19] This changed the kinds and ranges of tasks that comprise existing occupations, transforming them and generating new occupations and occupational activities to be learnt and, in many instances, doing so away from learning about the entire retinue of occupational tasks. It was the loss of these small and family businesses' roles in the development of skills, and the arrival of a range of new occupational practices, that precipitated the need for the occupations that were central to the emerging industrial economy to be prepared in hybrid educational institutions. This process progressed in different ways across nation states, depending upon their circumstances and historical moments. For instance, in Germany the need for these skills coincided with the formation of the new nation state and as well as developing the kinds and quantum of skills required by the nascent nation, there was also a focus on civic education to assist young people to become aligned with its values and sentiments.[20] Hence, there were more general educational provisions being advanced; at the same time, across modern society was the important step of having compulsory education for children. The initial focus on much of educational development across many nation states was on the education of young children. Yet, in distinct ways and through different institutional arrangements, this led later to the development of education provisions for occupational preparation largely being conducted within tertiary education institutions.[15]

So, with the advent of 'schooled societies' arose hybrid educational institutions and programmes designed to develop occupational capacities that were unlikely to remain remote from the circumstances of practice. It was concluded that the kinds of knowledge needed to perform occupations could best be developed through experiences in these kinds of settings.[4] Indeed, perhaps most humans now live in 'schooled societies' (i.e., those in which schooling is comprehensive and ubiquitous) where educational institutions are legitimised, and their discourse, precepts and practices are pervasive and often taken for granted as being the most efficacious way of learning. The discourse of education or 'schooling' can be limited in its explanatory reach, however, primarily because it focuses on what occurs within such hybrid institutions and through processes of instruction. It tends to privilege specific accounts of learning and knowing, and overly emphasises declarative forms of knowing (i.e., those that can be stated and written down) and the didactic or teacherly transmission of knowledge. A key and fundamental shift in the advent of these hybrid institutions was from an emphasis on individuals' learning, to them being taught, which overturned the evidence over millennia of how the development of occupational capacities might best progress. Moreover, what was to be learnt was determined by nation states, their bureaucracies or religious bodies.[21] Indeed, through this process, the concept of curriculum changed from being something about individuals' learning journey across the life course to being about achieving the goals of the institution where education occurred.[22]

It is noteworthy that, despite their longstanding contributions to advancing societal and personal needs, the processes of mimetic learning (i.e., observation, imitation and practice) that had served humanity well across the millennia often became viewed as a limited mode of learning. That is, it was associated with mimicry as mindless copying. Moreover, within the educational, governmental and related academic discourses, the mode of learning through practice frequently earned the erroneous moniker of 'informal' learning.[2,23] Consequently, a process that focused on intentional learning as directed by individuals and that often included demanding cognitive and physical engagement and appropriation was viewed as being posterior to the process of learning through teaching. That is, a process requiring individuals to understand what is to be learnt, then attempting to approximate and increasingly improve performance to perform as well as the observed task, became marginalised. Curiously, as the shortcomings of learning experiences in educational institutions tend to be understood and the lack of being able to adapt what had been learnt in the classroom to circumstances outside of it became apparent, a reappraisal of how learning had occurred through such processes occurred. For instance, within the model of reciprocal teaching and learning[24,25] and cognitive apprenticeships[26,27] that became prominent there was a revisiting of the kind of processes that had been displaced by schooled societies and the educational discourse. Anthropological studies of learning through practice became fashionable and were reinvigorated and engaged with at this time.[28–31] These accounts almost universally sought to emphasise active learning by individuals as meaning makers rather than as students being taught, and the importance of providing an environment and guidance to support their learning.[25,32] All of this is reminiscent of what had occurred across the past millennia in and through work. Yet, what this interest demonstrated was that a detailed, comprehensive account of this process of learning through work remains incomplete. Of necessity, advancing such an account necessitates identifying and elaborating factors that inform it on its own terms, not those of educational institutions and their discourses, which it predates.

These observations notwithstanding, the discussion here is not to downplay the important contributions that schooling, teaching and educational institutions play or the vital contributions that 'schools' and 'schooling processes' make to individuals' learning and development and societal progress. Sometimes the focus on learning through work is seen as being about undermining what occurs in education.[ii] Instead, the quest here is for other premises and models of educative experiences and learning processes to be embraced as being worthwhile, legitimate and purposeful, albeit in ways that are distinct from what occurs in, through and by educational institutions; that is, to acknowledge and optimise the worthwhile and adaptable learning that occurs outside of those institutions and programmes.[8] Importantly, it involves changing the perspective that views learning as being a product of hybrid process derived from teaching and intentional educational experiences, to an acceptance that there is no separation amongst doing, learning and the remaking of occupational practice.[33] There is often no need, on its own terms, to make learning happen because this occurs all of the time as individuals engage in thinking and acting. When they engage in intentional goal-directed activities, such as those at work, the legacies are twofold: (a) changes within individuals (i.e., learning) and (b) contributions to the ongoing remaking and transformation of cultural practices that comprise occupations. As individuals engage in activities shaped by particular circumstances and points in time, they are both learning through these experiences and contributing incrementally to the evolution of occupational practices, albeit enacted in particular circumstances of practice.[33] Prior to the advent of schooled societies and mass schooling, this form of learning through and remaking of occupational practice was almost solely responsible for ensuring human progress and continuity.[34] These processes were enacted across human history and realised innovation and development[35] not only to develop canonical occupational practice, but also to make changes to it in response to the everyday challenges that arise through practice. Consequently, we need to understand more about how those processes of learning through work or practice progressed so that we can understand, apply and support those processes in the contemporary era.

How learning through work progresses

We need to know more about how learning through work progresses. As indicated earlier in this chapter, records from Early Imperial China provide highly detailed descriptions of the bureaucratic ordering of work and workers, including who is allowed to produce what and where, and how it can be traded.[17] Yet, despite all these detailed records, there are seemingly no accounts of how these skilled workers developed their occupational capacities. Indeed, only a very few written accounts of the processes of skill development appear to exist in pre-modern societies. It has been suggested that perhaps these processes were not of interest to those who were able to write and those preparing such documents.[iii] Or perhaps what was ordinarily occurring through observation, imitation and practice was so obvious that it did not warrant mentioning. So, apart from the accounts referred to above, to date, few others have been identified reporting the processes of learning and support for that learning. An academic archaeologist specialising in excavating ancient kilns[iv] in China advised that rhymes and mnemonics may have been used within communities such as those producing pottery and porcelain to pass on processes and ways of achieving skilful outcomes. But, beyond that, little else is known.

However, there may also be a very plausible explanation for this lack of mentioning in these historical records. That is, this learning occurred as part of individuals' everyday engagement in their work activities, and as such it was not worthy of mention by societal elites who comprised aristocrats, theocrats, bureaucrats and academics who viewed such activities as being not worthy of serious consideration.[v] It was rarely the subject of any teaching or direct guidance or specialised training facilities and resources as we might expect in contemporary school societies. Instead, it was an outcome of novices' engaging in work, possibly within family or community, and where they had the responsibility to learn their occupation mimetically through work, rather than being taught by somebody. Indeed, as mentioned, much of this learning likely arose through active processes of observation and imitation, opportunities to practise and, occasionally, direct guidance of more informed co-workers (i.e., mimetically).[1]

In the anthropological literature, the few instances of direct guidance by more expert workers sometimes refer to a more experienced worker intervening when what needed to be learnt could not be achieved through discovery or observation and imitation. For instance, accounts of learning pottery[36] refer to more experienced potters verbalising the processes that they are engaged in completing so that novices can understand. There are references to experts placing their hands upon those of novices when trying to assist them to understand the feel for fashioning pots on a potter's wheel.[37] So, there were instances of direct guidance as and when this was required, although evidence of what would be taken contemporaneously as teaching seems to be largely absent. However, those forms of guidance were seemingly reserved for circumstances and tasks that were unlikely to be learnt through observation and imitation alone, rather than being a commonly provided means of support for learning by more experienced co-workers.

In sum, before schooled societies, which largely arose in late modernity as consequences of industrialisation and formation of modern nation states in Western countries and elsewhere, institutionalised educational provisions were limited to a few occupations, mainly those for elite professions. Yet, even then, much of students' learning occurred through engagement in practice and in circumstances of work practice. For instance, medical education in Hellenic Greece largely comprised students acting as assistants to medical practitioners and directly taking care of patients in their homes and in the absence of more experienced practitioners. Noteworthy here is that such a process was found to have limitations and led to the introduction of anatomy classes and the production of textbooks.[38] The lack of opportunity for learning physiology led to the need for anatomy classes; similarly, the lack of sustained interactions with medical practitioners and the limits of learning that could be secured through these interactions necessitated the codification of medical knowledge into textbooks, which then could be read by the students independently of their access to being able to observe and be guided by experienced medical practitioners.

These accounts suggest that when seeking to understand how individuals learn outside of educational provisions, in circumstances of practice for instance, the educational discourse may not be particularly helpful in describing these processes and their outcomes. However, its fundamental concepts and precepts can be helpful for articulating the forms, contributions and potential limitations of learning through practice in a way that can be understood more broadly. Also, in seeking to revitalise and emphasise the worthiness of learning through the circumstances of practice, adopting the educational discourse can be helpful in that process of legitimisation. In seeking to understand the geneses of these processes, it is worth noting the similarities of these processes across cultures and circumstances and what they comprise.

Learning through work practice: similarities, workplace affordances and individuals' engagement

This section offers a preview of how the processes of learning and the circumstances of practice have been enacted across history and culture, drawing attention to three key factors. First, these processes have been reported across history and culture. The second and third factors relate to what is afforded or provided in the practice circumstance, on the one hand, and on the other, how individuals come to engage in work and learning in developing the capacities for the enactment of the occupational capacities. The conceptual framework here of the duality between workplace affordances and individual engagement has been found to be useful in understanding learning through work in the contemporary era.[39] These processes are elaborated in later chapters. Here, they are introduced amongst other concepts to provide an initial overview of how learning in the circumstances of practice was supported and occurred in earlier times. These propositions arise from a review of historical and anthropological literature[40] and are used to illuminate how learning practices for occupations occurred across a range of cultures and countries, from which can be imputed how these occupations were learnt over time. Importantly, these accounts provide instances of how intentional learning activities occurred outside of educational programmes and institutions.

Similarities across time and cultures

Seemingly, quite consistently across continents, regions, and cultures, throughout human history learning through work has been the most common and central means for the initial and ongoing development of individuals' occupational capacities and for the continuity of key cultural practices. As noted, these have been essential for the existence and progress of societies and communities.[34] The similarities in how this learning occurred across Europe, Asia and, likely, elsewhere, are noteworthy. The most common sites for that learning in Europe, Scandinavia and Asia were within the family or local workplaces. Whether referring to learning to make pottery in India,[41] Japan[37] or China,[12-14] local family and community settings are commonly reportedly as sites of this learning and the reported processes of participation and learning appear to be quite similar. It seems that this mode of occupational preparation was orthodox and accepted and had largely been effective in engaging successive generations in the development of skilful work. Although transformed by industrialisation across these countries, workplace experiences still play an important role in the initial preparation of occupational skills and their further development across working lives.[42-45] The difference in the contemporary era is that, whereas previously this would have been taken as the most common and efficacious mode of educative processes, in the era of schooled societies, it is now often being seen as posterior to what occurs in educational institutions and through teaching. This can lead to its contributions being undervalued, misrepresented and not fully utilised. As is now being more broadly realised, this positioning comes at a cost in situations in which development of skilful knowledge is most important for meeting current needs and responding to emerging challenges in the requirements of occupational practice.

In the following sections, and in overview for what is elaborated in later chapters, primary consideration is given to duality: what is afforded by work settings in terms of opportunities, guidance and support that can assist individuals in those environments to learn the kinds of knowledge that are important for occupational practice and the specific requirements of those work settings. Those affordances, or invitational qualities when engaging in work activities and interactions, can be positive or negative, depending upon whether they hinder or assist in individuals' access experiences and guidance to effectively support their learning.[39] What is evident though is that these affordances are not wholly objective. That is, whether they are helpful or hindrances depends upon their utility for the individuals who either accept or reject the invitation to participate. What for one individual will be useful in structuring and guiding experiences might for another frustrate their efforts to learn. For one individual, a routine problem-solving activity will lead to the enhancement and refinement of what they know, can do and value, while for another individual the same task represents a nonroutine problem-solving activity that can variously extend what they know, can do and value or be so novel as to generate dissonance and being overwhelmed. This merely indicates that it is how individuals come to engage with what is afforded to them which is central to their learning and development in person-dependent ways. Hence, it is important to understand the kinds of personal practices that are most likely to be helpful in the development of their knowledge to practise effectively in work settings.

Experiences afforded by work settings (practice curriculum and educative experiences)

In considering what is afforded individuals to assist their learning, it may be helpful to divide them into two kinds. First, there are the activities and interactions that are afforded them, which includes the sequencing of experiences and how individuals are allowed to participate in them and for what purposes. This represents pathways of experiences that novices and more experienced workers progress along in moving from engaging in tasks that might have little consequences of harm through to those where error costs are far higher. It is referred to as the learning[30] or practice curriculum.[46] Invitations to participate in progress along this practice curriculum are likely to be mediated by workplace practices, including those of experienced workers and owners and managers of those work settings. Likely, most workplaces have some form of practice curriculum, although it may not be recognised as such, because it is accepted practice about how a novice would progress in that work setting; that is, not permitting novices to engage in activities that are beyond their competence as it might jeopardise the goods or services being provided. Second, there are the intentional experiences that are provided to augment and extend the experiences that come from participating in work activities and interactions. These are referred to as practice pedagogies and are often, but not always, distinct from the kind of teacherly approaches utilised in educational institutions. Indeed, these pedagogies are often embedded within work activities and interactions and are likely to be unhelpful if separated from them. That is, both concepts are inherently associated with what occurs within occupational practice, although not commonly referred to as such.

These bases of what is afforded through work settings in terms of activities and interactions that are goal directed, and how individuals come to engage with what is afforded them, are essential in elaborating an account of learning through practice, and understanding how support for that learning is afforded in the circumstances of practice. So, it is also helpful to discuss the nature of the occupational tasks to be learnt and how cultural and societal factors shape how this work and learning is and needs to be valued and organised.

Learning through work across human history

Within this chapter, it has been proposed that across human history, learning through work has been the overwhelmingly key source of the development of occupational competence, as have the innovations and advancements that have progressed what constitutes occupational practice and its requirements. These processes of learning and innovation have been essential for the progress of humanity, as well as for individual learning and development. We would not exist as a species had not learning and innovations of these kinds been exercised in responding to the needs of humanity for both the most basic requirements for survival and to enrich human life. These requirements and their learning through practice have been the key means for learning about, addressing and advancing human needs. These needs include securing nutrition, shelter and care, not to mention those capacities required by societies to function, progress and develop cultural and social practices. Seemingly, most of these have been learnt through work, until the most recent of times. For the majority of working individuals, across most of human history, these outcomes have been secured by learning through work. Even now in contemporary schooled societies, with educational institutions supporting much of the initial development of occupations through programmes in schools, vocational colleges and, increasingly, universities, there remains a strong need for practice-based experiences to support the required outcomes.[47] Moreover, beyond the initial provision of occupational skills, there is a need for ongoing learning across workers' lengthening working lives that will most likely be supported through learning experiences in workplaces and their work.[48]

The central point here is that these learning processes and innovations have most likely been secured as part of everyday work activities. Therefore, we need to acknowledge these contributions and reposition this process within the lexicon of learning and development and bring it more centre stage in processes such as educational provisions for initial and ongoing occupational development, not to mention considerations of lifelong learning and educational provision more generally. This chapter has set out an overall understanding of how these processes of learning have arisen through history, culture and situation and yet, surprisingly perhaps, have quite common formats and offer means by which in an era of schooled societies can be used to effectively illuminate, elaborate and advance arrangements to support learning for, through and across working lives.

Notes

i The phrase journeyman is misleading. Its origins appear to derive from the French term pertaining to a day – de jour – and refers to a period of day labour that apprentices were required to engage in which necessitated them of ten travelling distances to find that kind of work
ii A head of the nursing school tried to prevent my dissertation being made public, claiming that it would undermine recent efforts to have nurse education be undertaken within university settings.
iii This comment was made by the librarian at the Joseph Needham Centre at the University of Cambridge, John P.C. Moffett.
iv Prof Nigel Wood from the University of Oxford.
v When I submitted one of my first manuscripts from my PhD on situated cognition in hairdressing salons to a prestigious American journal, one reviewer wrote "hairdressing, what next door to door salesmen."

References

1. Billett S. *Mimetic learning at work: Learning in the circumstances of practice.* Dordrecht, The Nertherlands: Springer; 2014.
2. Marsick VJ, Watkins K. *Informal and incidental learning in the workplace.* London: Routledge; 1990.
3. Ellström PE. Practice-based innovation: A learning perspective. *Journal of Workplace Learning.* 2010;22(1/2):27–40.
4. Billett S. Learning in the circumstances of practice. *International Journal of Lifelong Education.* 2014;33(5):674–693.
5. Greinert WD. *Vocational education and training in Europe: Classical models of the 19th-century and training in England, France and Germany during the first half of the 20th.* Luxembourg: Office for Official Publications of the European European Communities; 2005.
6. Troger V. Vocational training in French schools: The fragile State-employer alliance. Paper presented at: Towards a history of vocational education and training (VET) in Europe in a comparative perspective, 2002; Florence.
7. Tennant M. Is learning transferable? In Boud, D. & Garric, J. (eds) *Understanding learning at work.* Routledge; 2012: 165–179.
8. Billett S. *Learning in the workplace: Strategies for effective practice.* Sydney: Allen and Unwin; 2001.
9. Royer JM, Mestre JP, Dufresne RJ. Introduction: Framing the transfer problem. In: Mestre JP, ed. *Transfer of learning from a modern multi-disciplinary perspective.* Washington: Information Age Publishing; 2005: vii–xiv.
10. Cleland J, Leaman J, Billett S. Developing medical capacities and dispositions through practice-based experiences. In: Harteis C, Rausch A, Seifried J, eds. *Discourses on professional learning: On the boundary between learning and working.* Dordrecht: Springer; 2014: 211–219.
11. Gimpel J. *The Cathedral builders.* New York: Grove Press; 1961.
12. Ebrey PB. *China: Illustrated history.* Cambridge: Cambridge University Press; 1996.
13. Barbieri - Low AJ. *Artisans in early imperial China.* Seattle, WA: University of Washington Press; 2007.
14. Ledderose L. *Ten thousand things: Module and mass production in Chinese art.* Princeton, NJ: Princeton University Press; 2000.

15. Hanf G. Introduction. Paper presented at: Towards a history of vocational education and training (VET) in Europe in a comparative perspective, 2002; Florence.
16. Portal J, ed. *The First Emperor; China's terracotta army*. London: The British Museum Press; 2007.
17. Kerr R, ed. *Chemistry and chemical technology: Part XII: Ceramic technology*. Vol 5. Cambridge: Cambridge University Press; 2004.
18. Greinert W-D. European and vocational training systems: The theoretical context of historical development. Paper presented at: Towards a history of vocational education and training (VET) in Europe in a comparative perspective; October, 2002; Florence.
19. Kincheloe JL. *Toil and trouble: Good work, smart workers and the integration of academic and vocational education*. New York: Peter Lang; 1995.
20. Gonon P. *The quest for modern vocational education: Georg Kerschensteiner between Dewey, Weber and Simmel*. Vol 9. New York: Peter Lang; 2009.
21. Print M. *Curriculum development and design*. 2nd ed. Sydney: Allen & Unwin; 1993.
22. Billett S. The personal curriculum: Conceptions, intentions and enactments of learning across working life. *International Journal of Lifelong Education*. 2023; 42(5):470–486.
23. Eraut M. Informal learning in the workplace. *Studies in Continuing Education*. 2004;26(2):247–273.
24. Palinscar AS, Brown AL. Reciprocal teaching of comprehension-fostering and comprehension-monitoring activities. *Cognition and Instruction*. 1984;1(2):117–175.
25. Brown AL, Palinscar AM. Guided, cooperative learning and individual knowledge acquisition. In: Resnick LB, ed. *Knowing, learning and instruction, essays in honour of Robert Glaser*. Hillsdale, NJ: Erlbaum & Associates; 1989: 393–451.
26. Collins A, Brown JS, Newman SE. Cognitive apprenticeship: Teaching the crafts of reading, writing and mathematics. In: Resnick LB, ed. *Knowing, learning and instruction: Essays in honour of Robert Glaser*. Hillsdale, NJ: Erlbaum & Associates; 1989: 453–494.
27. Newman D, Griffin P, Cole M. *The construction zone: Working for cognitive change in schools*. Cambridge: Cambridge University Press; 1989.
28. Lave J. Tailor-made experiments and evaluating the intellectual consequences of apprenticeship training. *Quarterly Newsletter of Institute for Comparative Human Development*. 1977;1:1–3.
29. Lave J. *Cognition in practice: Mind, mathematics and culture in everyday life*. Cambridge: Cambridge University Press; 1988.
30. Lave J. The culture of acquisition and the practice of understanding. In: Stigler JW, Shweder RA, Herdt G, eds. *Cultural psychology*. Cambridge: Cambridge University Press; 1990: 259–286.
31. Jordan B. Cosmopolitical obstetrics: Some insights from the training of traditional midwives. *Social Science and Medicine*. 1989;28(9):925–944.
32. Rogoff B. Observing sociocultural activity on three planes: Participatory appropriation, guided participation, apprenticeship. In: Wertsch JW, Alvarez A, del Rio P, eds. *Sociocultural studies of mind*. Cambridge: Cambridge University Press; 1995: 139–164.
33. Billett S, Smith R, Barker M. Understanding work, learning and the remaking of cultural practices. *Studies in Continuing Education*. 2005;27(3):219–237.

34. Billett S. The practices of learning through occupations. In: S.Billett, ed. *Learning through practice: Models, traditions, orientations and approaches.* Vol 1. Dodrecht: Springer; 2010: 59–81.
35. Epstein SR. *Transferring technical knowledge and innovating in Europe 1200–1800.* London: London School of Economics; 2005.
36. Gowlland G. Learning craft skills in China: Apprenticeship and social capital in an artisan community of practice. *Anthropology and Education Quarterly.* 2012;43(4):358–371.
37. Singleton J. The Japanese folkcraft pottery apprenticeship: Cultural patterns of an educational institution. In: Coy MW, ed. *Apprenticeship: From theory to method and back again.* New York: SUNY; 1989: 13–30.
38. Clarke ML. *Higher education in the ancient world.* London: Routledge & Kegan Paul; 1971.
39. Billett S. Learning through work: Workplace affordances and individual engagement. *Journal of Workplace Learning.* 2001;13(5):209–214.
40. Billett S. Learning in the circumstances of work: The didactics of practice. *Education and Didactique.* 2011;5(2):129–149.
41. Menon J, Varma S. Children playing and learning: Crafting ceramics in ancient Indor Khera. *Asian Perspectives.* 2010;49(1):85–109.
42. Berryman S. Learning for the workplace. *Review of Research in Education.* 1993; 19:343–401.
43. Billett S. Relevance of workplace learning in enterprise transformation: The prospects for Singapore. *Singapore Labour Journal.* 2023;2(01):6–21.
44. Colin K. Workplace's learning and life. *International Journal of Lifelong Learning.* 2004;4(1):24–38.
45. Tynjala P. Perspectives into learning in the workplace. *Education Research Review.* 2008;3(2):130–154.
46. Billett S. Workplace curriculum: Practice and propositions. In: F. Dorchy DG, ed. *Theories of learning.* London: Routledge; 2011: 17–36.
47. Billett S. Realising the educational worth of integrating work experiences in higher education. *Studies in Higher Education.* 2009;34(7):827–843.
48. Billett S, Dymock D, Choy S, eds. *Supporting learning across working life.* Dordrecht: Springer; 2016.

Part II
Foundations of learning through work

3 Learning through work

Personal processes and social contributions

Learning through work

A comprehensive explanatory account of the processes of learning through work is necessary for understanding how it arises and how it can be effectively guided and supported to achieve both workers' developmental outcomes and the realisation of workplace goals. This understanding necessarily extends to addressing issues associated with individuals' development and employability and its contributions to the effective performance of work tasks and sustaining the viability of the private and public sector enterprises that deliver the goods and services individuals and communities need.[1] At the conceptual level, the explanation is not so distinct from those used to describe learning in other kinds of social and physical settings and circumstances, such as through community activities, educational programmes or cultural practices. This is because it emphasises the fundamental roles of contributions to that learning afforded by the social world and its institutions (e.g., schools, workplaces), on the one hand, and the personal processes and practices of engagement by individuals, on the other. Together, and relationally, these contributions explain and elaborate the duality that comprises the processes of learning in and through engagement in educational institutions, workplaces, community affiliations and practices. That duality can best be understood through a consideration of affordances and engagements.[2] Affordances comprise the suggestions from the social world that constitute invitational qualities of these settings' activities and interactions, that is, the kinds of activities and interactions that individuals are invited to and can engage in within the social practice (e.g., workplace). These invitations can be positive (i.e., supportive, inviting and engaging) or negative (i.e., being denied opportunities and restricted in what they can do). Alternatively, individuals' engagement with what is afforded to them can be understood as how they elect to engage with such invitations. That engagement is premised upon their process of experiencing in work setting, construal of what they experience and their response to it. This process of construal and construction of what is afforded them (i.e., what they perceive) is informed and shaped by, and shapes, what individuals know, can do and value (i.e., what they learn). Importantly, the duality between these personal processes and those afforded by the work settings is relational, not uniform.[3] It is person-dependent, in so far as how the kinds of workplace activities and interactions are construed and constructed (i.e., mediated) by individuals, as well as how the affordances are suggested to individuals. Ultimately, that duality is foundational to explanations about the process of learning through work, as they are for learning through other social institutions (e.g., schools, colleges, universities, community practices). It is also highly consistent with understandings within the social sciences about the relationship between structure and agency,[4,5] albeit manifested in the processes of learning in and through work.[6] So, it is this range of social and personal factors and the relationships amongst them that assist in explaining the processes of learning through work and in offering bases for how that might be managed, directed for particular purposes or improved.

In making its case, this chapter draws upon a series of practical investigations into learning through work that occurred over time and that represent a process of generating the explanation advanced above. Those explanations are by philosophy, social cultural constructivist theory, cognitive science, anthropology, sociology and historical studies. But they are primarily framed within cultural psychology as a discipline that informs about relations between cognition and culture. To set out some of the key precepts above, this chapter briefly outlines the evolution of that explanation through an overview of earlier studies. Next, key explanatory elements associated with how individuals construe, construct and organise their knowledge through what is broadly referred to as cognition are advanced as they relate to learning through work. Then, the personal and social legacies arising from processes of engaging in and learning through work are elaborated and, finally, the premise of these conceptions is discussed in summary.

Evolution of an explanation

The conceptions and explanations of learning at and through work advanced here primarily arise from a series of practical investigations undertaken across a three-decade-long period commencing in the early 1990s. The outcomes of the first decade of those studies were captured in a 2001 monograph (*Learning in the workplace: Strategies for effective practice*: Allen and Unwin) as well as articles in refereed journals leading up to and extending beyond that time. So, the formation of the ideas explaining learning at and through work as advanced here arose through the application of concepts and practices to make findings and advance deductions from these practical inquiries in workplaces and with different kinds and categories of workers. These outcomes, as noted above, emphasise both the individual and social contributions to meaning making and knowledge construction. In overview, the programme of research identified: (i) strengths and limitations of learning through work from studies grounded in practice,[7] (ii) conceptual elaborations of these findings,[8] (iii) interdependencies between social and individual contributions, emphasising the centrality of co-participation and participatory practices in explaining learning through work[9] and (iv) relational interdependencies between personal and social contributions.[3] These are now described and discussed in the sections below.

Contributions and limitations of learning through work

The practical inquiries commenced with securing accounts – through interviews, observations, surveys and critical incident data – of how workers learnt their occupational practices across a range of industry sectors through work to identify what contributed to the learning through their work activities.[10] Those studies were conducted in a range of workplaces including coal mining, secondary processing, food manufacturing, hairdressing and a range of service-related occupations. From those initial investigations, four sources or contributions of that learning were identified. These were:

i the authenticity of the work activities in terms of the knowledge to be learnt and applied;
ii level and kind of engagement required to achieve workplace goals;
iii access to indirect guidance (e.g., observation and listening); and
iv access to direct guidance (e.g., mentoring, modelling) by more experienced workers.[11]

The key premise here is that there is a cognitive legacy (i.e., learning as change) arising from engagements in goal-directed activities and that engagement leading to change, and the degree to which it is mediated by the requirements of those activities and what the individual already knows, can do and values. So, work activities have particular legacies as was described by Rogoff and Lave[12] when stating that 'activity structures cognition.' That is, the kind of activities you engage in shape the organisation, structuring and recall of what arises through those experiences. Consequently, activities that are authentic in terms of those that are required to be recalled and applied in work settings are likely to be efficacious for learning work-related applications; in other words, how what is experienced is subsequently organised, structured and indexed is central to its recall and utilisation in work activities. The changes in which individuals know, can do and value are then of the kind that are aligned with what is needed to be learnt for occupational performance and the requirements of specific circumstances in which they are practised.[8] What is evident across these four contributions is that they comprise both something that is afforded through the activities and interactions in work settings, as well as something that needs to be engaged with by learners, and by degree and in ways mediated by what those individuals know, can do and value (i.e., their personal epistemologies).

The authenticity of the experience afforded is only potent in so far as the individual engages with it and utilises the knowledge learnt through their processes of construal and construction. That is, if individuals are not interested in the experiences or view them as not worthwhile, they are unlikely to develop rich learning outcomes from that experience. This is the difference between what Wertsch describes as appropriation – the active process of learning – and mastery – superficial acquisition of knowledge.[13] Also, the level and kind of engagement in these work activities is dualistic in terms of, on the one hand, how the workplace affords opportunities for the individual to engage, and on the other, how they, in turn, elect to engage with those activities. Then, being able to observe, listen and learn through indirect guidance is premised upon the degree by which the individual is invited or permitted to engage in those ways, and then direct guidance by more experienced co-workers will also be a duality. For instance, the degree by which novices take more experienced workers to be a credible source of knowledge will shape how they come to engage with them.[14] There can be no guarantee that somebody deemed to be a supervisor or trainer will be engaged with in the same way as somebody who has the reputation for being highly competent and being able to resolve problems. So, these four contributions that were identified in earlier studies emphasise the duality between affordances and engagements. Thus, more than the activities individuals engage in, the quality of the interactions is also important.

References to problem-solving, observation, listening and monitoring progress with activities all emphasise the active process of meaning making and knowledge construction by the individual, rather than the more passive process of being taught, particularly when that teaching is highly didactic (i.e., projected by individuals). Indeed, only the reference to direct guidance could be seen as being associated with proximal guidance or teaching. What was found in these studies has also been more broadly supported through the Programme of International Assessment of Adult Competence (PIAAC) data[15] that refer to adults reporting the frequency and kinds of their problem-solving activities in work settings and the processes of learning. Workers of all kinds and classifications report engaging in learning through both routine and nonroutine problem-solving activities in work settings. These are held to be generative of both the refinement, reinforcement and honing of what they already know, can do and value in the first instance, and the generation of new knowledge for the latter kinds of problem-solving.[16] However, whilst the data from these early studies indicated how learning arose through activities and interactions in work settings, they also identified a series of limitations associated with that learning. It is noteworthy that workplace affordances are the primary defining quality of these limitations (i.e., primarily affordances), which are listed as:

i the risk of learning unhelpful or inappropriate understandings, construction of inappropriate knowledge;
ii there might be limits in gaining access to authentic activities from which to learn and hone;
iii the reluctance of experts or more experienced co-workers to share insights, assist with procedural development and otherwise guide the learning;

Personal processes and social contributions 47

iv there being a lack of access to expertise because it is remote or does not exist in the workplace;
v the opaqueness of some knowledge to be learnt which makes gaining access to it quite difficult; and
vi limits in the access to instructional materials whilst working.[17]

Added here is the level of effort or intentionality with which workers might engage in their work activities and interactions as well as limits to which they engage effortfully, either intentionally or because of other commitments and activities that limit the scope of the conscious and active approaches to learning which is necessary for constructing new knowledge, and these are addressed below.

Constituting learning through work

Workplace activities and interactions have a range of potential qualities associated with learning premised on engagement in goal-directed activities. These activities are variously familiar or novel to individuals and there are particular processes of learning through work and interactions with others and through observing and taking account of the physical and social clues and cues about the conduct of work. Together, these contributions assist in the construction of the knowledge required for work performance. Importantly, the data from those studies indicated that changes (i.e., the learning) arising through engaging in these activities were primarily about reinforcing, refining and honing what is already known, or being generative of new knowledge. A precept here is that learning is nothing more or less than change in what individuals know (i.e., their conceptual knowledge), what they can do (i.e., their procedural knowledge) and what they value (i.e., their dispositional knowledge). Hence, those changes were mediated by work activities and interactions, as well as by individuals' engagement with them. Yet, this learning arises in ways needing to be understood in terms of both the activities and interactions, on the one hand, and individuals' engagement with them, on the other. It is also important to be reminded here that what constitutes the novelty of the activity, the kind of interactions that occur and the interpretations of the suggestions (i.e., clues and cues) from the social and physical world are, to some degree, person-dependent. That is, there is no objective basis for making claims about what is afforded individuals (e.g., novelty of activities, interactions, etc.) as these are essentially personally subjective. What is a rich and/or nonroutine learning experience for one individual is potentially a mundane and routine experience for another.

Therefore, individuals' engagement in tasks that are familiar to them is likely to lead to honing, refining and reinforcing what is already known, can be done and valued. However, engaging in tasks that are novel to individuals can lead to them transforming or extending what they know, can do and value. So, the latter is generative of new learning for individuals or extending or even transforming their cognitive structures (i.e., what they know), procedural capacities (i.e., what they can do) and dispositions (i.e., what they value). But the former is important for improving performance. Technically, this is referred to as engagement in increasingly mature approximations of modelled tasks.[18]

From a cognitive perspective, this is seen as being the difference between problem-solving that is routine (i.e., engaging in familiar tasks) and that which is nonroutine (i.e., engaging in novel tasks), and from a perspective associated with transfer is whether the new learning comprises 'near' or 'far transfer.'[19] The point here is that the degree by which the activities are familiar to the individual has consequences for their subsequent learning and can also be understood from the perspective of problem-solving and transfer. The person dependence is also salient here. That is, what for one individual is routine problem-solving, for another is nonroutine, and similarly with transfer being variously 'far' or 'near' depending upon the individual's experiences. For instance, for the medical students or recent interns who are working in an emergency department on a weekend, the confronting consequences of automobile accidents, drunken assaults or drug overdoses can be potentially overwhelming, because all of this is new and confronting. However, for the experienced emergency physician, these are almost routine tasks they confront every weekend, and they have well-honed procedures for treating these patients' conditions, and managing their own personal equilibrium (i.e., well-being).

One concern here is that if such experiences are too overwhelming, unhelpful learning outcomes might arise: dissonance, confusion and withdrawal. For instance, junior doctors, nurses, and the like are overwhelmed by experiencing stress and often elect to leave those occupations.[20] Hence, the issue of readiness becomes important for engagement in and effectively learning through workplace experiences. Added here also is the zone of potential development to which Vygotsky referred,[21] that is, the degree by which what is experienced can be comprehended and responded to in ways that have the potential to generate productive learning outcomes, or if the experience is so novel that it cannot be constructively engaged with within the scope of potential learning. This is then when the guidance of more experienced others and what is referred to as the Brunerian concept of zone of proximal development arises (see discussion below about these differences). For instance, the experienced emergency physician would need to help medical interns with the kind of procedures needing to be undertaken immediately to ascertain an accident victim's injuries to prioritise those that are potentially life-threatening over other injuries. Similarly, if new technologies or work processes that are totally novel are introduced, effective or constructive learning outcomes are unlikely to be realised without guidance. Many readers will have experienced travelling to a country whose language is different from the one or ones with which we are competent. Even the scant knowledge learnt though guidebooks and online language tutorials they have undertaken is rendered useless by how the language is being used and the speed of its delivery in ordinary daily practice.

It follows that readiness in terms of individuals' ability to engage productively with what they encounter in work settings is central to the kinds and qualities of meaning-making and construction of knowledge in which they engage. One element of readiness is the degree by which what is experienced and learnt in one setting is recognisable in another. For instance, a problem arises when the activities experienced in educational settings, with their particular social and physical environment, do not necessarily lead to outcomes that provide individuals with the ability to recognise and apply what they have understood and learned from a different environment to others, referred to as the 'transfer problem.'[22,23] So, generally recognisable bases for the application of that knowledge in other settings, such as in other workplaces, are important for the ability to adapt to circumstances other than those in which the knowledge has been developed.

Co-participation and participatory practices

As advanced and rehearsed above, the basis of the explanation of learning for and through work is premised upon a duality between personal processes of experiencing and responding, on the one hand, and what is afforded individuals in terms of work activities and interactions, on the other. This then led to the explanatory concepts of co-participation[24] and participatory practices.[25] These concepts emphasised the need to understand two kinds of participation: (i) how individuals are afforded opportunities to participate in workplace activities and interactions and (ii) how they elect to participate in them (e.g., based on effort, engagement, knowledge). This then led to the concept of participatory practices: the acknowledgement that there are bases within both the personal and the social situation that are both interdependent and relational.[26] Hence, in some situations, individuals are invited to participate and be supported, encouraged and guided; in other circumstances, this happens much less so, or they are even denied being able to participate in work activities and interactions. Equally, it is how individuals elect to participate that captures the other aspect of the duality. For instance, it was found that even workplaces that provided rich opportunities and support for learning did not necessarily lead to workers' enthusiastic engagement.[2] That usually only occurred if the individuals intentionally wanted to engage in that way; the interview data provided examples of individuals who rejected invitations to engage and learn, despite being offered guidance and support. All of this helped to explain that more than just considering sets of social and personal factors as shaping individuals' learning and development, it was the interdependence and relations between these factors that are essential to this explanation. Conceptually, this led to the concept of relational interdependence between the personal and the social contributions to learning in and through work.[3] That is, the interdependence between these two sets of factors is inherently relational.

Such an account is not, however, constrained to explaining learning in work settings. It applies equally to what occurs within educational settings (i.e., what activities and interactions are afforded students and how they come to engage with them) and processes such as assessment, recognition of learning, conceptions of curriculum and how participation in cultural activities can be understood. For instance, it can help in understanding how individuals with different experiences and knowledge come to engage in educational settings and how those settings are more or less invitational to them. It is also helpful for understanding how innovations in workplaces can be encouraged and enacted, and by whom (see Chapter 5). Ultimately, the duality that comprises the relationship between what is afforded to individuals in work settings, on the one hand, and how they come to engage with them, on the other, is central to explanations about learning through work.

Relational interdependence: individuals' engagement, learning and practice

Findings from these earlier practical investigations and explanations were generative of the realisation of the interdependence between what the physical and social environmental affords and how individuals came to engage in and learn from those experiences. However, that duality is not uniform, as it personally and situationally relational.[3] What for one individual will be a new or novel task will for another be quite familiar; and whereas the former has a potential for transforming their knowledge, for the latter it will be a process of honing and refining what is being progressively learnt. Equally, what is afforded can be engaged with differently based upon individuals' roles and position within the workplace and how they are pressed to comply and conform. For instance, the kinds of discretion afforded workers differ enormously upon their status and standing in the workplace which determines the scope of their activities, what they can make decisions and the kinds of tasks and problem-solving activities in which they are permitted to engage. Hence, the duality of personal and workplace factors is relational, in so far that it is person-dependent, including how the kinds of workplace activities and interactions are construed and constructed (i.e., mediated) by individuals.

It follows that a key quality of this constructive process of meaning making, indexing and recall is the degree by which individuals engage in those activities effortfully and intentionally.[27] These personal bases for the engagement in the construction of knowledge are central here. Both individual and social constructivist theories concur that meaning making is fundamentally undertaken by individuals.[28] So, as proposed above and indicated below, the mediation of social circumstances and settings are powerful and essential components to knowledge construction, organisation and recall. Yet, it is necessary to emphasise the personal processes of that construction, as it is individuals' effortfulness, agency, intentionality and direction and focus of their active engagement that ultimately mediate how and what they experience and therefore, what they learn. For instance, Wertsch[13] refers to two processes of individuals' engagement and meaning making and social and cultural contexts: mastery and appropriation. Whilst mastery is a form of learning in which individuals are uncommitted or lack belief, appropriation is a more engaged and active process of learning, usually arising from alignments between individuals' beliefs and what is being suggested to them.

So, these personal processes of learning are quite central to understanding how individuals learn in and through their work. Beyond the kinds of studies reported here, much if not the majority of learning across working life is mediated largely through individuals' own efforts. For instance, PIAAC data consistently indicate across a range of countries that workers report learning more from their own efforts than when being supported by other and more experienced workers.[15,16] In some ways, this finding is not surprising, given that the close guidance by others is not always available in work settings and workers will need to learn in response to new challenges and hone and refine what they know as they engage in their work tasks. However, that data are quite consistent in its reporting about the frequency of contributions to workers' learning in and through their work.[15] Beyond these processes, it is important to consider the kind of outcomes that arise from learning in and through work.

Personal and social legacies of learning through work

When individuals engage in their occupational practice, two kinds of legacies arise. First, as has been noted above, the process of engaging in thinking and acting is generative of change in individuals (i.e., learning and development). That change can comprise the generation of new knowledge (i.e., fresh concepts, novel perspectives, new means of achieving goals), which can quantitatively and qualitatively change what individuals know, can do and value. However, and second, beyond individuals' learning arising through those experiences, the activities they engage in are continually being remade or transformed through these processes.[29,30] So, social legacies in the forms of changes in work-related norms and practices also arise through individuals' learning in and through work. These two legacies are now briefly discussed.

Personal legacies of learning through work

As noted, the personal legacies of learning through work are shaped by social factors and contributions, but in ways that are personally mediated. Importantly, although the individual or the personal are often seen as being the antithesis of the social, quite the opposite is the case. That is, the personal is the epitome of the social.[21,31] As long acknowledged,[32] it arises through individuals' ontogenetic development. That comprises the ongoing negotiations amongst the contributions to the experiences individuals encounter when engaging with the suggestions of the social world and as mediated by what they know, can do and value, including that shaped by the brute factors of maturation.[33] As has been shown, what is suggested to individuals every day by the social world shapes what they know, can do and value, which also progressively and incrementally shapes their ontogenetic development across individuals' life histories.[34] In other words, individuals' processes of experiencing are themselves a product of earlier or pre-mediate experiences.[35] That development subsequently shapes how what occurs later is construed and constructed, and this pertains to individuals' sense of self and subjectivity as well as knowledge associated with occupations. As Harre[31] proposes,

> Personality becomes socially guided and individually constructed in the course of human life. People are born as potential persons, in the process of becoming actual persons takes place through the individual transformation of social experience.
>
> (p.373)

That is, these processes are person-dependent by degree. The cultural psychologist Valsiner[35] refers to everyday experience as being unique to individuals in some way. Central to the personal is the human intentionality[36] and agency[37] that shapes individuals' meaning making. To make that point, it is worthwhile distinguishing between occupations and vocations. Occupations are cultural practices that arise from historical sources and cultural variations and are manifested situationally. People and communities need doctors, nurses, hairdressers, carpenters and so on to meet their needs. Those occupations transform over time as social requirements and expectations change and practices of these occupations are transformed by new discoveries, technologies and ways of being practised. This means that occupations are what Searle refers to as institutional facts.[38] They arise and are manifested from these historical, cultural and situational imperatives.

In contrast, vocations are personal facts.[39] That is, individuals elect what constitutes their vocations and the degree by which they will exercise their effort and interests to engage with them. Essentially, individuals have to assent to an occupation being their vocation.[40] No amount of social pressure can alone make an individual want to engage wholeheartedly and effortfully with an occupational practice in which they are not interested and which they do not find fulfilling. More than that, not only is it assenting to accept an occupation as a vocation, but it is how it is enacted or practised. What individuals bring to the enactment of the occupation, their knowledge about it, capacities to enact and values associated with it, comprise the occupation in practice. Without the person, there is nothing being practised. What that person brings not only gives life to the practice but also shapes it in particular ways. Dewey[40] uses the example of a small room with nothing in it apart from a window and telescope to meet this point. He suggests that to a brute realist, the room seems relatively barren and constricted. However, to the astronomer who lives there, it opens up onto the entire universe.[41] Indeed, it is this personal mediation of experience – the process of experiencing – through which humans learn and come to practise, as has been advanced throughout. Factors associated with human capacities, intentionality and agency are those that shape what people do. Indeed, Valsiner[21] proposes that:

> Most of human development takes place through the active ignoring and neutralisation of most of social suggestions to which the person is subject in everyday life.
>
> (p.393)

He goes on to suggest that this process of mediating what is experienced is essential to buffer individuals' personalities against the constant demands of social suggestions. He continues,

> Hence, what is usually viewed as socialisation efforts (by social institutions or parents) is necessarily counteracted by the active recipients of such efforts and can neutralise or ignore a large number of such episodes, aside from single particularly dramatic ones.
>
> (p.393)

Moreover, Valsiner[35] invites a reconsideration of some precepts which have long been established within theorising about the social world and human development. As foreshadowed, he suggests that the popular portrayal of Vygotsky's concept of the zone of proximal development is quite counter to what was originally intended, which was to give licence to individuals' agency and intentionality through engagements in activities which they found interesting and engaging. Here, he proposed that Vygotsky was referring to the zone of potential development that is shaped by the exercise of interest, such as in play:

> In play, the child is always higher than his (sic) average age, higher than his usual everyday behaviour; he is in play as if a head above himself. The play contains, in a condensed way, as if in the focus of a magnifying glass, all tendencies of development; it is as if the child in play tries to accomplish a jump above the level of his ordinary behaviour.... Play is the resource of development, and it creates the zone of nearest development. Action in the imaginary field, in the imagined situation, construction of voluntary intention, the formulation of life plan, will motivate, this all emerges in play.[35,42]

As can be seen, this conception is the opposite of what was proposed through the concept of zone of proximal development in which the locus of the learning is premised upon interaction with a more experienced interlocutor, who can provide access to this knowledge. Vygotsky's contemporary, Leontyev,[43] referred to appropriation as individuals making their own from what they experience in the social world, which is quite different from being fully shaped by it.

Central here is the concept of individuals' ontogenies, that is, the development that has risen across their personal histories from the accumulation of personal processes of experiencing. Through having had experiences in particular social circumstances, individuals learn moment by moment (or microgenetically) from what they experience.[44,45] This process incrementally and over time shapes what they know, can do and value, and in ways which have to be person-dependent to some degree. This is because the set of experiences and individuals' experiencing of them, their accomplishments and how these are realised and the continual process of engagement, reconciliations, appropriations, accommodations and dissonances that they encounter are person specific. These occur, moment-by-moment, every day and in different ways across individuals' life histories. Consequently, there is an inevitability that individuals' mediation of construction of knowledge and their role in remaking occupational practices are person-dependent in some ways. This has been demonstrated when individuals generate concept maps of a common goal or task.[46] For instance, when hairdressers were given the task of generating concept maps from the same set of labels about hair structures and the procedure of colouring hair, it was possible to identify the different sources of experiences that had led to the very diverse concept maps they constructed.[47] So, human learning and development arise continuously through microgenesis, the moment-by-moment process of everyday experiences, and this process, incrementally, contributes to ontogenetic development (i.e., development across the life course) which in turn mediates what individuals know, can do and value as they engage microgenetically. Hence, the personal legacies of engaging in work activities are both incremental learning and contributions to individuals' ontogenies. Collectively, serially and accumulatively, these experiences are inevitably person-dependent and, as a collective set of experiences, come to constitute what comprise their personal curriculum.[48]

Social legacies of learning through work

Given that occupations are cultural practices that arise through history, culture and situation[49] and are transformed by, and co-occur with, human learning and development,[50] these practices offer useful platforms to consider the social legacies of learning through work. What is proposed here is that occupational practices are transformed through history in response to human needs, are shaped by specific cultural needs and mores and are manifested in particular circumstances (i.e., the preferred and required practices of workplaces).[51] For instance, the need for occupations for cutting human hair arose across human history but took on different forms for males and females (i.e., hairdressing for females and barbering for males). Moreover, there are particular practices and practical considerations for hairdressing and barbering across cultures (e.g., beading in African countries, removal of facial hair in Southeast Asia). Yet, the particular workplace may have specific emphases on hairdressing (e.g., fashionable cuts or catering to elderly ladies) that constitute its focus and continuity.⁵² However, the existence, advancement and enactment of these practices are also shaped by how individuals engage with, remake and transform them. Hence, explanations of the geneses, manifestations and advancement of these practices need to account for the contributions of both institutional (i.e., those of the social world) and personal factors (i.e., those pertaining to individuals' development) and, of course, the relations between them. Sitting within all of this are also brute facts (i.e., those of the natural world) that shape the needs for many occupations, on one hand, and yet on the other is how humans come to engage, enact and learn through them. Accounting for these factors includes those associated with maturation, which shapes how individuals engage with the world as they experience it. So, more than the social suggestion, consideration of what constitutes occupational practice and how it is engaged and advanced necessarily includes a consideration of personal and brute factors and relations amongst all three. The educational implications here are powerful and enduring. Sites and circumstances of practice, and individuals' engagement in them, have been the key source of that learning across human history.⁵¹ The advancement of the human species has, in some ways, been largely premised upon how individuals learn through their occupational practice and innovate. These processes have been supported by practice curriculum (see Chapter 6) and pedagogies (see Chapter 7), and as directed by their personal epistemologies, as they learn, practise and innovate (see Chapter 8).

So, in sum, the occupations that individuals practise and that are needed by their communities are shaped by history, culture and situation. As noted, they comprise cultural practices that are dynamic and responsive to historical developments (e.g., new technologies), new cultural practices (e.g., requirements for particular occupations, ways of working) and situational requirements (e.g., those imperatives that arise locally and may be quite situationally distinct). Yet, they are enacted in specific circumstances of practice and in ways of responding to routine or nonroutine tasks, and it is through responding to the nonroutine tasks that these occupations are remade in the circumstances of practice.⁵⁰ This consideration emphasises the importance of how culture is sustained and advanced through its enactment. Importantly, for a consideration of occupational practice, there is a co-occurrence between individuals' learning and the remaking of the occupational practice.⁵³ It has been proposed that as individuals engage in their occupational practices incrementally, individually and collectively, they are contributing to a process through which occupations are continually being remade as requirements for occupational practice either slowly change or are transformed by new technologies. In this way, rather than change in occupational practices being characterised as a tsunami of change sweeping all before it, it is more like thousands of small waves of different kinds and intensity bringing about occupational change. For instance, an occupation like nursing is increasingly confronted not only by an ageing population of patients but also by increased frequency of demented patients. It is predicted that soon, as many as a third of all patients in hospitals in Western countries will have issues of dementia beyond the particular health-related issue for which they are being treated. Moreover, engagement in practice can also lead to the transformation of that practice as new circumstances arise and requirements change. Awareness of environmental impact has led to changes in practice associated with disposal of refrigerants or oil waste; understanding the dangers arising from construction workers encountering asbestos has led to transformations in renovation work. Some of these transformations can arise quite rapidly. For example, during the Covid-19 pandemic, patient care practices had to change quickly and radically. In some situations, instead of having patients being directly treated by numerous healthcare practitioners, the number of those in close contact was reduced to minimise the risk of infection to healthcare workers. Yet, these solutions had to be generated and implemented locally and quickly by healthcare staff. In this way, the practices of disease control work transformed. So, as Lave reminds us, 'knowledge always goes through reconstruction and transformation in use' (p.8).

Thus, individuals need to access and engage with the occupational knowledge that arises through history, culture and situation. Yet, the future development and learning of that occupational knowledge is dependent upon individuals acting on and with it in responding to requirements for the occupation in particular circumstances. Hence, cultural practices such as occupations co-occur with individuals' learning, with both processes being mediated by personal factors. Through that engagement and learning process with its legacies for individuals arises the remaking of occupational practices to address contemporary needs and requirements and, over time and through particular instances, the remaking of those occupational practices in response to emerging imperatives.

Learning through work

In sum and conclusion, what has been proposed above is an explanatory account for understanding learning through the circumstances of practice. First, some conceptual premises for understanding the phenomena of learning through work were advanced, emphasising the duality between, on the one hand, what is afforded by workplace settings, and on the other, how individuals come to elect to engage with them. This then led to a consideration of that duality in terms of it being both relational and interdependent. All of this emphasises the importance of considering not only the physical and social settings of the workplace, but also the personal history and readiness of individuals who come to engage in those settings. That then suggests that it is difficult to make judgements about work, learning and development without a consideration of both sets of factors, and the relationality between them. This discussion has emphasised that learning and development are two separate concepts best captured in the distinction between microgenetic and ontogenetic forms of development. However, central here has been found to be the intentionality, capacities and engagement of individuals in ultimately mediating what they experience and learn.

These processes have been illuminated, elaborated and exemplified through empirical inquiries into learning through work. It is those inquiries that have identified that the social and personal legacies arising from both are founded on an interdependence between the person and the physical and social world they encounter. It was the search to understand the phenomena of learning through work that engaged and developed explanatory concepts. This included the basis of learning and development through work as being bidirectional and mediated by social sources and those from the brute world, and individuals' personal epistemologies and their mediation of what they experience. Third, this theorising contributes to our understanding of the socio-genesis of knowledge and, more broadly, human and societal development. It extends a consideration of the social origins and contributions of knowledge and knowing to individuals' personal histories and ontogenies. It also sought to balance understandings and to challenge some existing precepts, for instance, that there is nothing more social than the personal or the individual. It also questions the Vygotskian premise of knowledge arising firstly on the social plane and then becoming an intra-psychological attribute: How can anything be experienced if there is no basis for that experiencing? To deny the innate contributions of individuals' cognitive, neural and sensory systems, let alone what they have learnt across their lives – the capacities and understanding they have developed – suggests a very poor theorisation, as Wertsch and Tulviste[54] proposed earlier. Indeed, all of this suggests that inter-psychological processes cannot be understood without a consideration of the intra-psychological.

Finally, in consideration of learning occupational practice, all of this elaborates these practices as being mediated relationally across culture, situation and personal facts, including brute facts, which are part of our own personal experiencing. As stated in the introduction to this chapter, beyond understanding about how learning through work progresses and might be enhanced, a consideration of learning and development arising through everyday activities through engagement in culturally derived activities and interactions situated in specific circumstances also offers a means by which an understanding of human learning, cultural change and phylogenetic development arises.

References

1. Scribner S, Beach K. An activity theory approach to memory. *Applied Cognitive Psychology.* 1993;7:185–190.
2. Billett S. Learning through work: Workplace affordances and individual engagement. *Journal of Workplace Learning.* 2001;13(5):209–214.
3. Billett S. Relational interdependence between social and individual agency in work and working life. *Mind, Culture and Activity.* 2006;13(1):53–69.
4. Giddens A. Sociology. 3rd ed. Cambridge: Polity Press; 1997.

5. Hays S. Structure and agency and the sticky problem of culture. *Sociological Theory.* 1994; 12(1):57–72.
6. Billett S. Learning throughout working life: A relational interdependence between social and individual agency *British Journal of Education Studies.* 2008; 55(1):39–58.
7. Billett S. Situated learning – a workplace experience. *Australian Journal of Adult and Community Education.* 1994;34(2):112–130.
8. Billett S. Situated learning: Bridging sociocultural and cognitive theorising. *Learning and Instruction.* 1996;6(3):263–280.
9. Billett S. Learning through work: Workplace participatory practices. In: Rainbow H, Fuller A, Munroe A, eds. *Workplace learning in context.* London: Routledge; 2004: 109–125.
10. Billett S. Guided learning at work. *Journal of Workplace Learning.* 2000;12(7): 272–285.
11. Billett S. Workplace learning: Its potential and limitations. *Education and Training.* 1995;37(5):20–27.
12. Rogoff B, Lave J, eds. *Everyday cognition: Its development in social context.* Cambridge, MA: Harvard University Press; 1984.
13. Wertsch JV. *Mind as action.* New York: Oxford University Press; 1998.
14. Billett S. Towards a model of workplace learning: the learning curriculum. *Studies in Continuing Education.* 1996;18(1):43–58.
15. Organisation for Economic Co-operational and Development. *OECD skills outlook 2013: First results from the survey of adult skills.* Paris: OECD; 2013.
16. Billett S. Work, discretion and learning: Processes of learning and development at work. *International Journal of Training Research.* 2015;13(3): 214–230.
17. Billett S. *Learning in the workplace: Strategies for effective practice.* Sydney: Allen and Unwin; 2001.
18. Collins A, Brown JS, Newman SE. Cognitive apprenticeship: Teaching the crafts of reading, writing and mathematics. In: Resnick LB, ed. *Knowing, Learning and instruction: Essays in honour of Robert Glaser.* Hillsdale, NJ: Erlbaum & Associates; 1989: 453–494.
19. Royer J. Theories of the transfer of learning. *Educational Psychologist.* 1979;14:53–69.
20. Australian Institute for Health and Welfare. Challenges for the health workforce. In: Health Do, ed. Canberra: Australian Institute for Health and Welfare; 2024: 14–15.
21. Valsiner J. *The guided mind: A sociogenetic approach to personality.* Cambridge, MA: Harvard University Press; 1998.
22. Pea RD. Socializing the knowledge transfer problem. *International Journal of Educational Research.* 1987;11(6):639–663.
23. Royer JM, Mestre JP, Dufresne RJ. Introduction: Framing the transfer problem. In: Mestre JP, ed. *Transfer of learning from a modern multi-disciplinary perspective.* Washington: Information Age Publishing; 2005: vii–xiv.
24. Billett S. Coparticipation at work: Affordance and engagement. In: Fenwick T, ed. *Sociocultural perspectives on learning through work.* Vol 92. San Francisco, CA: Jossey Bass/Wiley; 2001.
25. Billett S. Learning throughout working life: Interdependencies at work. *Studies in Continuing Education.* 2001;23(1):19–35.
26. Billett S, Barker M, Hernon-Tinning B. Participatory practices at work. *Pedagogy, culture and society.* 2004;12(2):233–257.

27. Ericsson KA, Simon HA. *Protocol analysis – verbal reports as data*. Cambridge, MA: MIT Press; 1984.
28. Billett S. Mimetic learning at work: Learning through and across professional working lives. In: Billett S, Harteis C, Gruber H, eds. *International handbook of research in professional and practice-based learning*. Dordrecht: Springer; 2014.
29. Ellström PE. Practice-based innovation: a learning perspective. *Journal of Workplace learning*. 2010;22(1/2):27–40.
30. Hoyrup S, Bonnafous-Boucher M, Hasse C, Lotz M, Molller K, eds. *Employee-driven innovation: A new approach*. Basingstoke: Palgrave-McMillan; 2012.
31. Harre R. The necessity of personhood as embedded being. *Theory and Psychology*. 1995;5:369–373.
32. Baldwin JM. Personality-suggestion. *Psychological Review*. 1894;1:274–279.
33. Billett S. Sociogeneses, activity and ontogeny. *Culture and Psychology*. 2003;9(2):133–169.
34. Hodkinson P, Billett S, Bloomer M. The significance of ontogeny and habitus in constructing theories of learning. *Studies in Continuing Education*. 2004;26(1):19–43.
35. Valsiner J, van der Veer R. *The social mind: The construction of an idea*. Cambridge: Cambridge University Press; 2000.
36. Malle BF, Moses LJ, Baldwin DA. Introduction: The significance of intentionality. In: Malle BF, Moses LJ, Baldwin DA, eds. *Intentions and intentionality: Foundations of social cognition*. Cambridge, MA: The MIT Press; 2001: 1–26.
37. Archer MS. *Being human: The problem of agency*. Cambridge: Cambridge University Press; 2000.
38. Searle JR. *The construction of social reality*. London: Penguin; 1995.
39. Billett S. Personal epistemologies, work and learning. *Educational Research Review*. 2009;4 (3):210–219.
40. Dewey J. *Democracy and education*. New York: The Free Press; 1916.
41. Higgins C. Dewey's conception of vocation: existential, aesthetic, and educational implications for teachers. *Journal of Curriculum Studies*. 2005;37(4):441–464.
42. Vygotsky LS. Play and its role in the mental development of the child. *Soviet Psychology*. 1966;5(3):6–18.
43. Leontyev AN. *Problems of the development of the mind*. Moscow: Progress Publishers; 1981.
44. Siegler RS. Microgenetic analyses of learning. *Handbook of Child Psychology II* 2007;3(11).
45. Scribner S. Vygostky's use of history. In: Wertsch JV, ed. *Culture, communication and cognition: Vygotskian perspectives*. Cambridge: Cambridge University Press; 1985: 119–145.
46. Novak JD. Concept maps and vee diagrams: Two metacognitive tools to facilitate meaningful learning. *Instructional Science*. 1990;19:29–52.
47. Billett S. Subjectivity, learning and work: Sources and legacies. *Vocations and Learning: Studies in Vocational and Professional Education*. 2008;1(2):149–171.
48. Billett S. The personal curriculum: conceptions, intentions and enactments of learning across working life. *International Journal of Lifelong Education*. 2023;42(5):470–486.
49. Billett S. Situation, social systems and learning. *Journal of Education and Work*. 1998;11(3):255–274.
50. Donald M. *Origins of the modern mind: Three stages in the evolution of culture and cognition*. Cambridge, MA: Harvard University Press; 1991.

51. Billett S. Learning in the circumstances of work: the didactics of practice. *Education and Didactique*. 2011;5(2):129–149.
52. Billett S. Knowing in practice: Re-conceptualising vocational expertise. *Learning and Instruction*. 2001;11(6):431–452.
53. Billett S, Smith R, Barker M. Understanding work, learning and the remaking of cultural practices. *Studies in Continuing Education*. 2005;27(3):219–237.
54. Wertsch JV, Tulviste P. L. S. Vygotsky and contemporary developmental psychology. *Developmental Psychology*. 1992;28(4):548–557.

4 Occupations, situations and knowledge required for work

Knowledge required for occupations and work

It is important to understand what capacities are required for effectively performing work tasks because these become the goals for learning through practice. To inform how the processes and outcomes of learning through and for work might be evaluated, identified and optimised, it is necessary to understand how they are aligned with generating the knowledge required for the effective workplace performance, including dealing with new challenges. Through understanding what constitutes those performance requirements and the kinds of knowledge enabling them, it is possible to inform and evaluate the efficacy of work-related learning processes and how curriculum considerations, pedagogical practices and workers' personal practices can be best organised, enacted and evaluated. The delineation and detailing of these requirements are informed by precepts and propositions from studies of expertise and situational accounts of work performance requirements derived empirically. These sources suggest that effective work performance is premised on (i) a base of canonical occupational knowledge (i.e., needs to know, do and value) and (ii) situated requirements for performance in particular work settings, and adaptive capacities to respond to changes in both.[1] The first is associated with concepts, procedures and dispositions developed over time for the enactment of cultural practices referred to as occupations. There is also a need to account for the specific work performance requirements as these are not uniform across the circumstances in which those occupations are enacted, given the diversity and situated character of those requirements. At a more executive level is, third, the need for adaptability within both the canonical and situational domains of occupational knowledge, that is, the capacities that need to be developed by individuals either individually or in teams to perform in ways that can effectively realise those outcomes as well as remake and transform the occupational practice as new requirements emerge. To outline and elaborate these requirements in greater detail, three forms of knowledge central to that performance are advanced and discussed. These are domain-specific conceptual, procedural and dispositional knowledge, and the interdependence amongst them. Domain specificity, within the cognitive account of expertise, is aligned with a domain of occupational activity,[2-4] whereas within sociocultural accounts, it also refers to the situated domain of knowledge required for performance in a particular work setting.[5] As noted, added here is the capacity to adapt that knowledge to respond to new challenges and to change the practice itself. Importantly, it is both these domains of knowledge that individuals come to construct as their personal domain of knowledge that drives their work performance. However, there are distinct means through which each of these forms of knowledge (i.e., conceptual, procedural and dispositional) is likely to be constructed. Understanding how these forms of knowledge are constructed offers a platform to inform the requirements of occupational practice and situated performance and how curriculum, pedagogic and personal practices associated with learning through work are enacted.

In making its case, this chapter first elaborates and discusses the need for an informed account of what constitutes occupations and performance in work through an elaboration of considerations outlined above. This commences by proposing why an account of what constitutes work performance is necessary, because much of how work has been valued in the past is based upon supposition and biases of societal elites, rather than accounts informed by empirical investigation. The following section elaborates what constitutes the importance of canonical occupational knowledge, its situated and personal manifestation, making the case for considering these as specific domains of knowledge based upon such enquiries. In making this case, this chapter first elaborates these three domains of competence and processes underpinning their construction. The first two are essentially institutional facts (i.e., those arising from social institutions),[6] whereas the latter comprises personal facts (i.e., those arising from personal interest, capacities and processes).[7] So, whilst outlining the canonical and the situational, particular emphasis is given here to occupational competence being a personal domain. Following this, the three forms of knowledge that underpin that performance (i.e., conceptual, dispositional and procedural) and their interdependence are elaborated and discussed. Finally, considerations for the learning of that knowledge are advanced as a basis to understand how learning through everyday activities occurs, and how best it might be improved and elaborated.

Historical discourses of occupational practice

It is necessary to understand what constitutes the requirement for effective work practices based on informed and evidence-based accounts. This is important because across human history many of the earlier as well as current accounts of what constitutes the qualities and worth of occupational knowledge have been based upon suppositions and biases derived from speculation and societal privilege. Only in recent times have theoretically informed and evidence-based accounts of what constitutes those practices been available and accessible. Prior to discussing what constitutes the forms and structures of the occupational knowledge required for work performance and how it is learnt, it is necessary to emphasise why such informed understandings about what constitutes that knowledge are important. That is, there is a need to delineate the key kinds and categories of knowledge and their qualities objectively to inform and evaluate how they can effectively be learnt. In addition, there is a need to identify how that process can occur within and through work activities and interactions.

Put plainly, the standing and worth of occupational practice is deeply rooted in societal values and relations and these are rarely premised on empirically informed accounts. Across human history, it has been 'privileged others' (i.e., aristocrats, theocrats, bureaucrats and academics) who have influenced and shaped the worth of occupational practice and assumptions about what they constitute as well as how they need to be learnt.[8] Quite frequently, views about what constitutes occupational practice have been advanced in the absence of the voices of those who practise. This situation has led to distorted understandings and uninformed bases of what constitutes these practices, the knowledge required to practise these occupations and how this knowledge might be learnt.

For instance, many Western traditions and precepts about work and education for work emanate from Hellenic Greek philosophers.[8] In a highly socially segmented and gendered society largely owing its existence to slavery, in which societal elites viewed most forms of work with disdain, it is unsurprising that occupations were categorised hierarchically, as were the means of learning about them. For instance, Plato distinguished among three kinds of work: (i) artisans, (ii) artists and (iii) professions. Artisans engaged in activities such as building, carpentry, pottery and weaving, leading to the generation of tangible products or services. Artists comprise musicians, painters, poets and those who produced things that were concrete and also aesthetic. The professions were those occupations such as practising medicine, law, theology or military activities. Yet for Plato,

> Artisans' and artists' work belonged to that side of life which the average free born Greek citizen regarded as 'banausic' and unworthy of his serious attention.[9]
>
> (p.15)

These occupations were deemed to be unworthy of the efforts of free-born Greek males. Later, and similarly, Aristotle proposed that

> The citizens must not lead the life of mechanics or tradesmen, which is ignoble and far from conducive of virtue.[10]
>
> (p.167)

More than viewing these occupations as being low status were the qualities associated with individuals who performed those tasks. For instance,

Aristophanes referred to potters as 'stupid buffoons' because of the work they do; Plato suggested that the nurse and the tutor were of no worth for anything else. That is, what they knew was restricted, concrete and not adaptable elsewhere. Consistent with this view, Plato claimed that artisans were incapable of generating new ideas themselves. Instead, 'they have to wait for God to invent a solution' to the problems[11] (p.105). Plato, as a consequence, considered the lowest level of education was for those who worked with their hands and not with their minds,[9] categorising that work as technical, from the Greek *techne* – to make. It was also suggested that only a limited number of professions (e.g., medicine, law, military, and philosophy) were to be prepared for through a formalised provision of education. There were to be no such provisions for artists and artisans as they were not deemed sufficiently worthwhile to warrant such an education. These kinds of sentiments were not restricted to Hellenic Greece. For instance, in Imperial Rome, Cicero stated:

> Now in regard to trades and employments, which are to be considered illiberal and which mean, this is the more or less accepted view. ... all craftsmen are engaged in mean trades, for no workshop can have any quality appropriate to a free man. Least worthy of all are those trades which cater to the sensual pleasures: 'fishmongers, butchers, cooks, poulterers and fishermen' Cicero – De officiis (On Duties) 1.150 trans Finley.
> (1973/1999)[12]

It is noteworthy that Socrates, Plato and Aristotle all deemphasised the importance of human senses that are so central to performing arts and craft,[13] whilst emphasising reasoning of a particular kind, including that required of the professions. Perhaps, this was because senses were quality that all humans possessed, including women and slaves. Therefore, acknowledging the worth of senses would diminish their special standing as elites, based on supposedly higher order functions associated with reasoning which only they could perform. So, there are distinct cultural and societal valuings of the kinds of work undertaken, their worth and conduct and arrangements for their learning.

Yet, what this kind of supposition overlooks is that the development and enactment of skills through honing and refining of highly specific skills is required. Likely, most of those skills were developed through learning through observation, imitation and practice (i.e., mimetically),[14] as reported elsewhere in anthropological accounts[15] and also contemporary investigations of how individuals learn through their everyday work activities.[5] Possibly because much of the kinds of procedural knowledge required for those kinds of occupations had to be learnt in this way, without access to specialised educational provisions, this led to conclusions that such occupations were easy and did not require dedicated educational interventions. Moreover, we now know that the development of conceptual knowledge can also arise through these kinds of learning processes.[16] The kind of rehearsal required to develop many of the specific procedural skills of playing musical instruments and making artefacts could only arise through the concerted efforts and intentionalities of those who came to practise them. Essentially, these processes are underpinned by dispositions of rehearsal and rote kinds of learning that we now highly value in people able to learn such processes. Today, we refer to these processes as the intentional engagement in increasingly mature approximations of modelled performance.[17] Also not fully understood was that such learning arose not through solitary processes alone, but through being immersed in the circumstances of practice. It is within these circumstances that novices progressed through a series of activities aligned with their developing capacities (i.e., practice curriculum).[18] When doing so, they also had access to models of how work tasks need to be conducted and their outcomes,[19,20] and sometimes close guidance of more experienced co-workers (i.e., practice pedagogies).[15,21] In this way, they were likely engaging in a set of educative experiences structured by the work setting, although it was unlikely to be considered by them in these terms.[22,23]

Perhaps unsurprisingly, there were similarities in the valuing of skilled work in Imperial China and Hellenic Greece. Both societies were hierarchical, with elites who would never engage in the kinds of work undertaken by artisans and craft workers. Yet, in Imperial China, personal merit was valued so competent individuals could potentially enjoy elevated opportunities in ways unimaginable in Hellenic Greece. Also, skills such as calligraphy were a competency required for the merit-based public examination used for secure employment and promotion in the public service.[24] Those skills included demonstrating diligence and practice required not only to master the ideographic skills needed for written communication but also aesthetic and cultural prowess of the kinds that were disavowed within Hellenic Greece. It is noteworthy that Confucius was renowned as a competent archer. This valuing of skilful work also seems to be sufficient to warrant a questioning of the kinds of knowledge privileged by elites: declarative kinds. The Daoist philosopher Zhuangzi (369–286 BC) used a parable of a wheelwright talking to a learned general to describe the power of procedural knowledge over the concepts found in books:

> I see things in terms of my own work. When I chisel at a wheel, if I go slow, the chisel slides and does not stay put; if I hurry, it jams and doesn't move properly. When it is neither too slow nor too fast, I can feel it in my hand and respond to it from my heart. My mouth cannot describe it in words, but there is something there. I cannot teach it to my son, and my son cannot learn it from me. So, I have gone on for seventy years, growing old chiselling wheels. The men of old died in possession of what they could not transmit. So, it follows that what you are reading are their dregs.[24]
>
> (p.49)

This parable says much about the importance of procedural capacities learnt over time and through effort, the role that human senses play in the conduct of skilful work, and also the dispositions associated with the patience and diligence to develop those capacities and then their use. This parable also provides an early example questioning the privileging of declarative or discursive knowledge that has been and continues to be privileged in Western educational discourses. It is important to note that even today, much of what is seen as being knowledge is restricted to declarative knowledge in that discourse.

Indeed, emphasised are forms of knowledge and ways of knowing such as those exercised through kinds of haptic and sensory capacities that are not acknowledged or privileged in discourses of schooling and school societies, that is, their emphasis on declarative forms of knowledge and knowing (i.e., facts, concepts, propositions). Yet, it is the collective contributions of procedural, conceptual and dispositional capacities that are central to effective performance in occupational practices, not just the professions.[25] Importantly, most of these kinds of capacities are not easily taught didactically: they have to be learnt.[26] Yet, these aristocrats proposed that not only was the work undertaken by these practitioners of low worth, but also that they themselves were of low worth and incapable of demanding complex thought.

Similarly, theocrats, as another class of powerful social elites, also expressed sentiments about the worth of work based on their own suppositions, not based on any evidence. The word 'vocation' has its Latin root as *vocare*, which is to call – a summons, a bidding, an invitation to a particular way of life. However, that invitation was premised on views and beliefs about what constituted worthwhile work. For instance, some economic activities were seen as being distinctively more 'perilous to the soul' than others and the more commercial the motive, the more dangerous the activity became[27] (p.130). Hence, some work activities were held to be unworthy. With Calvinism, work was set to reshape the world in the fashion of the divine kingdom coming through one's dedicated labours to prove oneself as directed towards that view of fashioning.[28] Within such traditions, daily work became the design for what was characterised as the so-called Protestant or puritan work ethic; that is, for individuals to labour unquestioningly and without disrupting the status quo, which included religious beliefs and values. Noteworthy, Marx critiqued the concept of work ethic as workers being duped into false consciousness.[29] What he proposed was that this societal sentiment was reducing workers to being mere ciphers and subject to the demands of societal elites and directly contributing to their own servitude. Whilst containing elements of truth, what such a sentiment proposes is that if individuals found satisfaction, interest and fulfilment in their work, then they were being duped. If, however, workers were dissatisfied with their work and resisted and rebelled, they were being socially emancipated. This binary is conceptually satisfactory; what it denies, however, is how individuals come to see value and view the worth of their work and what potentially becomes their vocation.[28] Again, this rehearses the views of a societal elite that fails to account for the perspective of those who practice.

In more recent times in modern nation states, it has been bureaucratic mandates that have served to make distinctions and allocate worth across occupations. The formation of these nation states led to the rise of bureaucratic control associated with securing and maintaining that state. So, although a key outcome of modernity was the rise of individualisation, there was a desire for state-sponsored activities such as education to be aligned with the interests of the state, which included delineating occupations into hierarchies to serve its needs.[30] Moreover, entities such as occupations had to be ordered and calibrated in some way, and for specific reasons. For instance, the development of what are now referred to as professions arose from a concern to delineate and create occupational hierarchies. This included generating a set of occupations associated with science and technology that reflected changes in the kinds of work to be undertaken. Moreover, there were social motives behind such delineations. With the growing possibilities of individual emancipation, there was a societal process to distinguish those occupations deemed to be societally acceptable, as proposed by these elites, and efforts to preserve such occupations for the elites. Those seen to offer clean and decent work were to be reserved for societal elites and a growing middle class, and the pathway to those occupations became privileged and often only accessible by certain kinds of educational success. So, across human history, there has been a pattern of social elites influencing how occupations were to be valued, being subject to educational processes and who was able to access them. These seemingly had particularly lasting legacies in Western societies.

It is noteworthy that what occupations are seen as being desirable in the 20th century were not similar to suppositions advanced at the time of Plato, as indicated in Table 4.1. In this table, a scale of the social desirability of occupations[31] is presented. In the left-hand column are how they are classified, with Roman numeral I being the highest and VII the lowest. It is noteworthy that the hierarchy of desirability is characterised by the so-called mental-manual divide, and that the knowledge required to make things (i.e., techne) through skilful work features in the lower levels of desirability. Note, for instance, that in Class III, work involving routine non-manual activities (e.g., clerical work) is seen to be more socially desirable than the work of the self-employed, technicians and skilled manual workers, which in many instances would require far higher levels of occupational capacities. Within such delineation and hierarchies of work also come different demands and requirements for the recognition of work and the discretion afforded to workers.[32]

The point made here is that across human history, it has been privileged others who made judgements about occupations, usually without any informed basis. Moreover, these views have extended into considerations of what kind of work is deserving of organised educational provisions. It might be easy to view this as being an issue of the past, but as the examples above indicate, they have resonance today.

However, many academics have also contributed to delineating standing of work through different set of suppositions, often based on speculation rather

Table 4.1 Occupational social desirability[31]

Class	Occupations
Class I	High-grade professionals, managers, administrators and large proprietors
Class II	Lower grade professionals and managers, and higher-grade technicians
Class III	Routine non-manual workers
Class IV	Small proprietors and the self-employed
Class V	Lower grade technicians and supervisors of manual workers
Class VI	Skilled manual workers
Class VII	Semi-skilled and unskilled manual workers

than evidence. This is despite having the means by which such evidence can be secured. For instance, in ways reminiscent of Plato's propositions, the sociologist Bauman[39] states that

> The majority of people [are] locked into meaningless and degrading work that offers little opportunity for notoriety or fulfilment.
> (p.36)

He goes on to suggest that such activities are not worthy of individuals' key life projects. Yet, it is doubtful that such views were formed through engaging in discussions with individuals to whom he refers. Possibly, at the time that he was writing this book in Leeds, England, nearby were communities affected by the closure of coal mining sites that had a huge impact upon individuals and their communities. Miners and their families were publicly protesting about the way that their work was no longer valued even though it was clearly highly skilful and potentially challenging work.

Elsewhere, Wright-Mills,[40] who did interview some workers, came up with similar conclusions:

> For most employees, work has generally an unpleasant quality. If there is little Calvinistic compulsion to work among propertyless factory workers or clerks, there is also little bit of Renaissance exuberance in the work of the insurance clerk freight handler, or department store sales lady.
> (p.3)

Yet, he seemingly never interviewed enough informants to make conclusions about entire classes of workers and those who work. Fortunately, others offer different perspectives. For instance, Dewey was far more circumspect. He proposed that the worth of occupational practice is essentially what it means to those who enacted it and also their associates. He stated

> A vocation means nothing but such direction in life activities has rendered them perceptibly significant to a person, because of the consequences they accomplish, and are also useful to his (sic) associates.
> (p.307)

Pusey,[41] whose research projects interviewed and surveyed large numbers of middle-class Australian workers, also reached similar conclusions, claiming that:

> For nearly everyone work is a social protein, a buttress for identity and not a tradable quality.
>
> (p.2)

Similarly, Noon and Blyton (1997) refer to the diversity of work and the ways in which workers' experiences emphasise both satisfaction with work and alienation from it, and how this is expressed through patterns of cooperation and resistance to work.

These kinds of sentiments seem to be more closely aligned with the findings of recent projects about individuals' engagement with work and working life. Many individuals employed in forms of work that others might find to be low status and demeaning, such as aged care,[42] production processes[43] or wholesale fruit and vegetable market[44] workers, claim satisfaction in their work and find meaning within it. Moreover, these workers often reported taking pride in what they do and being seen as effective in that work. Furthermore, across these studies was not only the extent of discretion that workers have; they also needed to perform their work effectively, requiring the exercise of their agency. Hence, out of necessity, even occupations that would be viewed as having low status and seemingly precarious forms of employment afforded levels of discretion that were engaged with by those who were interviewed.

Such findings are also supported by those from the Programme of International Assessment of Adult Competence (PIAAC)[45] that indicate all kinds and classifications of workers engage in problem-solving in and through their work, and much of it of the kind that requires higher order thinking capacities and is, in turn, generative of those capacities.[32] This finding contradicts some common assumptions about the requirements of work and workers. For instance, it was found that technicians engage more frequently in nonroutine problem-solving than those classified as professional workers. This questions not only what Plato and others stated a long time ago, but also how occupations are presented in contemporary qualification frameworks that purport to advise about the different kinds and levels of knowledge required to perform work tasks. These frameworks are used by governments to allocate time and resources for the development of those occupational capacities. This is not to suggest that all individuals' work is rewarding or that individuals find worth within it. Indeed, many are likely not to adopt their work or occupations as their vocations, as did some of the aged care workers.[42] However, these differences in individuals' personal valuing of their work's worth to them suggests there is a need to go beyond the assumptions of social elites and societal sentiments and to engage with more broadly informed accounts about what constitutes the standing and worth of specific occupations; that is, not to view it in terms of being societally unworthy or the product of false consciousness, but rather as what it means to those who perform those occupations and the recipients of their enactment. So, this opening section has suggested that rather than relying upon the societal biases, assumptions of elites and suppositions of theologians, bureaucrats and academics, considerations of occupational requirements and worthiness need to be based upon a combination of empirical work and considered analysis.

Domains of knowledge: Occupational competence and work requirements

What constitutes domains of knowledge is important for capturing what constitutes the requirements for work performance, as foreshadowed. Competence is usually aligned with specific domains of activities that can be demonstrated through individuals' performances.[46] In particular, the idea that human competence is related to particular domains of activities was emphasised and evolved across three decades of research within cognitive psychology to understand what comprises human expertise and expert performance in fields such as work.[25,47] In essence, it was found that human performance, whilst having some levels of generalisability (i.e., cleverness or ability to manipulate knowledge), is associated with abilities for performing effectively within a particular domain of activities.[2,3,48,49] Hence, the idea of general performance measures or competences that can be applied across fields of practice has been found to be lacking.[3] Yet, outside of that domain, or if the rules of it were changed, even competent individuals would not necessarily perform any better than novices. For instance, expert chess players possessed a range of particular domain-specific skills, heuristics, organisation of knowledge and retinue of solution strategies that were essential for the performance;[4] however, when the rules of chess were changed, experimentally, these experts performed no better than novice players.[50] Importantly here, games like chess are associated with general capacities (i.e., ability to plan, think and act logically). Yet, the basis of effective performance was related to the specific practices of chess playing, not to general cleverness and adaptability to other activities and domains (i.e., the ability to manipulate what they know). From the literature on differences between novices and experts, the key attributes of experts' performance have been identified as their ability in terms of (i) effective categorisation of problems by likely solution strategies, (ii) effective monitoring of problem resolutions, (iii) seemingly instantaneous application of cognitive processes to problem-solving, (iv) accurate diagnosis of problems based on domain-specific principles and (v) effective use of solution strategies.[26] These are very useful for considering how experiences in work and educational settings can potentially develop these capacities.

Considerations of domains of knowledge and activities are not, however, restricted to cognitive psychological accounts of expertise: they are far more widely acknowledged. The cultural psychologist Scribner[51] refers to work activities as being sets of cultural practices 'involving socially organised domains of knowledge and technologies, including symbol systems' (p.13), thereby emphasising occupations as specific domains. Similarly, discussions on apprenticeship learning associated with particular domains of activities are also advanced by the sociocultural psychologist Rogoff.[52] Educational researchers concerned with developing specific capacities also refer to particular domains, such as when considering the learning within and for particular circumstances of practice,[53] such as the learning of problem-solving skills in mathematics[54,55] and literacy.[56] The same goes for those researchers who were seeking to address the issues of the lack of transfer from what is learnt within educational settings such as through cognitive apprenticeships,[49,57] reciprocal teaching and learning,[58] worked examples[54] and other instructional processes.[59,60] Here, domains of knowledge provide bases for understanding the scope and which knowledge can be adapted, and what constitutes those domains. Moreover, those focusing on the development of occupational capacities similarly refer to learning domain-specific knowledge.[17,61] Indeed, these perspectives are particularly helpful when considering occupational practices and what comprises competent performance at work, that necessarily introduces the idea of a particular domain of activities shaped by the work practices, settings and those participating in them.

A consideration of domains of knowledge, therefore, is helpful for understanding what constitutes performance in work roles. Occupational practices comprise quite specific sets of activities that have developed across human history arising from human, cultural and societal needs.[62] As noted, these practices have been delineated on the basis of societal esteem, standing and practicalities associated with their enactment.[63] As such, they represent sets of culturally derived understandings, procedures and dispositional qualities (i.e., values associated with their enactment). Occupations are, therefore, usually identified as a specific field of activities that have particular societal standing and personal meaning associated with their relationship to cultural or societal sentiments.[64,65] These extend to socially derived affiliations that include identifiable occupations (e.g., trades, crafts, professions, etc.), and occupational (e.g., trade unions, professional associations) and even geographical communities (e.g., farming or coal mining communities). In addition, there are the personal meanings including individuals' vocations that arise through association with particular occupations and become part of individuals' subjectivity or sense of self,[65] that is, the degree by which individuals come to identify with the occupation they practise. So, fundamentally and foremost, as occupations arise from the social world, they are institutional facts (i.e., that of society),[6] not the creation of individuals. However, through their engagement, individuals can assent to the occupations they practise becoming their vocations;[64] these are personal facts.[66] What the presence of these two distinct sets of facts suggests is that occupational competence needs to be considered on both the societal or social plane (albeit at the canonical and situational levels) and the personal one, all of which extends to the formation of that knowledge.

Common to these three kinds of domains is that they are constituted by three kinds of interrelated domain-specific knowledge: (i) conceptual – what people know, (ii) procedural – what they can do and (iii) dispositional – how

Table 4.2 Forms of knowledge and their characteristics

Form of knowledge	Characterisation and qualities
Domain-specific conceptual knowledge	– 'knowing that'[33] (i.e., concepts, facts, propositions – surface to deep; e.g., Glaser[34]) – what individuals need to know
Domain-specific procedural knowledge	– 'knowing how'[33] (i.e., specific to strategic procedures; e.g., Anderson,[35] Sun et al.[36]) – what individuals need to do
Dispositional knowledge	– 'knowing for'[33] (i.e., values, attitudes) related to canonical and instances of practice (e.g., Perkins et al.[37]), includes criticality (e.g., Mezirow[38]) – what individuals need to value

they are valued. These forms of knowledge are presented in Table 4.2. In this table, the forms of knowledge are presented in the left-hand column, and the right-hand column provides an overview of their characteristics and qualities. Clear distinctions are made between the forms of knowledge that permit 'knowing that,' 'knowing how' and 'knowing for,' premised upon what we know (i.e., conceptual knowledge), what we can do (i.e., procedural knowledge) and what we value (i.e., dispositional knowledge). This listing builds upon and expands and refines earlier taxonomies of knowledge such as Bloom's.[67] Those refinements include extending what counts as knowledge beyond the declarative or conceptual knowledge that often dominates definitions of what constitutes such taxonomies, to include procedural and dispositional forms of knowledge. In departing from those earlier constructs, what is often referred to as skills is captured within conceptions of procedural knowledge. That is, it accounts for both cognitive and psychomotor procedures, thereby acknowledging what Ryle referred to much earlier as the ghost in the machine.[33] Also distinguished from earlier constructs are other kinds of knowledge that shape how concepts and procedures are valued and engaged with, premised upon individuals' interests and values (i.e., their dispositions).[37,68]

Whilst able to be categorised as being distinct and having their own characteristics, qualities and levels, as discussed below, when engaged in thinking and acting, these three forms of knowledge are essentially interdependent. The arrows in Figure 4.1 depict the inherent interdependencies amongst these three kinds of knowledge. That interdependence is likely to be person specific and related to individuals' personal domain that comprises how these have been constructed and what individuals have come to value or find less useful in their experiences. For instance, in one study, a hairdresser had a negative experience with chemicals that are used to straighten hair. An outcome was that he, dispositionally, was reluctant to engage in straightening hair using such chemicals and discouraged others, including apprentices, from doing

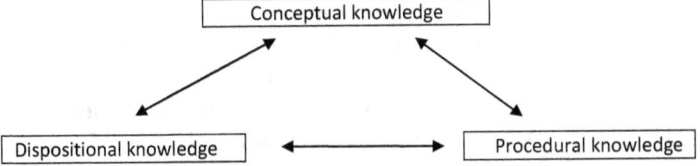

Figure 4.1 Interdependence amongst conceptual, procedural and dispositional knowledge.

so. In this way, a particular experience shaped how he came to view the concept of straightening hair, how that might be achieved and what would be the most efficacious means of achieving that outcome. Another person might have had quite different experiences and the organisation of that knowledge and dispositions towards that process might be quite different.

This interdependence is perhaps most noticeable in how individuals come to use these forms of knowledge as organised and shaped by their personal domains of knowledge. As with the above examples, these have been refined and transformed through those experiences, that is, when individuals conceptualise something that entails the process of engaging procedures in its recall and alignment with what is being considered, and these processes are underpinned by dispositions (i.e., how the individual values the concepts and exercises intentionality in enacting them). Equally, when exercising procedures, it is shaped by how they are conceptualised in terms of the goals to be achieved and the worthiness of those goals, which extends to the amount of effort to be directed towards achieving them, and in what ways. Moreover, our dispositions are shaped by concepts and the process of valuing and making decisions is shaped by the exercise of procedures, as with the above examples. Consequently, our everyday thinking and acting draw upon the interdependence amongst these three forms of knowledge, albeit in ways that are interdependent and likely to be person-dependent. That is, the experiences leading to the construction of personal domains of knowledge are shaped by an interaction amongst these three kinds of knowledge and that process continues as we have new experiences and engage in those that are familiar to us. However, that knowledge is relational and can only be understood through individuals' personal domains.

Importantly, these three kinds of knowledge and their interdependence underpin the requirements for occupational performance (i.e., the canonical), the kinds of concepts, procedures and dispositions that are appropriate to a particular circumstance of practice (i.e., the situational) and what individuals construe, construct that knowledge, including its organisation in memory, in ways that are person specific. The first (i.e., canonical domain of occupational knowledge) is a product of gathering perspectives and assembling them in way that represents what these practitioners need to know, do and value. The second is a grounded construct (i.e., situational domain of occupational knowledge) that is shaped by the circumstances in which the occupation needs to be performed and to realise goals germane to those circumstances. The third is constructed by individuals as shaped by their earlier experiences, beliefs, interests and aspirations (i.e., the personal domain of knowledge) that is shaped by individuals' processes of experiencing.

As noted, the kinds of experiences are likely to be generative of each of these kinds of knowledge. In the chapters on models of practice curriculum (see Chapter 6), practice pedagogies (see Chapter 7) and workers' personal practices or epistemologies (see Chapter 8) are indicated the kinds of knowledge that are likely to be generated through these practices. That is, some kinds of activities and interactions are more or less likely to be able to develop specific kinds and classifications of conceptual, procedural and dispositional knowledge.

The knowledge required for work and its learning

In sum, in considering learning through work and achieving the kinds of outcomes that enterprises need and nation states want from workforces, the imperative here is to capture: (i) what constitutes the canonical occupational knowledge (i.e., which any occupational practitioner needs to know, do and value); (ii) the situational requirements for performance in particular work settings, including the capacities to be adaptive within the canonical and situational domains of occupational knowledge; and (iii) how that knowledge is constructed and constitutes individuals' personal domain of occupational knowledge. The first is associated with concepts, procedures and dispositions that have developed over time through the emergence, further development and refinement of cultural practices that are labelled as occupations. These practices arise because of societal needs for them, and they are transformed over time as needs and requirements change and are manifested within settings such as communities, workplaces and other institutions within nation states. Considerations of how occupations are manifested quite differently across workplaces, countries and cultures are noteworthy here. This acknowledges that practice and performance requirements for these occupations are not uniformly manifested in work settings. Instead, there is significant diversity and variety in the requirements for the occupational practice depending upon the goals, focuses, clientele, patients and so on of the circumstances in which the occupation is being practised and the kind of goals that it needs to achieve. So, there is also a need to acknowledge and be informed about the situational requirements for occupational performance, presented here as the situational domain. Associated with both the canonical and situational domains of occupational knowledge is the need for adaptability: the capacity to apply, extend and, in some cases, transform the occupational practice as novel requirements emerge and new challenges need to be addressed. It is these that become essential qualities of the personal domain that individuals construct and then need to apply and adapt as circumstances change. Yet, in considerations of how they might be learnt, considering them separately and in terms of their particular levels and forms is important for identifying and progressing how they might be learnt in workplaces and educational settings. These are the issues that are addressed within Chapters 6 and 7, as are the kinds of knowledge likely to be developed through practice curriculum models, a selection of pedagogic practices and the personal practices of the workers. So, in this way, these three domains and the three forms of knowledge stand to be those that learning through work needs to address. This is because they not only provide a platform for understanding the requirements of occupational practice and situated performance but they are also helpful in guiding curriculum and pedagogical considerations associated with learning through work.

References

1. Billett S, Harteis C, Gruber H. Developing occupational expertise through everyday work activities and interaction. In: Ericsson KA, Hoffman RR, Kozbelt A, eds. *Cambridge handbook of expertise and expert performance*. 2nd ed. New York: Cambridge University Press; 2018: 105–126.
2. Chi MTH, Glaser R, Farr MJ. *The nature of expertise*. Hillsdale, NJ: Erlbaum; 1982.
3. Ericsson KA, Smith J. *Towards a general theory of expertise*. Cambridge: Cambridge University Press; 1991.
4. Charness N. Expertise in chess and bridge. In: Klahr D, Kotowsky K, eds. *Complex information processing: The impact of Herbert A. Simon*. Hillsdale, NJ: Erlbaum; 1989: 183–204.
5. Billett S. Knowing in practice: Re-conceptualising vocational expertise. *Learning and Instruction*. 2001;11(6):431–452.
6. Searle JR. *The construction of social reality*. London: Penguin; 1995.
7. Billett S. Personal epistemologies, work and learning. *Educational Research Review*. 2009;4(3):210–219.
8. Billett S. *Vocational education: Purposes, traditions and prospects*. Dordrecht: Springer; 2011.
9. Lodge RC. *Plato's theory of education*. London: Kegan Paul, Trench, Trubner; 1947.
10. Elias JL. *Philosophy of education: Classical and contemporary*. Malabar, FL: Krieger Publishing; 1995.
11. Farrington B. *Greek science*. London: Pelican; 1966.
12. Finley MI. *The ancient economy*. Berkeley and Los Angeles: Univ of California Press; 1999.
13. Robinson DN. *An intellectual history of psychology*. Madison: Univ of Wisconsin Press; 1995.
14. Billett S. *Mimetic learning at work: Learning in the circumstances of practice*. Dordrecht: Springer; 2014.
15. Pelissier C. The anthropology of teaching and learning. *Annual Review of Anthropology*. 1991;20:75–95.
16. Billett S, Rose J. Securing conceptual knowledge in the workplace. In: Murphy P, ed. *Learners, learning and assessment*. London: Sage Publications; 1999: 329–344.
17. Gott S. Apprenticeship instruction for real-world tasks: The co-ordination of procedures, mental models, and strategies. *Review of Research in Education*. 1989;15:97–169.

18. Lave J. The culture of acquisition and the practice of understanding. In: Stigler JW, Shweder RA, Herdt G, eds. Cultural psychology. Cambridge: Cambridge University Press; 1990: 259–286.
19. Singleton J. The Japanese folkcraft pottery apprenticeship: Cultural patterns of an educational institution. In: Coy MW, ed. *Apprenticeship: From theory to method and back again*. New York: SUNY; 1989: 13–30.
20. Bunn S. The nomad's apprentice: Different kinds of apprenticeship among Kyrgyz nomads in Central Asia. In: Ainely P, Rainbird H, eds. *Apprenticeship: Towards a new paradigm of learning*. London: Kogan Page; 1999: 74–85.
21. Gowlland G. Learning craft skills in China: Apprenticeship and social capital in an artisan community of practice. *Anthropology and Education Quarterly*. 2012;43(4):358–371.
22. Marchand TH. *The pursuit of pleasurable work: Craftwork in twenty-first century England*. London: Berghahn Books; 2022.
23. Lave J. *Apprenticeship in critical ethnograhic practice*. Chicago, IL: University of Chicago Press; 2011.
24. Ebrey PB. *China: Illustrated history*. Cambridge: Cambridge University Press; 1996.
25. Stevenson J. Vocational expertise. In: Stevenson J, ed. Cognition at work. Adelaide: National Centre for Vocational Education Research; 1994: 7–34.
26. Billett S. *Learning in the workplace: Strategies for effective practice*. Sydney: Allen and Unwin; 2001.
27. Rehm M. Vocation as personal calling: A question of education. *The Journal of Educational Thought*. 1990;24(2):114–125.
28. Dawson J. A history of vocation: Tracing a keyword of work, meaning, and moral purpose. *Adult Education Quarterly*. May 2005;55(3):220–231.
29. Pines CL. *Ideology and false consciousness: Marx and his historical progenitors*. Albany: SUNY Press; 1993.
30. Quicke J. *A curriculum for life: Schools for a democratic learning society*. Buckingham: Open University Press; 1999.
31. Goldthorpe JH, Hope K. *The social grading of occupations: A new approach and scale*. Oxford: Clarendon Press; 1974.
32. Billett S. Work, discretion and learning: Processes of learning and development at work. *International Journal of Training Research*. 2015;13(3): 214–230.
33. Ryle G. *The concept of mind*. London: Hutchinson University Library; 1949.
34. Glaser R. Expertise and learning: How do we think about instructional processes now that we have discovered knowledge structures? In: Klahr D, Kotovsky K, eds. *Complex information processing: The impact of Herbert A. Simon*. Hillsdale, NJ: Erlbaum & Associates; 1989: 289–317.
35. Anderson JR. Problem solving and learning. *American Psychologist*. 1993; 48(1):35–44.
36. Sun R, Merrill E, Peterson T. From implicit skills to explicit knowledge: A bottom-up model of skill development. *Cognitive Science*. 2001;25:203–244.
37. Perkins D, Jay E, Tishman S. Beyond abilities: A dispositional theory of thinking. *Merrill-Palmer Quarterly*. 1993;39(1):1–21.
38. Mezirow J. A critical theory of self-directed learning. In: Brookfield S, ed. *Self-directed learning: From theory to practice*. San Francisco, CA: Jossey Bass; 1985: 17–30.
39. Bauman Z. *Work, consumerism and the new poor*. Buckingham: Open University Press; 1998.

40. Wright Mills C. The meaning of work throughout history. In: Best F, ed. *The future of work.* Englewood Cliffs, NJ: Prentice Hall; 1973: 6–13.
41. Pusey M. *The experience of Middle Australia.* Cambridge: Cambridge University Press; 2003.
42. Somerville M. Who learns?: Enriching learning cultures in aged care workplaces. Paper presented at: 11th Annual International conference on post-compulsory education and training: Enriching learning cultures, 2003; Gold Coast.
43. Billett S. Learning throughout working life: A relational interdependence between social and individual agency *British Journal of Education Studies.* 2008;55(1):39–58.
44. Smith R. *Necessity in action: The epistemological agency of the new employee* [Master of Education]. Brisbane: Faculty of Education, Griffith University; 2004.
45. Organisation for Economic Co-operational and Development. *OECD skills outlook 2013: First results from the survey of adult skills.* Paris: OECD; 2013.
46. Mulder M. Conceptions of professional competence. In: Billett S, Harteis C, Gruber H, eds. *International handbook of research in professional and practice-based learning.* Vol 1. Dordrecht: Springer; 2014: 107–137.
47. Ericsson KA. The influence of experience and deliberate practice on the development of superior expert performance. In: Ericsson KA, Charness N, Feltowich PJ, Hoffmann RR, eds. *The Cambridge handbook of expertise and expert performance.* Cambridge: Cambridge University Press; 2006: 685–705.
48. Glaser R. Education and thinking – the role of knowledge. *American Psychologist.* 1984;39(2):93–104.
49. Lajoie S. Developing professional expertise with a cognitive apprenticeship model: Examples form avionics and medicine. In: Ericsson KA, ed. *The development of professional expertise.* Cambridge: Cambridge University Press; 2009: 61–83.
50. Wagner RK, Sternberg RJ. Tacit knowledge and intelligence in the everyday world. In: Sternberg RJ, Wagner RK, eds. *Practical intelligence – nature and origins of competence in the everyday world.* Cambridge: Cambridge University Press; 1986: 51–83.
51. Scribner S. Studying working intelligence. In: Rogoff B, Lave J, eds. *Everyday cognition: Its development in social context.* Cambridge, MA: Harvard University Press; 1984: 9–40.
52. Rogoff B. *Apprenticeship in thinking – cognitive development in social context.* New York: Oxford University Press; 1990.
53. Brown AL, Palinscar AM. Guided, cooperative learning and individual knowledge acquisition. In: Resnick LB, ed. *Knowing, learning and instruction, Essays in honour of Robert Glaser.* Hillsdale, NJ: Erlbaum & Associates; 1989: 393–451.
54. Renkle A. Worked-out examples: Instructional explanations support learning by self explanation. *Learning and Instruction.* 2002;12(5):529–556.
55. Sweller J. Should problem solving be used as a learning device in mathematics? *Journal of Research into Mathematics Education.* 1989;20(3):321–328.
56. Sticht TJ. *Functional context education.* San Diego, CA: Applied Cognitive and Behavioural Science; 1987.
57. Collins A, Brown JS, Newman SE. Cognitive apprenticeship: Teaching the crafts of reading, writing and mathematics. In: Resnick LB, ed. *Knowing, learning and instruction: Essays in honour of Robert Glaser.* Hillsdale, NJ: Erlbaum & Associates; 1989: 453–494.
58. Palinscar AS, Brown AL. Reciprocal teaching of comprehension-fostering and comprehension-monitoring activities. *Cognition and Instruction.* 1984;1(2):117–175.

59. Schmidt HG, Rikers RMJP. How expertise develops in medicine: Knowledge encapsulation and illness script formation. *Medical Education.* 2007;41: 1133–1139.
60. Sutherland L. Developing problem solving expertise: The impact of instruction in a question analysis strategy. *Learning and Instruction.* 2002;12:155–187.
61. Groen GJ, Patel P. The relationship between comprehension and reasoning in medical expertise. In: Chi MTH, Glaser R, Farr R, eds. *The nature of expertise.* New York: Erlbaum; 1988: 287–310.
62. Scribner S. Vygostky's use of history. In: Wertsch JV, ed. *Culture, communication and cognition: Vygotskian perspectives.* Cambridge: Cambridge University Press; 1985: 119–145.
63. Billett S. Mediating learning at work: Personal mediations of social and brute facts. In: Harteis C, Rausch A, Seifried J, eds. *Discourses on professional learning: On the boundary between learning and working.* Dordrecht: Springer; 2014: 75–93.
64. Higgins C. Dewey's conception of vocation: Existential, aesthetic, and educational implications for teachers. *Journal of Curriculum Studies.* 2005;37(4):441–464.
65. Rehm M. Emancipatory vocational education: Pedagogy for the work of individuals and society. *The Journal of Education.* 1989;171(3):109–123.
66. Billett S. Conceptualising learning experiences: Contributions and mediations of the social, personal and brute. *Mind, Culture and Activity.* 2009;16(1):32–47.
67. Bloom BS, Engelhart MD, Furst EJ, Hill WH, Krathwohl DR. *Taxonomy of educational objectives: The classification of educational goals.* New York: Longmans; 1956.
68. Tobias S. Interest, prior knowledge, and learning. *Review of Educational Research.* 1994;64(1):37–54.

5 Being innovative

Aligning learning and workplace innovations

Work, workers and innovations

Work and occupational practice are characterised currently by the need to address constantly changing requirements for the goods and services they produce. This is the case for both private sector enterprises as well as public enterprises serving the social and healthcare needs of communities. Such a need has led not only to employees' requiring ongoing learning, but also to innovations in the goals and procedures of those enterprises. This situation seems unlikely to change in the future. Both kinds of changes (i.e., workers' learning and changes to work practices) necessitate responding to emerging technologies, different ways of working and adaption and transformation of the activities and interactions needed for individuals' employability and enterprise viability. Perhaps, the majority of these innovations are in some ways workplace specific.[1] This means that, as in the past,[2,3] much of the goals for and procedures of workplace and occupational innovations need to be realised through activities in those workplaces and through employees' agency and activities.[4] This is because responding to the changing requirements of occupational and workplace practices often requires initiating and enacting work-related innovations germane to the specific enterprise's circumstances and needs.[4] This occurs regardless of whether the impetus for change is initiated in the workplaces or from practices or technologies outside of them. In both instances, there will inevitably be the need for novel practices to be identified, adapted, fitted in or merely enacted in the work setting. Those processes inevitably require and bring about changes in what workers know, can do and value (i.e., their learning).[5] So, there is a co-occurrence between innovations and learning through work.[6] Consequently, in different ways and by degree, through these processes, employees' learning will arise interdependently. Through identifying responses to work-related problems or challenges, selecting and generating appropriate responses and enacting and monitoring them, these processes are generative of employees' learning and development.

Together, these processes require employees to engage in problem-solving and adaptability through which changes in their thinking and acting arise (i.e., learning).[7,8] Engagement in goal-directed activities, such as those associated

DOI: 10.4324/9781003519416-7

with those new workplace practices, leads to change in what individuals know, can do and value.[9-11] In these ways, much of that learning arises from individuals adapting what they know, can do and value through processes that are referred to as problem-solving.[8,9] It is through this co-occurrence that occupational, workplace and work practice changes can be enacted, remade and transformed interdependently, as has occurred in the past.[2,12]

Consequently, understanding further how employee-directed and employee-driven innovations (EDIs) coalesce is central to advancing how the changing occupational requirements and bases for workplace performance can be addressed through work-related processes. This includes generating the kinds of learning required by working-age adults to remain employable and be innovative in current, emerging and future work. As foreshadowed, and importantly, innovations promoting the viability and advancement of the goods and services that enterprises produce are not just about profitability. It is also about the kinds and qualities of human services that public sector enterprises provide that are central to effectively meeting the health and social care needs of individuals and communities.[13,14] It was to advance this understanding that two investigations into the relationship between innovations and workers' learning were undertaken and whose findings inform the discussion in this chapter.

The concept of EDIs[5] offers a starting point to examine this relationship. It elaborates and illustrates innovations that are initiated, enacted, monitored and evaluated by employees. Drawing on the findings of an investigation into how innovations in Singaporean small-to-medium-sized enterprises (SMEs) are initiated and enacted, it was possible to identify and delineate three different types of innovations (i.e., strategic, workplace practices and procedural).[1] This included identifying the degree by which and how employees were involved in the initiation and enactment of these types of innovations and the potential for the kinds and extent of learning arising through them. The qualities of initiation, authorisation, enactment and adoption, and the learning required for and arising from each of these three kinds of innovations, shape the zones of potential development (i.e., the potential scope and qualities for learning). The three zones of development are advanced as a means of illustrating and elaborating how workers' learning and workplace change can be understood and advanced together. This elaboration includes (i) the interdependence of innovations and workers' learning, (ii) the different scope of the learning potential from kinds of innovations, (iii) processes through which those innovations and workers' learning can co-occur and (iv) how such processes can be supported within workplaces.

In advancing these points, this chapter commences with a consideration of EDIs, what they constitute and their potential for both workplace innovations and learning in, for and through work. Then, findings from two investigations conducted in SMEs about the enactment of innovations and learning required for and arising through them are presented and discussed. The first investigation explored under what circumstances the initiation, enactment and evaluation of innovations can occur in five SMEs. The second investigation sought to elaborate the co-occurrence of innovations and learning through identifying the processes and outcomes of change processes in seven enterprises of different kinds. Through this investigation, three distinct zones of development associated with the kind and scope of innovations were identified, premised upon the extent and degree of engagements and discretion workers were able to exercise and which shaped their learning. These zones are held to be indicative of how the concurrence of learning and innovations can be understood in work settings.

Employee-driven innovations

The proposition that employees (i.e., workers) can and should initiate innovations in and through work is longstanding and central to the evolution of both occupations and work practices.[2,15,16] When invited to contribute to their workplaces' viability and advancement, workers often make positive and essential contributions.[5,13,17,18] Conversely, when workplace support for innovating is not forthcoming, even workers' best efforts may be insufficient to realise effective learning and workplace innovations.[19,20] It follows that securing effective alignments between workers' learning and innovations in their workplace requires both the employees' efforts, and the agency of and invitations from within the workplace that invite and support their participation in these activities. The alignment and the co-occurrence between these processes of learning and remaking practice are central to securing individual employability, workplaces' ongoing viability, the provision of goods and services that individuals, communities and societies want and, collectively, realising important economic and social goals.

As mentioned, across human history and cultures, workers have been generative of many, if not most, of the innovations that have sustained, extended and advanced the occupational practices serving societal, community and personal needs[2,21,22] and societal progress. Although some large enterprises have developmental teams, product development processes and strategically planned innovations, many innovations are likely still to arise through employees' everyday work activities as they respond to challenges, problems and workarounds.[23] The value of workers' involvement was famously highlighted by the Hawthorne experiment which, among others, indicated that when workplaces take an interest in and grant discretion to workers, they can return that interest through heightened problem-solving and enhanced productivity. The absence of discretionary roles seemingly leads to the opposite outcome – low morale and productivity – as in Taylorist type of production work.[24] In the economic reconstruction efforts following the Second World War, employee engagement and innovations were central to national efforts. Against expectations, Japan and Germany emerged with strong economies in the post-war period. In both countries' reconstruction efforts, optimisation of their workforces occurred, leading to high productivity and innovations, albeit in different ways. Although adopting distinct approaches, common to both were the engagement and efforts to optimise workers' capacities and creativities, particularly workers on the front line of production. The suggestion here is that how employees are engaged in workplaces and exercise their discretion influences outcomes associated with productivity, innovations and opportunities for learning aligned with their employability.

Recent data from the Programme of International Assessment of Adult Competence (PIAAC)[25–27] indicates that the level of discretion afforded workers differs across countries and, seemingly, those granted high levels of discretion enjoy more productive outcomes. The data from countries with entrenched social democratic ethos and practices indicated high levels of discretion. Swedish workers reported higher levels of discretion in selecting and completing work tasks, compared with countries in which such discretion was not extended,[25] for instance. In contrast, the findings from the 2015 PIAAC survey in Singapore indicated relatively low levels of discretion being reported by working-age adults.[26] This led in 2016 to the Singaporean Government actively encouraging enterprises to afford greater discretion and openness to their workforces.[28] For this nation state, the capacities and innovative qualities of its workforce are central to remaining economically viable and competitive in an increasingly globally competitive environment. Unlike many other countries, Singapore has very limited natural resources to draw upon. Much more than many other nations, it requires workforces that are currently competent, adaptable, and able to innovate to sustain and extend their workplaces' viability.[12] More generally, workers' discretion, problem-solving abilities and being innovative are core qualities for contemporary workers now and in the foreseeable future.

The Scandinavian concept of EDI was used to propose how workers' interests, capacities and abilities could be most effectively deployed to achieve workplace viability.[5] Scandinavian countries have demonstrated the worth of fostering collaboration among government, capital and labour as directed towards differentiated but common goals associated with working life, and engaging employees in driving innovations is often viewed as orthodox and necessary practice.[29] This foundational premise raises questions about the degree by which such practices can be exercised across nation states with other societal and cultural sentiments. For instance, in Singapore, as perhaps in other Confucian heritage countries, there are concerns that some workers view themselves as 'rank-and-file' and whose roles or responsibilities as employees are to follow orders and not extending to suggesting and driving innovations. These are, instead, viewed as others' roles and responsibilities.

However, this is no longer a viable proposition given the changing requirements for employability and the need for enterprise sustainability when confronting changes. The evidence from across human history suggests that all kinds and classifications of workers have the capacities to drive innovations[2,13,16,30] and learn through problem-solving activities, such as indicated in the recent PIAAC data.[25–27] That is, they are capable of identifying and enacting solutions to workplace tasks that may be, by degree, novel to them. The PIAAC data suggest that all classes and kinds of workers are frequently engaged in workplace innovations,[26] thereby making the ability to be innovative a core quality of contemporary work capacities.[31] Indeed, such innovations at work are defined by central government agencies as:

> ... the implementation of a new or significantly improved product (good or service) or process, or a new organizational method in business practices, workplace organisation or external relations.[32]
>
> (p.46)

Yet, some will suggest that not all occupations and forms of work are well aligned to accommodating EDIs. For instance, the highly codified and regulated 'command and control'-based occupations such as emergency services, police and military may not encourage or reward such innovations. Yet, these kinds of workers also need to quickly adapt to changing circumstances (i.e., be innovative),[33] albeit with care, particularly in those circumstances for when innovations must be trialled and carefully tested prior to being adopted (e.g., healthcare, aviation and some aspects of engineering). Then, there are risks associated with incautious adoption of innovations.

Hence, whilst being a necessary quality of all kinds and levels of contemporary employees, including owners and managers, in their workplaces, the processes of initiation, authorisation and evaluation of innovations arise in and through all kinds of work. Innovations with significant implications for the viability of the workplace, such as a change in the products or services, and how these are produced, likely require initiation and authorisation from senior levels in the enterprise. So, there are quite different kinds of innovations that have potentially major or minor implications in terms of risks, threats to viability of and potential benefits for enterprises' direction and focus. These qualities can also be quite different in terms of their scope and the extent of remaking or transforming practices and the potential learning that is required and can arise through them.

Co-occurrence of learning and workplace innovations

As noted, there are dual considerations for understanding how innovations can be encouraged and supported, how learning arises through them and the interdependence between innovating and learning.[1,12] Little attention has been given to how those changes can change workplace norms, forms and practices. Learning, that is, changes in what individuals know, can do and value arises as a result of their participation in work activities.[34–36] Yet, as noted, the activities through which individuals learn can also realise changes in workplace practices and how work activities are performed.[4] In short, when engaging in goal-directed workplace activities, workers not only learn but also change occupational and workplace practices either incrementally or transformationally through processes of remaking of their norms, forms and practices.[23] That remaking is a necessary process as workers or groups of workers engage daily in activities and interactions to meet the evolving needs of the goods or services they produce. For instance, with ageing populations in many countries, the incidence of health and social care workers engaging with patients with underlying delirium and dementia is increasing and becoming commonplace in healthcare settings. These workers are advancing understandings, procedures and dispositions to effectively engage with such patients and their family members. So, there are co-occurrences and reciprocity between the innovations required to meet the needs and learning of these health and social care workers as they identify and enact innovations to provide clinical care.

Thus, more than focusing on individuals' learning and development, there is an associated need to understand how work practices can also reciprocally be transformed to meet changing work performance: innovations. This co-occurrence of learning and innovations warrants greater acknowledgement as it is fundamental to how cultural practices, such as the occupations that serve communities' needs, can be utilised to enhance the dual outcomes of workers' learning and workplace continuity and advancement. Aligning workplace innovations and workers' learning offers a means for effective and adaptive workplaces and workers' occupational development.[1] Such co-occurrences also indicate how culture and cognition come together[37] to be advanced as personal and cultural practices, such as occupations, are formed and transformed as societal, technological and brute imperatives change[38-40] through individuals' engagement with them.[41] In these ways, the dual processes are, therefore, at the heart of the continuity and advancement of the socially and culturally derived practices that are central to progressing the human species. This co-occurrence may well help explain how humans have reached this point in our evolutionary history through the interaction between individual ontogenetic development and advancing the cultural practices in which we engage to meet our needs and secure our continuity and that of the communities in which we engage.

There is nothing particularly novel here, except its rehearsal and illumination in the context of work innovations and learning. It is perhaps only in recent times that innovations have become associated with laboratories, research and development units, and geeks. Before that, and still today, most occupational and workplace innovations have likely been the product of workers' innovations and learning. As has been reported in the empirical studies, far from all workplace innovations are de novo (i.e., wholly novel) or technologically initiated. Many are about adapting what already exists to emerging needs and workplace requirements,[42] including accommodating workplace-specific requirements and factors. Even de novo changes, when generated elsewhere, require adapting to specific workplace situations and practices. Such innovations often cannot be merely implemented in workplaces. Instead, they require workers to adapt them to specific workplace practices and goals. This emphasises the situated nature of innovations, as found in a study of small businesses implementing a nationally uniform taxation system.[43] Workers in these small businesses had to respond in quite different ways to this de novo process (i.e., strategic innovation), depending upon the nature of the business, existing financial accounting systems and competencies and the delineation of responsibilities within those workplaces. In every instance, it reportedly led to change in some individuals' work within those small businesses.

The duality of workers' engagement and learning, on the one hand, and workplace practices, on the other, offers tentative premises to explore and elaborate the development of capacities for innovative work performance.[44,45] Workers' learning and innovations are, however, not wholly a product of what is afforded by workplaces. Individuals' interests, agency and commitment are also essential elements in both learning and innovation processes. Without accounting for these personal factors, the co-occurrence of innovations and learning cannot be fully understood. These processes will likely differ across workplaces and professional practices, as evident in the study of learning and innovations in healthcare and precision-engineering small businesses discussed below.[46] Rather than seeking fixed guidelines about how to align learning and innovations in workplaces, informed principles and practices will likely need to be understood situationally in terms of factors assisting or inhibiting workers and their workplaces to optimise opportunities for learning and innovations.[47] It is the two case studies discussed in the following that inform and elaborate these points.

> **Case study 1 Elaborating on initiation, enactment and support of workplace innovations**
>
> How workers' learning and innovations can co-occur was illuminated in an initial investigation undertaken in five SMEs in Singapore. The practical inquiries comprised interviews with workers and managers/supervisors, as well as observations of these workplaces. SMEs were selected as learning and innovations are central to their viability. Importantly, as the need for innovations extends to the quality of services, SMEs in both manufacturing and the provision of services were selected as sites for this research. The five enterprises comprised three from the healthcare sector (i.e., home health, residential home and care home) and two from advanced manufacturing (i.e., 3D printing and precision engineering). Advanced manufacturing has an ongoing need to maintain and improve the quality of its products amongst changing circumstances to enhance productivity and engage with new technologies. The service sector SMEs also are required to innovate in response to changing client or patient needs and in more effective ways. With its ageing population, Singapore has an ongoing imperative to address the needs of a burgeoning aged care sector.

Procedures

The data-gathering comprised structured interviews with between three and five workers and their supervisors or managers in each of these SMEs, using a schedule of questions about (i) recent changes in work activities and (ii) how those changes had been initiated, supported and enacted in the SMEs. A survey was also used to identify factors supporting the initiation, enactment and rewards for innovations. The interviews identified instances of workplace innovations through informants reporting and discussing instances of changes in their workplace and using these instances when responding to the questions and scales, thereby enhancing data validity. Items also included those used in PIAAC surveys about (i) the kinds of discretion workers enjoyed, (ii) the frequency and kinds of problems solved and (iii) the engagement in and support for learning that are standard items within the survey.[25] These data were subjected to thematic analyses to identify workers' engagement with those innovations.

Findings

The factors shaping initiating, engaging in and rewarding innovative actions in these workplaces were found to be close or proximal to these workers. That is, the actions of and interactions with supervisors/managers and co-workers and workers themselves were identified as being central to these processes of learning and workplace innovations. These were found to be far more salient than more remote factors such as education provisions and government policies. The analysis identified patterns aligning both innovations and learning as being interdependent and co-occurring. There is no distinction between thinking and acting, and learning and actions – such as initiating and enacting innovations – are generative of learning,[9,48] particularly higher orders of procedures and linking of conceptions. Therefore, understanding what supports and sustains the initiation and enactment of these innovations is also central to elaborating learning arising through these innovations.

Elaborating the co-occurrence between work and learning here is premised on the duality of affordances and engagement.[49] As noted, affordances are what is provided, offered or made available to individuals (i.e., workers) as innovators and learners. Essentially, these affordances were largely provided by bosses/managers, supervisors and co-workers and, to a lesser degree, outside of those workplaces that included accessing educational programmes. Engagement is that exercised by workers as they participate in these activities. Hence, through using grounded instances of work activities, it is possible to identify the importance of factors that support or inhibit opportunities to workers (i.e., affordances) and those associated with how workers initiated and enacted innovations at work, through which they also learn. In these five SMEs, the combination of proximal factors, on the one hand, and workers' engagement on the other was found to represent the interdependence between workers' engagement and the discretion and support provided by the workplace that is central to effective co-occurrence of learning and innovations.

Importance of workers' engagement

Findings indicated the key role of workers and co-workers' engagement in undertaking work tasks, identifying potential innovations and supporting their enactment as being central to innovations and innovative practices in these five SMEs. Although the affordances extended to these workers and their abilities to be innovative differed across the SMEs, the evidence across measures of initiating and enacting innovations were largely by these workers. Managers and supervisors were central to distributing opportunities and rewards for initiating and enacting innovations. Yet, the engagement and actions of workers and co-workers were most salient, thereby positioning them centrally in innovations at work. Some of the variations in the degree of discretion and exercise in innovations were explained by specific kinds of practices within the enterprises. For instance, in home health, the health workers perform their roles in relative social isolation in clients' homes. The reach and control of managers and supervisors was inevitably weakened, and workers' agency and discretion were central in these circumstances. They needed to respond to clients' particular needs shaped by the home circumstances (e.g., physical and social setting). In this form of work, adaption and workarounds are inevitable. So, high levels of discretion to initiate and exercise innovations were necessary in such circumstances. Yet, in other SMEs in the healthcare sector (e.g., aged care residences), the workers were less able to exercise discretion because of institutional work hierarchies and practices and supervision requirements associated with elderly care.

Proximity to managers and workers

A key finding was the degree by which discretion is shaped by enterprise size. SMEs have distinct configurations, organisation and decision-making processes. Also, the closeness to those who supervise and authorise (e.g., owners, managers, supervisors) may lead to different kinds and scope of workplace discretion than in larger workplaces. It is noteworthy that in people-intense working environments, such as healthcare and manufacturing SMEs, managers and supervisors were most central to initiating, enacting, supporting and rewarding innovations. These hierarchical management arrangements are aligned with the care of the aged or sick. However, confounding this orthodoxy is that the home care workers had greater autonomy in clients' own homes. That is, they are not under the direct supervision and control of others in the workplace. So, factors of size and circumstance seem central here.

This first investigation's findings indicate that (i) workers as active and directed agents are central to initiating innovations; (ii) managers and supervisors are central to authorising opportunities for innovations; (iii) the support for innovations in the workplace was from immediate and local actors (i.e., supervisors, co-workers, workers); (iv) engaging in workplace innovations is premised upon workers (i.e., workers themselves and co-workers); and (v) rewards for innovations were reported as being largely afforded by managers and supervisors.

Case study 2 Investigating innovations at work

The second investigation comprised seven case studies of Singaporean SMEs from a range of industry sectors, including service provisions (i.e., removalists, maintenance, cleaning, education), food production, storage and logistics and auditing work. The enterprises identified, approached and agreed to participate in this project had recently won business awards for innovations. These awards indicated they had recently or were currently engaged in significant workplace changes. Enterprises engaging in such changes were seen to be able to provide examples of changes and informants who had experienced these processes of change and could provide data with high validity grounded in events they had recently experienced. In each of the seven enterprises, a vertical sample of up to ten staff was interviewed. These SMEs comprise (i) Peace – a family-owned removal company that removes and transports household contents both within Singapore and overseas; (ii) Forrest – a family-owned food production company that produces, markets, and distributes its own brand of steamed buns; (iii) Education School – a privately run educational provider for overseas school-aged children; (iv) Storage Hub – a privately run enterprise providing warehousing and transport logistics for Singaporean enterprises; (v) Audit Central – a privately owned company providing auditing and accounting services to both public and private sector organisations; (vi) Best Maintenance – a privately run company providing maintenance services across a number of buildings; and (vii) Corporate Cleaning – a privately run company providing cleaning services to offices, airports, shopping centres and other facilities.

For each enterprise, two rounds of interviews were undertaken with informants. Following requests that a vertical slice of employees be selected by the enterprise for interviews, each informant was interviewed individually and, occasionally, in pairs of peers. Across these enterprises, first interviews were conducted with 58 employees, and a slightly smaller number in the second round due to workplace attrition/separation. Those interviews comprised questions about the informants' workplaces, work activities, roles and responsibilities, and describing the innovations and changes in workplace goals, processes and activities over the last few years, along with demographic information (i.e., duration of service, roles, educational levels). The informants were pressed to provide instances of how changes in the workplaces (i.e., innovations) have been initiated, enacted and evaluated and the kinds of learning associated with those innovations. The analysis identified different kinds of innovations that occurred in these enterprises and the scope and possibilities for employees' involvement in initiating and enacting them. From these, it is possible to deduce how these employees have initiated, enacted and evaluated workplace innovations, and under what circumstances they could exercise their capacities in so doing. It was also possible to delineate different kinds of innovations and particular roles that employees exercised within their initiation, enactment and evaluation of innovations.

Kinds of innovation

Three distinct kinds of innovations were identified through the interview data, based on their scope and scale, as the innovations were enacted and experienced by the informants. These were labelled as (i) Strategic, (ii) Work practice and (iii) Procedural innovations. Each of these three kinds of innovations is quite distinct in terms of their scope or scale, as well as indicators of how they are initiated, endorsed, enacted and sustained. This delineation is pertinent as the innovations reported were of different scope and scale not only of the change required, but also the potential learning through those processes. Those comprising *Strategic* changes included major changes to the enterprise's goals, business direction or processes; changes to *Work practices* and *Procedural* changes were more specific to the operational aspects and processes of the work being undertaken. Consequently, innovations that were identified as representing major shifts in the enterprise's goals or processes (i.e., *Strategic, Work practice*) and those with potential positive or potential negative impacts were most likely to be initiated by senior management or owners and needing to be carefully considered, trialled and monitored by them or supervisors. Then, there are those changes comprising refining what already occurred, with more limited potential benefits and risks, which are perhaps most likely to be initiated by employees engaged in related tasks. It is often those employees who confront and need to find ways of addressing practical problems and emerging challenges.[5] As such, these different kinds of innovations offer explanatory categories for understanding the degree by which employees can become involved in, and the distinct role of employees within, different kinds of innovations. In brief, they comprise:

> *Strategic innovations* – innovations shaping changes in the enterprise's direction or fundamental operation, including the work undertaken and how it is undertaken. These are usually reported as being initiated and endorsed by senior management.
>
> *Work practice innovations* – innovations changing how work in the enterprise is undertaken, including its organization and enactment, which are usually initiated and endorsed by senior management, but enacted by operational staff.

Procedural innovations – innovations comprising enhancements, improvements, or transformations of actual working practice – often initiated by operational staff but endorsed by management/supervisors/'keymen' and enacted by operational staff.

Procedural innovations were those identified as being most closely aligned with EDIs as per their original conception proposed for Scandinavia.[5] These are innovations in which the operational or rank-and-file workers and/or lower level supervisors exercised their discretion to innovate as they conducted their work, solved problems and advanced ways of working to accommodate new or emerging challenges. This set of three distinct kinds of workplace innovations and kinds and levels of workers' engagement and discretion potentially stand as bases for analysing innovations of different kinds and potential scope of learning through their initiation, endorsement, enactment and monitoring. In this way, each of these kinds of innovations had their own zones of innovations, that is, how they are initiated, endorsed and enacted, and which can be used to predict the kinds of learning likely to arise through employees' participation in them.

Zones of innovations: processes for initiating, endorsing, and implementing

Each of these kinds of innovations had their processes of initiation, endorsement and implementation. As indicated above, *Strategic innovations* are largely initiated by the executive. This is unsurprising as they usually first need to be initiated and endorsed by senior management after they have been trialled and judged effective. The implementation of these innovations is realised through operational staff being informed, consulted and encouraged to engage, adopt and adapt them as part of their work practices. There is nothing particularly novel here, as it is a quite common practice in both large and small enterprises and particularly those with hierarchies (e.g., government, health, command and control, public service, aviation). This is referred to as bounded agency:[50] the degree of agency and discretion that workers can engage in and conduct, within institutional boundaries (i.e., those associated with viability, workplace performance, and management of risk). However, employees' adoption of these initiatives is premised on those at the operational level becoming committed to them, particularly when those workers are not closely monitored or supervised.[51]

Work practice innovations are, similarly, largely initiated and endorsed by the executive or senior managers but, at Peace removalists, they included consultation with workers, down to the supervisor level (i.e., 'keyman'). This kind of innovation likely requires a higher level of engagement at the operational level. This is because these work practices will need to be engaged in and adopted by workers, including their nuanced understandings about the requirements for work tasks and how these might best be realised. That is, they impinge more directly on and are contingent upon employees' work activities.

The initiation and enactment of *Procedural innovations* are more broadly distributed across these workforces, including those at the operational level (i.e., frontline workers). These kinds of innovations and workers' engagement with them rehearse the original conception of EDIs more than the other two kinds. The initiation of these innovations was often reported as being founded in workers' responses to problems they encountered that had complicated or confounded their work. However, despite their initiation, some of these innovations required processes of consultation, evaluation and eventual endorsement within the enterprise before being enacted (e.g., requiring financial investments; safety and health regulations being met). Yet, there were others for which endorsements were not required, for various reasons.

So, different processes of initiation, evaluation, authorisation and implementation of these three kinds of innovations were required. But, more common across the three was a need to gather information to justify prospective changes and to seek permission and support for bringing about those changes at levels beyond the procedural matters. Much of that permission-seeking is to justify and validate the worth of the innovation before being endorsed within the SME and enacted by its employees. For most employees, seeking permission for *Work practice* innovations requires a case being made to management, underpinned by an appraisal of its worth; that is, engaging in an appraisal, constructing justifications and making a considered case, albeit in an oral or written form. All these processes are also helpful for supporting learning, as seeking information, building a justification and making a case press worker into extending what they know, can do and value through these activities. Hence, across all three kinds, the innovations arise through processes of workers' problem-solving that leads to learning and development,[9,48] albeit associated with the capacities required for tasks associated with storage, removalists, disposal and so forth. The point here is that worker discretion, problem-solving and enacting innovations operate within sets of agreed workplace principles and practices that shape the scope and kind of decision-making they enact (i.e., bounded agency).[50]

Explaining co-occurrence of workplace learning and innovations

The explanation of the co-occurrence of learning and innovations advanced here is broadly social constructivist. It emphasises the interdependence between personal and social contributions to thinking and acting.[52] It holds that individuals' ways of knowing and acting (i.e., their personal epistemologies) and suggestions from the social world are interdependent when enacting goal-directed activities at work. Those epistemologies arise through individuals' personal histories (i.e., ontogenies) and how they have, over time, developed what they know, can do and value. This is referred to as their ontogenetic development, the accumulation of what they have learnt through processes of experiencing across their lives.[53] Hence, individuals' earlier (i.e., premediate) experiences come to shape their immediate experiences.[54] That development is necessarily person-specific as it arises through the myriad and person-particular ongoing processes of each individual's moment-by-moment learning (i.e., microgenetic development)[55] that is shaped by their premediate or earlier experiences. These are referred to here as their personal curricula.[56] This process of ongoing learning occurs as each individual engages with what they experience, construes that experience based on what they know, can do and value and then constructs meaning from it:[57] the process of experiences and experiencing.

Hence, these processes can lead to person-particular ways of knowing and doing that, whilst not being wholly idiosyncratic, shape how individuals construe and construct knowledge in subsequent events such as those suggested by the social world.[53] The social suggestion here comprises the historically, culturally and situationally generated activities and interactions workers undertake, the problems and other challenges they confront and the expectations for work performance that are subject to both occupational and situational requirements (i.e., desired outcomes).[36] These are all institutional facts:[58] that is, they arise through the social world. The brute suggestions are those of nature[58] and include adults' maturation, for instance. So, maturation might bring changes in sensory perception, but also repertoires of experiences and ontogenetic development associated with occupational tasks and work requirements. These processes of learning and innovations need to account for the contributions and relations amongst the person, the social suggestion and brute factors.

As noted, innovations cannot be implemented from outside of workplaces or enacted without accommodating situational factors and requirements, and employees' agencies and intentionalities.[59] Even when pressed to engage in new practices, unless individuals appropriate them (i.e., value and actively construct), their engagement and legacies will be potentially superficial – what Wertsch[60] refers to as mastery (e.g., learning they are not committed to). Thus, rather than proposing guidelines to align learning and innovations in workplaces, informed principles and practices are likely needed to accommodate situational factors in assisting workers and their workplaces to optimise opportunities for learning and innovations.[47]

The co-occurrences between learning and innovations deserve greater elaboration and explanation to identify how these dual outcomes can be more effectively realised. Together, these relations shape both individuals' development across their life courses, and the remaking and transformation (i.e., innovations) of the culturally derived practices that comprise occupations through work and in response to specific challenges.[61] To date, much attention has been given to how inter-psychological processes (i.e., those between individuals' contributions and suggestions of social and physical environments) shape individuals' learning and development. Yet, these analyses rarely address how individuals' contributions shape continuity and change in the form of socially derived norms, forms and practices, such as work activities and interactions through which they learn. So, these considerations of co-occurrence between learning and innovations address gaps in our understanding of the interdependencies between how social institutions and settings (i.e., workplaces) and practice (i.e., ways of working)[58] change through processes of personal transformations (i.e., learning). This is a fundamental issue for human societies, as securing continuity and responding productively to changes that constantly emerge are essential for the continuity and transformation of societies. Investigating and illuminating these changes in socially derived, personally engaged activities, such as workplace innovations, offers the basis for understanding further these phenomena.

Aligning innovations and learning at work

In sum, more than individuals' learning in and through work just being directed towards their needs and employability, there are also important implications for workplaces. These include assisting in maintaining their viability over time and their development in the face of constant changes for the goods and services they provide. In an era in which the requirements for work performance and the need to respond to customers, clients, patients and so on have intensified, that viability often resides in enterprises being adaptive and innovative. This chapter has drawn on two recent studies and conceptual appraisals to elaborate how the co-occurrence of learning and innovations in and through work can achieve the dual goals of individuals' employability and workplace change. It advances concepts of zones of development that arise from different sorts of changes or innovation in workplaces and the diverse kinds and qualities of learning potentials that arise from different types and levels of engagement in identifying, initiating, enacting and monitoring innovations in and through work. The findings from the interview data from the seven SMEs in the second study provide tentative explanatory accounts about the need to consider innovations as having different kinds and scope. Moreover, delineated here are bases by which employees can participate variously in the processes of initiation, enacting and appraising them as comprising zones of discretion, agency and learning bounded by workplace imperatives. These boundaries are shaped by workplace norms, forms and practices and employees' capacities to successfully enact innovations and negotiate those boundaries. In this way, the personal consequences of learning through work and their potential societal contributions have been brought into alignment.

Inevitably, bringing about change in workplaces or initiating and enacting innovations requires not only the capacities of those who work within them to change and adapt or support these new initiatives, but also that through those processes learning arises. Hence, there is interdependency between change in workplaces and workers' learning. So, the co-occurrence between these two phenomena is interdependent. Learning through work not only generates outcomes for individuals (i.e., learning); it is also aligned with workplace change and innovations. The implications from the five SMEs (i.e., Case Study 1) are that, ultimately, it is factors within the workplaces themselves that are likely to be the key source shaping the opportunities for, engagement in, and support for innovations and learning through them in these workplaces. Whilst governments sometimes seek to bring about change externally, here it is suggested that policy and practices to bring about change need to focus on and centre their efforts within workplace settings. It is such workplace practices and bases by which workers are engaged that are central to the co-occurrence of both learning and innovations. Hence, there are practices that can be enacted at the workplace level that can promote these dual outcomes.

References

1. Billett S, Tan J, Chan C, Chong WH, Keat J. Employee-driven innovations: Zones of initiation, enactment and learning. In: Lee WO, Brown P, Goodwin L, Green A, eds. *International handbook of education development in Asia Pacific*. Dordrecht: Springer; 2022: 1–19.
2. Epstein SR. *Transferring technical knowledge and innovating in Europe 1200–1800*. London: London School of Economics; 2005.
3. Halvarsson Lundkvist A, Gustavsson M. Conditions for employee learning and innovation – interweaving competence development activities provided by a workplace development programme with everyday work activities in SMEs. *Vocations and Learning*. 2018/04/01 2018;11(1):45–63.
4. Billett S. Explaining innovation at work: A socio-personal account. In: Pederson SH, ed. Employee-driven innovation: A new approach. London: Palgrave-MacMillan; 2012: 92–107.
5. Hoyrup S, Bonnafous-Boucher M, Hasse C, Lotz M, Molller K, eds. *Employee-driven innovation: A new approach*. Basingstoke: Palgrave-McMillan; 2012.
6. Billett S. The co-occurrence of work, learning and innovation: Advancing workers' learning and work practices. In: Malloch M, Cairns L, O'Connor B, Evans K, eds. Sage handbook of learning and work. London: Sage; 2020.
7. Voss JF. Learning and transfer in subject matter learning: A problem-solving model. *International Journal of Educational Research*. 1987;11(6):607–622.
8. Shuell TJ. Phases of meaningful learning. *Review of Educational Research*. 1990; 60(4):531–547.
9. Anderson JR. Problem solving and learning. *American Psychologist*. 1993;48(1): 35–44.
10. Glaser R, Bassok M. Learning theory and the study of instruction. *Annual Review of Psychology*. 1989;40(1):631–666.
11. Mayer EC. *Employment-related key competencies for post-compulsory education and training – A discussion paper*. Canberra: Australian Government Printing Service; 1992.
12. Billett S, Yang S, Chia A, Tai JF, Lee M, Alhadad S. Remaking and transforming cultural practices: Exploring the co-occurrence of work, learning and innovation. In: Collin K, Glaveanu V, Lemmetty S, Forsman P, eds. *Creativity and learning: Contexts, processes and impact*. London: Palgrave McMillan; 2021: 219–244.
13. Wegener C. Driving forces of welfare innovation: Explaining interrelations between innovation and professional development. In: Billett S, Dymock D, Choy S, eds.

Supporting learning across working life: Models, processes and practices. Dorchrecht: Springer; 2017: 113–127.
14. Anvik C, Vedeler JS, Wegener C, Slettebø Å, Ødegård A. Practice-based learning and innovation in nursing homes. *Journal of Workplace Learning.* 2020;32(2):122–134.
15. Ellström PE. Practice-based innovation: A learning perspective. *Journal of Workplace Learning.* 2010;22(1/2):27–40.
16. Epstein SR. Craft guilds, apprenticeship, and technological change in preindustrial Europe. *The Journal of Economic History.* 1998;58(3):684–713.
17. Rowden R. How attention to employee satisfaction through training and development helps small business maintain a competitive edge: A comparative case study. *Australian Vocational Education Review.* 1997;4(2):33–41.
18. Lemmetty S, Billett S. Employee-Driven Learning and Innovation (EDLI) as a phenomenon of continuous learning at work. *Journal of Workplace Learning.* 2023;35(9):162–176.
19. Darrah CN. Complicating the concept of skill requirements: Scenes from a workplace. In: Hull G, ed. *Changing work, changing workers: Critical perspectives on language, literacy and skills.* New York: CUNY Press; 1997: 249–272.
20. Darrah CN. *Learning and work: An exploration in industrial ethnography.* New York: Garland Publishing; 1996.
21. Barbieri – Low AJ. *Artisans in early imperial China.* Seattle: University of Washington Press; 2007.
22. Gimpel J. *The Cathedral builders.* New York: Grove Press; 1961.
23. Billett S, Smith R, Barker M. Understanding work, learning and the remaking of cultural practices. *Studies in Continuing Education.* 2005;27(3):219–237.
24. Taylor FW. *The principles of scientific management.* New York: Harper; 1906.
25. Organisation for Economic Co-operational and Development. *OECD skills outlook 2013: First results from the survey of adult skills.* Paris: OECD; 2013.
26. Organisation of Economic and Cultural Development. *Skills matter: Further results from the survey of adult skills.* Paris: Organisation of Economic and Cultural Development; 2016.
27. OECD. *Do adults have the skills they need to thrive in a changing world?: Survey of adult skills 2023.* Paris: OECD; 2024.
28. Ministry of Manpower. *Singapore PIAAC data.* Singapore: Ministry of Manpower, Singapore; 2016.
29. Scott A. *Northern lights: The positive policy example of Sweden, Finland, Denmark and Norway.* Melbourne: Monash University Publishing; 2014.
30. Bertrand O, Noyelle T. *Human resources and corporate strategy: Technological change in banks and insurance companies in five OECD countries.* Paris: Organisation for Economic Co-operation and Development; 1988.
31. Billett S. Work, discretion and learning: Processes of learning and development at work. *International Journal of Training Research.* 2015;13(3): 214–230.
32. OECD., Eurostat. *Oslo manual: Guidelines for collecting and interpreting innovation data.* 3rd ed. Paris: OECD; 2005.
33. Chatham RE. The 20th century revolution in military training. In: Ericsson KA, ed. *The development of professional expertise.* Cambridge: Cambridge University Press; 2009: 27–60.
34. Lave J. The practice of learning. In: Chaiklin S, Lave J, eds. *Understanding practice: Perspectives on activity and context.* Cambridge: Cambridge University Press; 1993: 3–32.

35. Rogoff B, Lave J, eds. *Everyday cognition: Its development in social context.* Cambridge, MA: Harvard University Press; 1984.
36. Scribner S. Studying working intelligence. In: Rogoff B, Lave J, eds. *Everyday cognition: Its development in social context.* Cambridge, MA: Harvard University Press; 1984: 9–40.
37. Cole M, Engestrom Y. A cultural-historical approach to distributed cognition. In: Salomon G, ed. *Distributed cognitions: Psychological and educational considerations.* Cambridge: Cambridge University Press; 1997: 1–46.
38. Harteis C. Machines, change, work: An educational view on the digitalization of work. In: Harteis C, ed. *The impact of digitalization in the workplace: An educational view.* Cham: Springer; 2018: 1–10.
39. Ingold T. *The perception of the environment: Essays on livelihod, dwelling and skill.* London: Routledge; 2000.
40. Lave J. Situating learning in communities of practice. In: Resnick LB, Levine JM, Teasley S, eds. *Perspectives on socially shared cognition.* Washington, DC: American Psychological Association; 1991: 63–82.
41. Schatzki T. Practices and learning. In Grootenboer P, Edwards-Groves, C, Choy S (eds) *Practice theory perspectives on pedagogy and education: Praxis, diversity and contestation.* Singapore: Springer; 2017:23–43.
42. Bailey T. Organizational innovation in the apparel industry. Industrial Relations. 1993;32(1):30–48.
43. Billett S, Ehrich L, Hernon-Tinning B. Small business pedagogic practices. *Journal of Vocational Education and Training.* 2003; 55(2):149–167.
44. Barkey D, Kralovec E. *Learning and work: New possibilities.* Boston: North Eastern University; 2005.
45. Dore RP, Sako M. *How the Japanese learn to work.* London: Routledge; 1989.
46. Billett S, Harteis C, Gruber H. Developing occupational expertise through everyday work activities and interaction. In: Ericsson KA, Hoffman RR, Kozbelt A, eds. *Cambridge handbook of expertise and expert performance.* 2nd ed. New York: Cambridge University Press; 2018: 105–126.
47. Howard A, (ed). *The changing nature of work.* San Francisco, CA: Jossey-Bass Publishers; 1995.
48. Greeno JG, Simon HA. Problem solving and reasoning. In: Aitkinson RC, Hormiston RJ, Findeyez G, Yulle RD, eds. *Steven's handbook of experimental psychology and education, Vol 2.* New York: Wiley; 1988: 589–672.
49. Billett S. Learning through work: Workplace affordances and individual engagement. *Journal of Workplace Learning.* 2001;13(5):209–214.
50. Shanahan MJ, Hood KE. Adolescents in changing social structures: Bounded agency in life course perspective. In: Crockett LJ, Silbereisen RK, eds. *Negotiating adolescence in times of social change.* Cambridge: Cambridge University Press; 2000: 123–136.
51. Mclaughlin MW, Marsh DD. Staff development and school change. *Teachers College Record.* 1978;80(1):69–94.
52. Goodnow JJ, Warton PM. The social bases of social cognition: Interactions about work and their implications. *Merrill-Palmer Quarterly.* 1991;37(1):27–58.
53. Billett S. Sociogeneses, Activity and ontogeny. *Culture and Psychology.* 2003;9(2):133–169.
54. Valsiner J. *The guided mind: A sociogenetic approach to personality.* Cambridge, MA: Harvard University Press; 1998.

55. Scribner S. Vygostky's use of history. In: Wertsch JV, ed. *Culture, communication and cognition: Vygotskian perspectives*. Cambridge: Cambridge University Press; 1985: 119–145.
56. Billett S. The personal curriculum: Conceptions, intentions and enactments of learning across working life. *International Journal of Lifelong Education.* 2023;42(5):470–486.
57. Billett S. Personal epistemologies, work and learning. *Educational Research Review.* 2009;4(3):210–219.
58. Searle JR. *The construction of social reality*. London: Penguin; 1995.
59. Malle BF, Moses LJ, Baldwin DA. Introduction: The significance of intentionality. In: Malle BF, Moses LJ, Baldwin DA, eds. *Intentions and intentionality: Foundations of social cognition*. Cambridge, MA: The MIT Press; 2001: 1–26.
60. Wertsch JV. *Mind as action*. New York: Oxford University Press; 1998.
61. Billett S. *Work, Change and workers*. Dordrecht: Springer; 2006.

Part III
Practice-based learning and educative experiences

6 Practice curriculum

Before James became a sales representative for the cardboard box producing company, he undertook a set of workplace experiences to inform him about the processes required to make the boxes, the different kinds of materials and the variations of boxes that could be produced to serve customers' needs. This required him to work across the production facility and engage in a range of roles, using equipment and producing boxes. It was these experiences that allowed him, later, to work with enterprises in designing the kind of boxes they needed for their businesses.

Beau learnt much of his knowledge about garment manufacturing from working through the trouser, waistcoat and jacket production lines. He commenced making belt loops and pocket facings and progressed onto overlocking, hemming, and then seaming, and then on to producing fly openings and then waistbands in the trouser production line. Then, he moved on to making the lining of waistcoats, welt pockets, and then backing out the waistcoats, inserting buttonholes and buttons. After that, in working across the jacket production line he learnt how to apply interfacings, chest canvases, sewing the slippery linings, preparing and inserting sleeve ropings, pocket components and then inserting flaps into pockets and completing pocket bags, before finally being able to sew the collars onto jackets, and then pressing off on finishing. At the end of all of this, beyond being able to operate effectively a whole range of sewing machines and being able to perform all of these specific procedures, what he also learned was the logic of production, that is, the strategic knowledge associated with organising and enacting the production of garments.

Practice curriculum

This chapter focuses on describing and elaborating the organisation and sequencing of experiences in work settings that support effective learning of occupational practice and workplace requirements. It is referred to as the workplace[1] or practice curriculum.[2] It sets out the bases by which experiences in work settings might be organised and sequenced and when specific work interventions in the form of practice pedagogies are likely to be required.[3] This set of considerations is particularly germane because, to be effective, learning through work settings often needs to follow a pathway of experiences premised upon the sequential development of occupational capacities and/or the requirements of the work practice. Many such pathways are already established within the norms and practices of workplaces and are often informed by tradition and previous experiences. There are at least two kinds of considerations being enacted here through this sequencing. The first is exposing novices or newcomers to experiences through which they can incrementally and in a structured way build the capacities required for occupational performance and meeting workplace requirements. The second is how these might be sequenced and organised in ways that address individuals' readiness to progress along this pathway of experiences in ways that permits the building of that knowledge effectively, that is, developing their personal domain of occupational practice and workplace requirements. So, whilst learning through and for work is realised through combinations of access to and engagement in workplace activities and interactions, there are ways to sequence these experiences to optimise their learning potential.[4] Through engaging in these authentic work activities, workers access the kinds of knowledge needed to be learnt and applicable for occupational and workplace purposes.[5] This is because the kinds of activities and interactions with which individuals engage are generative of legacies (i.e., learning) related to the kind of thinking and acting required for those purposes.[6] As Rogoff and Lave succinctly stated: 'activity structures cognition.'[7] There are cognitive legacies arising from the kinds of activities in which individuals engage. As proposed in Chapter 1, when aligned with the requirements for work performance and occupational practices, these kinds of learning experiences can potentially be quite potent. Consequently, that potential for learning can be realised when those experiences are sequenced in ways that optimise those outcomes. This is why practice curriculums have been utilised across human history and remain pertinent today.

In considering how these outcomes can be realised through these experiences, the practice curriculum offers three key attributes: (i) immersion in work activities and interactions – learning through engaging in the lived experiences of a work community,[7–10] (ii) deliberate structuring of learning experiences that provide access to and engage with the knowledge required to be learnt and (iii) sequencing experiences in ways that incrementally assist individuals to learn that knowledge and build their personal domain of knowledge.[8,11–13] These elements are all quite consistent with the original conception of curriculum.

The origin of the term curriculum refers to 'a track to progress along' or 'course to follow' (i.e., *currere*).[14,15] The term has arisen from young males' participation in physical activities of the gymnasium in Hellenic Greece, referring to the course to progress along or the pathway of experiences. However, this concept has been adopted within the educational discourse largely to describe the kinds and pathways of experiences in and through educational institutions and as directed towards meeting prespecified educational outcomes. Indeed, in one of the first comprehensive texts theorising curriculum in 1949, Tyler[16] claimed that the purpose of curriculum was to achieve the goals of the 'school.' A broader interpretation of these pathways and purposes is quite well aligned with a curriculum founded in work settings that is largely aligned with meeting the needs of those occupations being practised or requirements of work settings. Importantly, Bobbitt,[17] who is seen as the founder of curriculum theory, defined it quite broadly as the 'entire range of experiences, both directed and undirected, concerned with unfolding the abilities of the individual' (p43). That is, it was intended to include the entire range of experiences encountered that shape individuals' learning and development, and not just those seen as being intentionally educational. Similarly, Dewey referred to 'unconscious education' that acknowledged much of individuals' learning arising through the everyday activities and interactions that constitute daily life; of course, for working age adults, these also comprise working life. These foundational concepts of curriculum are consonant with the range of contributions and kinds of day-to-day experiences in work settings as emphasised in anthropological studies.[8,11,18,19] Indeed, these processes have occurred over human history and across cultures.[13,20–24]

These pathways of experience are often part of the processes through which newcomers are introduced to norms and practices of work settings.[25] For instance, a key premise for that sequencing is progressing from activities in which, if errors are made, the consequences are limited, to those in which error costs are greater. Referred to by Lave as the 'learning curriculum,' examples of this model of sequencing are to progress from activities with low error risk to those where consequences of errors are greater, as with tailors,[18] hairdressers,[6] production workers,[26] doctors[12] and potters.[13] However, there are other models of practice curricula that are shaped by the kinds and circumstances of the occupational and work practice. These models of practice curriculum are largely derived from anthropological studies, which also inform work-based learning processes and interventions referred to as practice pedagogies (see Chapter 7). In the following, a range of models of practice curricula are advanced as a means of presenting options and demonstrating how learning through work can be organised and experiences enacted, being directed towards achieving the kinds of goals demanded by workplaces.

Foundations of practice curriculum

Accounts of individuals' learning to practise their occupations from anthropological studies have emphasised the foundational role of engagement in activities and interactions

  i within the lived experience of communities – the lived world comprising processes of everyday experiencing and enactment of that culturally derived practices;[8–10,27] ii intentional structuring of experiences – specific arrangements outside of that lived world that provide access to knowledge that otherwise would not be accessible in those communities.[8,12,13,27,28]

So, there are the kinds of learning arising through participation in the ordinary everyday activities and interactions, albeit in workplaces, homes or community settings, on the one hand, while on the other are circumstances created to intentionally provide access to and the development of specific kinds of capacities that cannot be learnt through the everyday experiences to which individuals have access. Elaborating these two kinds of experiences and their ordering assists in identifying how both kinds of experiences can be afforded to secure the kinds of learning required for those capacities.[29] Consequently, the concept of a practice curriculum as advanced here refers to the progression through everyday lived experience within a particular practice of community[30] or culture of practice[31] where the occupation is enacted. Yet, in some instances, the deliberate structuring of experiences is required to assist the knowledge to be learnt, and in ways that might not otherwise occur. These two dimensions of the learning curriculum are now discussed in turn.

The lived experience of a community

When individuals engage in the lived experiences in circumstances of work practice (e.g., construction sites, hospitals, schools and factories), learning associated with that practice arises through their participation in the everyday goal-directed activities and interactions that occur in those circumstances, largely mediated by learners' efforts and internationalities.[10,23,32] For instance, Bunn[8] identifies a range of skills learnt by children within nomadic Kyrgyzstan communities through the process of living and participating in community roles. These include being able to ride horses, herd and milk animals, harvest and utilise their skins and produce cheese and other food products, all of which are learnt mimetically through engaging in activities within those communities. So, as with language learning,[33] these capacities arise through active learning processes of engaging with and mediating what is experienced,[29] rather than being taught. Quite distinct pathways also exist in these communities based on gendered divisions of labour. The lived experience in these communities then reflect and reproduce those divisions by allocating different tasks to young boys and girls. Jordan[11] describes Mexican birth attendants' learning through growing up and living in the community and engaging with birthing women: roles (i.e., midwives) that would have been unavailable to males. Much of the learning reported in her study arose from novices' participation in the community and instances of birthing that were used in the developmental process. Here again, a societal more (i.e., gendered segmentation of occupations) was remade through this practice-based curriculum, highlighting the capacity to reproduce cultural practices. Yet, on its own, that reproduction may also be antithetical to progressing the needs of individuals or their communities.

For Rogoff,[7] apprenticeship is a term describing learning through participating in a community's everyday tasks and activities, whether learning language in villages or communities or girl scouts' annual cookie selling for fundraising. This is also the case for Singleton[13] who observed the same phenomena in Japanese pottery workplaces. Such is the ubiquity of this process when learning tailoring in Angola that Lave[34] states that whenever she encounters practice, she also finds learning. In her research on apprentices,[18] she describes learning progressing through apprentices being immersed in the practice of tailoring. It was through this work that she identified some key premises for the practice curriculum.[18] She found the sequencing of experiences afforded novice tailors was shaped by the requirements of practice and that they engaged in a sequence of tailoring tasks with little, if any, direct instruction occurring. Hence, she referred to this as the learning curriculum. The apprentices observed tailors and their working and used artefacts such as completed garments or those under construction, to guide their own approximations of what they had to achieve from what they had seen modelled (i.e., what they have observed).[18] The apprentices progressed along a pathway of tailoring activities shaped by the tailoring workshops' productive processes. They were not directly intentional or guided by more experienced practitioners but reflected the sequence of production of garments. This commenced with ironing and finishing garments in a sequence that was inherently pedagogic. Those processes allowed them to see the required qualities of finished garments that they had to emulate. Next, they progressed to making children's undergarments where, if mistakes were made, it would not be problematic, then on to adults' undergarments. Following that, they progressed to eventually being allowed to engage in making ceremonial garments where errors could be quite costly. In this way, their pathways of activities included initially engaging with tasks where errors could be tolerated and progressed by engaging progressively in tasks that were commensurate with their levels of tailoring competence (i.e., where their errors would not jeopardise the garments that they were making).[18] Importantly, throughout, there was no intentional engagement; rather, the activities were structured as part of the everyday practice of the workplace.

The processes of learning hairdressing were also found to progress from novice hairdressers keeping the hairdressing salon tidy, greeting clients and asking them whether they would like tea or coffee, with or without sugar and milk (i.e., 'tea and tidy'). The apprentices commenced hairdressing work by washing customers' hair, and then, later, washing the residues of chemicals and dyes from clients' hair.[4] From there, they progressed to placing rollers and curlers in hair and would practise on male clients before cutting females' hair. Beyond the progression from low to high error risks, there were other dimensions to the learning through this sequencing of experiences. Communicating and negotiating with clients is an important competence for hairdressers; hence, engaging in those processes of negotiating beverages and then having conversations with them when washing their hair are parts of the process of developing these occupational capacities. So, this sequencing of activities within hairdressing salons progressively engaged in tasks that were not only commensurate with the learners' readiness and technical competence but also provided experiences to progressively develop capacities of learning to communicate and negotiate with clients.

Similar patterns of progression of workplace activities and learning were identified in food manufacturing workers, hotel room attendants and medical doctors.[4] In the former, the progression of tasks was from the packaging area 'backwards' into the work area that organised and prepared breakfast cereals and made up the contents into bags which fitted within the cereal packages. The principle here was that workers needed to know what comprised the end product (i.e., getting the pouches of cereals into boxes, stacking them, placing them on pallets for delivery) as this shaped how work needed to progress earlier in the process. With the hotel room attendants, they first learnt how to prepare the room to an acceptable standard and pace in rooms that were checked out (i.e., had no guests), before progressing to working in rooms with guests. Also, with training medical doctors, novice interns were first asked to repeat the medical history taking and condition of patients that had already been undertaken by more experienced practitioners, with whom they then compared their diagnoses.[12] As well as being enacted across a range of these occupations, contemporaneously, these kinds of processes have been long-standing historically and, potentially, across cultures.

From earlier times in ancient India, Menon and Varma[24] report the discovery of miniature ceramic objects at an archaeological site. They propose that while some of these objects are toys, made by children, others were rough and immature versions of the objects made by adults found at those sites. That is, these versions were objects being made by novices as they attempted to improve the quality of their work. This process has been referred to by Gott[35] in more contemporary work situations as moving from immature to more mature approximations of the modelled task; this is the pottery pieces adults were producing. It is possible to trace the development or maturing qualities of objects made by children at this site, suggesting that the fashioning of these objects indicates a level of engagement by children in occupationally related play activities aligned with goals associated with contributing to the pottery work conducted within their families. These objects, which have no commercial purpose or value, could also be seen as bases through which the practice for work was developed. Clear levels of differentiation were identified in the skills exhibited in these miniature objects; these differences suggest a progressive development of skill amongst child crafters and may reflect age differences.

In these ways, the pathways of learning in the lived experiences within these locally and possibly family-run work settings were based on stages of maturation and moderated by gender segmentation and societal mores, in ways consistent with what Bunn[8] reports. In essence, there were courses to follow – tracks to progress along shaped by workplaces' productive requirements and through participating in a workplace community. Given the lack of evidence that any direct instruction or teaching occurred, the other notable quality about immersion within a particular practice community is that it was experienced and learnt mimetically, that is, largely through the active meaning-making and construction by the learner through observation, imitation and practice.[29] This process was also observed in Marchand's study of minaret building in Africa in which the apprentices were not instructed or taught but had to actively 'steal' the knowledge they needed to learn masonry tasks.[23] Part of achieving this outcome was to position themselves closely to the experienced masons so that they could observe and learn from them. That process of observation was enabled by the apprentices providing the masons with the kinds of stones and mortar they needed and when they were required. All of this occurred as part of the everyday lived experiences in these circumstances of practice and processes of learning. Yet, these processes of learning are intended to be initiated and exercised by apprentices.[32] This is directly aligned to what Singleton found in his study of apprentices learning pottery in Japan.[13] In this way, and as Coy[10] proposes, apprentice learning processes are part educational, part economic and partly about (reproducing) social relations.

> Apprenticeship is a form of gate-keeping. It is the gate through which a few are permitted access to a craft and its skills and secrets. On one side of this gate is everyday social and economic life; on the other side of this gate is membership in the craft. The concept of membership is indeed important in this respect ... craftsmanship implies not only a set of specialized skills, but a code of conduct as well ... occasionally embodied in a corpus of craft law.[10]
>
> (p.10)

It is these kinds of engagement and opportunities afforded through day-to-day work activities and interactions that shape opportunities for learning through the lived experiences of a work community. What this emphasises is that there are situational performances aligned with the norms and practices of work settings that also support the development, remaking and progression of capacities required for that setting. As Coy[10] suggests, it is about the continuity and regeneration of the work community that affords these opportunities and, where they are practised positively, including opportunities for learners. Similarly, studies of learning through work in Japanese corporations found that there were inherent practices of identifying tasks that novices could learn from and that provided them with the opportunity to do so.[36] However, there was one important caveat: the supervisors who provided these experiences were protected from being usurped and replaced by the workers whom they were supporting because advancement was based on seniority. A problematic issue in workplaces that provide less job security is that there might be caution about providing learning experiences for novices out of fear of being displaced by them. So, whereas these processes have the capacity to support the continuity of workplaces and the development of workers' capacities, there is also the risk that the experiences might be restricted and opportunities for novices limited on the basis that they may represent a threat to workers who might be replaced by them.

So, much learning occurs through immersion in everyday activities in work communities through sequenced engagement occurring within situations where affordances may be variously restricted, resisted or, alternatively, made widely accessible. This emphasises the role that this structure of experience plays in shaping practice curriculums. Whilst these experiences can permit participation and provide opportunities for observation and imitation, feedback and practice, they can be either promoted or constrained by the practices of those communities where they occur. This factor points to the important conclusion that whilst learning through day-to-day experiences is a key element of the practice curriculum, there are factors that can either inhibit or support that learning. Building upon this, and as indicated above, the second element of the practice curriculum comprises the intentional structuring of experiences.

Intentional structuring of experiences

Beyond the learning that occurs through everyday work activities and interactions is the deliberate structuring of experiences to intentionally promote and support learning that might not otherwise occur. Sometimes, everyday work experiences are unable to provide access to the knowledge required for occupational practice. For instance, in Hellenic Greece, medical education largely occurred through medical students caring for patients in their homes, having been briefed by the doctor by whom they were being supervised. However, these experiences were inadequate for all of the learning required to practise medicine. Consequently, two hybrid experiences were developed: first, the need for access to the codified knowledge of the medical domain, and this was made available through what became referred to as the textbook. These texts provided students with access to canonical knowledge of a particular field (e.g., medical knowledge) upon which they could draw when caring for patients. This assists in developing a personal domain of occupational knowledge. The second was the need for observing vivisections so medical students could learn about human anatomy, which was otherwise unavailable to them. So, these two kinds of hybrid learning experiences were deliberately introduced into practice-based medical education to provide access to experiences that otherwise would be unavailable in the circumstances of practice.

These kinds of intentional experiences were also utilised in circumstances where the required knowledge could not be acquired through family business or familiars. For instance, Bunn[8] identified four occupations within Kyrgyzstan communities whose development was not possible within the lived experiences of ordinary families: blacksmithing, yurt making (i.e., the tents nomadic people live in), traditional storytelling and falconry (i.e., hunting using an eagle). Each of these occupations necessitated engaging intentionally in specific sets of learning experiences outside of the everyday practices of these nomadic communities. The apprentice blacksmith had to work and learn by living in the blacksmith's family. The process of learning to make yurts was also structured in a similar way, because these were made within the family of the yurt maker, requiring long-term participation in making those tents. Similarly, the craft of telling traditional stories required spending time living and travelling with the storyteller to learn those stories and how to perform them. Developing skills in falconry required the raising of an eagle chick and teaching it how to hunt and return the prey to the falconer. So, when occupations have experiences that need to be accessed outside communities' everyday lived experiences, specific arrangements need to be enacted.

As stated in the introduction, in a recent study, one worker was employed by a packaging company to be a sales representative.[37] However, before being allowed to work in that role, he was provided with a set of structured experiences within the company's design and manufacturing areas. This entailed first working with the design team to understand the requirements of boxes for packaging different kinds of products (e.g., ones that were moist which required watertight installation, held products or were for exported goods). From understanding the design of these boxes and the use of different materials, he then progressed to work across the manufacturing plant, learning how to operate machines and important quality points in box manufacturing. All this was important as the sales job was not just to sell existing packaging, but to design and manufacture packaging for individual customers. This necessitated knowing how the boxes needed to be constructed and of what materials, what could or could not be printed on the outside of them, and how best they need to be constructed to meet customers' needs.

As noted, Marchand[23] also refers to apprentice minaret builders engaging in a process of intentional structured learning, albeit one where learners commenced by mixing mortar and fashioning stones before getting to supply the masons with materials and then coming to observe and, ultimately, practise stone-laying on the inside of the minaret being built. Only when they had honed their masonry skills through working on the inside of the minaret were the apprentices permitted to assist in placing stones on its outside. This task is most critical for the overall appearance of the minaret. All of this was learnt through participation and unobtrusive observation,[13,23] thereby emphasising the interdependency between the practice curriculum and personal epistemological actions.

Singleton[13] identified five stages through which apprentices progressed when working in a traditional Japanese pottery making high-quality teapots. These stages were (i) pre-practice observation, with the apprentice engaging in menial tasks in the workshop and household whilst observing how work was undertaken and the quality and standard of products been prepared; (ii) tentative experiments on the pottery wheel during lunch breaks or after the end of working days; (iii) being assigned regular practice at the wheel to develop and improve skills; (iv) being assigned production tasks at the wheel; and (v) a period of subsequent work in the shop as repayment for the training received. These apprenticeship stages were premised on access to and learning on the potter's wheel and these imperatives shaped the learning curriculum. This model of apprenticeship was different from those premised on progression from low to higher error cost,[18] as it involved gaining access to a piece of equipment whose priority was productive purposes (i.e., making pottery). Apprentices' access to pottery wheels had to be carefully managed as production was prioritised. The rough clay pots that were made during this period of practice were usually discarded and returned to the clay pit to be re-used the following day for productive purposes. Yet, this model of apprenticeship included ways of developing the skills and techniques required for making pottery.[13] This is because it provided opportunities to become competent in:

> ... the basic preparation and wedging of clay, methods of pottery forming other than those using the wheel, the preparation and application of decorative slips and glazes, styles of surface decoration, the careful techniques of firing, the intricate construction of kilns, aesthetic standards for judging one's own and others' work, strategies for marketing and displaying the ware that will build an artistic reputation, and the rituals and philosophies of pottery making and use.[13]
>
> (p.20)

Similarly, there was an ordering to the experiences of learning to make lace.[38] This ordering comprised (i) initial learning of the most basic stitches, (ii) using stitches to turn corners and (iii) making lace in the round and in a serpentine fashion. This sequencing or pathway of activities was justified as the means not just to make one weave, but also to become competent in the process of lace making. Hence, there were clear imperatives in the structuring of experiences to learn these occupational practices through models of different kinds of participation and pathways that are products of the occupational capacities to be developed and the exigencies of the circumstances of practice.

Educative access and reach: A caveat

There is an important caveat that needs to be introduced here. There are limits to the kinds of experiences that can be provided through work settings because of issues of access and availability of those experiences. The limited opportunity of access to the potter's wheel is just one example of the imperatives of production and the need to optimise time, artefacts and resources within work settings that restrict opportunities for developing occupational capacities. There are also experiences that cannot be found in work settings because they are simply unavailable, or in the kind of scale required for the number of novices. These are some of the reasons for establishing educational

Practice curriculum 111

institutions and experiences for developing occupational capacities with the formation of modern nation states.[39–41] Consequently, either some structured experiences within the workplace or provisions outside of them may be required, and increasingly. For instance, the growing need for accessing and comprehending the kinds of symbolic and conceptual knowledge required for contemporary working life represents such a challenge. The fact that much of this knowledge is relatively opaque (i.e., hard to access in work situations) suggests a growing need for both the structuring of work experiences and also efforts to make accessible knowledge which might otherwise remain inaccessible to the learner.[25] These requirements need to be addressed through engagement in specific educative experiences, yet also linked or aligned to experiences where those occupations are practised. So, the growing focus on work-integrated education seeks to provide and integrate the two sets of experiences (i.e., those in the education setting and workplace). These kinds of experiences may well be these that need to be increasingly pursued in the future, as is proposed in Chapter 9.

It would also be wrong to ignore and not be explicit that workplaces are contested environments. Access to experiences and close guidance can never be assured and may even be denied for organisational or personal reasons. In some instances, individuals will need to act agentically and with persistence to overcome these barriers.[26] Consequently, the interplay between affordances and individuals' engagement is central here. So, just as some individuals will reject or ignore invitations to participate as they are not motivated or interested or have other plans, equally, some individuals must exercise considerable agency to secure the experiences, guidance and support required to access and learn the kinds of knowledge that they need.[26] Thus, within a framing of the duality between affordances and engagements, what is discussed here offers models of the practice curriculum founded in empirical work which are consistent with many curriculum concepts and practices used in educational sciences.

Models of practice curriculum

Beyond the two broad approaches to the practice curriculum outlined above (i.e., the lived experience and intentionally organised ones), there are a range of models that are quite distinct in some ways because of their particular focus, the circumstances in which they need to be enacted and the processes of support for them. These provide instances that can be used as examples that might apply in other work contexts and that indicates their potential broader utilisation. In this section, these models are briefly described and broadly characterised. These qualities include the kind and ordering of experiences providing opportunities to engage progressively within a domain of occupational practice. They also include means for gaining access to, identifying, and securing goal-states (i.e., requirements for practice), comprising what was to be achieved. Nevertheless, they have distinct qualities.

As mentioned earlier, the ordering of experiences within the circumstances of tailoring practice has been referred to as the learning curriculum,[18] which is premised upon movement through tasks where error cost is a key consideration. Although this pathway was premised upon error cost, it was also inherently pedagogic and strong as it provided a set of structured experiences for the apprentices to understand the requirements for their work and then progressively engage in activities that developed tailoring capacities. Similarly, the activities of hairdressing apprentices were structured for them to incrementally develop occupational capacities through a pathway of experiences.[25] Again, there are important pedagogic qualities in terms of incremental development of skills, including the ability to communicate and negotiate with clients. Then, as noted, the path of activities was also identified in a food production plant, progressing in the reverse order to the production process.[26,42] So, the pathway of experience was to meet workplace imperatives. Similarly, as previewed, in a large and five-star hotel, novice room attendants progressed along a similar pathway. In this way, they had developed the capacities and understanding of their roles without having to be concerned with meeting the needs of any guests they might encounter and could begin to engage with them in English if required. The concern here was to manage the cognitive load[43] of the trained attendants as they developed the required capacities to perform the work.

From these examples, it might be concluded that these pathways of learning are restricted to occupations that have relatively low standing, and skills that are easily learnt through everyday practice. However, there are pathways of activities that professionals also must negotiate. Junior doctors sometimes have sequenced experiences through which they progress in hospitals when developing the capacities required for effective medical practice.[12] For instance, they might initially engage in admissions, history taking and examinations of new patients, repeating what had been done by the admitting doctor. Having conducted the history-taking and diagnosis, these junior doctors then consult with that doctor to compare their processes and outcomes. This is a highly engaging educational experience that is pedagogically rich[44] (i.e., has high learning potential). Having learnt and honed these skills, they progress to other kinds of activities, building upon foundational capacities of understanding patients and diagnosing their conditions.[12,45]

There is the process of parallel practice in medical education that is structured in ways to provide students with opportunities for patient history taking and diagnosis yet is set within clinical supervision.[46] In an example of this model, the first period of time (e.g., six weeks) comprised the medical student sitting in with the general practitioner during consultations, if the patients agreed. The doctor would sometimes use questioning and have students engage in activities as part of the history taking and diagnosis. Then, after this period of observation and partial engagement, students were provided with their own consulting room and with the agreement of patients they would conduct the history taking and diagnosis. Then the doctor would be consulted prior to finalising diagnoses and treatments. An important quality of this model is that medical students are provided with the opportunities to observe practice, understand how to conduct themselves as doctors and how to interact with patients and then engage in the clinical reasoning. Hence, this process engages them in active meaning making.

Similarly, Jordan[11] identified the temporal ordering of skill acquisition of the Mexican birth attendants mentioned earlier. They moved through phases of practice associated with developments within the prenatal phase, then onto the birthing process and postnatal support. Such traditions appear to be widely practised across cultures and practices, albeit shaped by specific kinds of activities and opportunities afforded by different kinds of occupations and circumstances of practice.

Table 6.1 presents and synthesises different kinds of sequencing of experiences – practice curricula, such as those mentioned above. This table presents the model of workplace curriculum, a description of its characteristics, and the kind of purposes it can secure. In the right-hand column are referenced how these experiences provide access to the forms and kinds of conceptual, procedural and dispositional knowledge that were advanced and discussed in Chapter 4. It is these forms of knowledge that are central to the performance of occupational tasks and meeting workplace requirements. Here, an attempt is made to indicate the kinds of knowledge likely to be provided by these models of practice curriculum. Although far from comprehensive, the range of models here indicates that there are options for pathways depending upon the kind of work being learned and the kinds of circumstances in which that working and learning occur. A consideration of the particular kinds of experiences is proposed as being likely to be generative of these forms of knowledge, based upon earlier and highly detailed analyses of how activities and interactions in work settings led to specific kinds of outcomes.[6,47]

The learning curriculum[18] is perhaps the most well-known and acknowledged pathway in which the sequencing of activities involves movement from novices engaging in activities in which there are few consequences if errors are made (i.e., low error risk) to those activities in which the consequences of errors are greater (i.e., high error risk).[18] Lave also identified the progressions of tailors' apprentices based on this principle. Her work also identified the pedagogic qualities and intents in this sequencing that was in many ways analogous to what occurs in educational settings.[25] Similar pathways were evident for hairdressers, production workers and hotel room attendants. Equally, the study of junior doctors also indicated progression of activities and learning premised on this principle.[12]

However, not all practice curriculum pathways are premised upon considerations of error risk. For instance, the stages or pathways associated with learning to be a potter are premised on access to artefacts (i.e., the potter's wheel) and materials,[13] with learning opportunities only occurring when the potter's wheel is not used for productive purposes, requiring a different kind of participation by novices. That is, rather than being involved directly in the

Table 6.1 Workplace curriculum practices – qualities and ordering of experiences for effective work and learning

Practice	Description	Purposes	Knowledge
Apprenticeship as a way of life	Engaging individuals in the lived experience of workplaces by participating in their everyday activities and interactions[8,11] to understand the practices and requirements for performance[18,38]	Identifying goals for workplace performance and learning procedural and conceptual knowledge, including honing procedures, forming propositional associations and developing strategic procedures	DP/C; PS/H; CS/D
Ordering of experiences	Providing access to and ordering of experiences required to learn occupational capacities not acquired through everyday work. Might entail skill acquisition in stepwise manner, from those that are easy to learn to more difficult	Offering a pathway of experiences through which occupational capacities (i.e., conceptual, procedural and dispositional) can be developed	DP/C; PS/H; CS/D
Learning (practice) curriculum	Organising access to work activities from those that have low consequences when errors occur, to those where error costs are high, commencing with observations to understand goal states and then progressing through activities of increasingly demanding work requirements.[18] In work where all components carry salience (e.g., midwifery,[11] junior doctors[12]) learning might be acquired in a linear order	Organising a pathway of experiences whose ordering is based on pedagogic and practice-based considerations, such as increased complexity or error cost	DP/C; PS/H; CS/D
Learning activities as work conditions permit	Learning staged around workplace imperatives (e.g., learning pottery relies on access to potter's wheel): (i) pre-practice observation with apprentice engaged in menial work activities, (ii) tentative experiments with wheel (when not used for productive purposes), (iii) assigned regular practice at wheel, (iv) assigned production tasks at wheel and (v) a period of work to repay training[13]	A pathway of experiences based upon access to other workers, equipment, resources that bring together the imperatives of work, workplace and learning	DP/C; PS/H; CS/D
Parallel practice	Individuals engaging in an occupational practice and being monitored and checked by a more experienced partner at key point in task's completion[48] e.g., doctors – seeing patients, taking histories and conducting examinations, often in parallel to what has been done by a registrar[12]	Opportunities to engage in authentic activities whilst being monitored and checked by a qualified practitioner	PS/H; CS/D

Note. Factual conceptual knowledge (CS); Deep or interlinked conceptual knowledge (CD); Specific procedural knowledge (PS); Strategic or higher order (PH); Personal dispositions (DP); and cultural norms, societal values or sentiments (DC).

production of pots, during periods of production, the novices' role was to provide support and engagement to the potters. The example of parallel practice provides a different kind of model, one that permits novices to engage in authentic clinical activities including clinical reasoning. And before they conclude their diagnosis, they must check and assure the doctor that their conclusions and any treatments are consistent with what the doctor might have concluded and prescribed themselves.

These instances illustrate how different and distinct kinds of practice curricula are conceived, organised and structured and, thereby, how they provide opportunities for learning. A fundamental premise is that learning and work co-occur, and specific opportunities for practice must fit within the requirements for productive work activities. In all, the focus on learning is premised upon work settings providing experiences that afford learners the opportunities to incrementally engage to develop the capacities required for effective performance in those settings.

Practice curriculum in conclusion

This chapter has discussed the role that practice curricula play in organising and enriching learning experiences in workplaces. Consistently, they are either the product of the lived experience in workplaces or the intentional structuring of experiences to achieve specific outcomes. Yet, there are diverse ways of sequencing and structuring experiences across different kinds of occupational practice and work settings. Given the emphasis on a pathway of experiences in workplaces, the practices that variously invite, structure, support and guide workers in the kinds of thinking, acting and learning are important for effective outcomes from these curricula.

Understandings about the processes of engaging in and learning through socially situated practices more generally are also important not only for workplaces, but also for educational institutions, community organisations and families. That engagement seeks to secure the continuity of that practice and is shaped and complicated by circumstances in which different interests and power relationships are embedded and enacted. So, the deliberations here comprise foundations from which to consider, plan and evaluate practice curricula across the diverse social settings in which individuals participate in work and engage in learning throughout their working lives.

In conclusion, the following principles arise from considerations about practice curricula. These comprise:

- the need to engage in the lived experience of work over time and through authentic work activities;
- progression along a pathway of activities exposing individuals to the processes of and goals for effective work, and progressively furnishing experiences that incrementally develop the understandings, values and procedures required for effective work performance;

- identification of and providing access to particular kinds of experiences to develop capacities which will not be learnt through engaging in the lived experience of the workplace; and
- ordering and sequencing of experiences in ways which most effectively support individuals' learning.

This then leads to considerations of how these experiences can be enriched through practice pedagogies and individuals coming to engage effectively in them. These are the topics of the following two chapters.

References

1. Billett S. Constituting the workplace curriculum. *Journal of Curriculum Studies.* 2006;38(1):31–48.
2. Billett S. Learning through work: premises, conceptions and practices. In: Tierney RJ, Rizvi F, Ercikan K, eds. *International encyclopedia of education.* 4th ed. Oxford: Elsevier; 2023: 381–389.
3. Billett S. Workplace pedagogic practices: Co-participation and learning. *British Journal of Educational Studies.* 2002;50(4):457–481.
4. Billett S. Workplace curriculum: Practice and propositions. In: F. Dorchy DG, ed. *Theories of learning.* London: Routledge; 2011: 17–36.
5. Billett S. Authenticity and a culture of workpractice. *Australian and New Zealand Journal of Vocational Education Research.* 1993;2(1):1–29.
6. Billett S. *Learning in the workplace: Strategies for effective practice.* Sydney: Allen and Unwin; 2001.
7. Rogoff B. *Apprenticeship in thinking – Cognitive development in social context.* New York: Oxford University Press; 1990.
8. Bunn S. The nomad's apprentice: different kinds of apprenticeship among Kyrgyz nomads in Central Asia. In: Ainely P, Rainbird H, eds. *Apprenticeship: Towards a new paradigm of learning.* London: Kogan Page; 1999: 74–85.
9. Chan S. Learning through apprenticeship: belonging to a workplace, becoming and being. *Vocations and Learning.* 2013;6(3):367–383.
10. Coy MW, ed. *Apprenticeship: From theory to method and back again.* New York: SUNY; 1989.
11. Jordan B. Cosmopolitical obstetrics: Some insights from the training of traditional midwives. *Social Science and Medicine.* 1989;28(9):925–944.
12. Sinclair S. *Making doctors: An institutional apprenticeship.* Oxford: Berg; 1997.
13. Singleton J. The Japanese folkcraft pottery apprenticeship: Cultural patterns of an educational institution. In: Coy MW, ed. *Apprenticeship: From theory to method and back again.* New York: SUNY; 1989: 13–30.
14. Marsh CJ. *Key concepts for understanding curriculum.* London: Routledge-Falmer; 2004.
15. Pinar WF. The method of "Currere" (1975). *Counterpoints.* 1994;2:19–27.
16. Tyler RW. *Basic principles of curriculum and instruction.* Chicago, IL: University of Chicago Press; 1949.
17. Bobbitt F. *The curriculum.* Boston: Houghton Mifflin; 1918.
18. Lave J. The culture of acquisition and the practice of understanding. In: Stigler JW, Shweder RA, Herdt G, eds. *Cultural psychology.* Cambridge: Cambridge University Press; 1990: 259–286.

19. Lave J, Packer M. Towards a social ontology of learning. In: Nielsen K, Brinkmann S, Elmholdt C, Tanggaard L, Musaeus P, Kraf G, eds. *A qualitative stance*. Aarhus: Aarhus Universitetsforlag; 2008: 17– 46.
20. Kovach SA. *An Artisan's Tale: T'ang dynasty pottery*. New York: Teachers College, Columbia University; 1987.
21. Lodge RC. *Plato's theory of education*. London: Kegan Paul, Trench, Trubner; 1947.
22. Gowlland G. Learning craft skills in China: Apprenticeship and social capital in an artisan community of practice. *Anthropology and Education Quarterly*. 2012;43(4):358–371.
23. Marchand THJ. Muscles, morals and mind: Craft apprenticeship and the formation of person. *British Journal of Education Studies*. 2008;56(3):245–271.
24. Menon J, Varma S. Children playing and learning: Crafting ceramics in Ancient Indor Khera. *Asian Perspectives*. 2010;49(1):85–109.
25. Billett S. *Work, Change and workers*. Dordrecht: Springer; 2006.
26. Billett S. Guided learning at work. *Journal of Workplace Learning*. 2000; 12(7):272–285.
27. Rogoff B. Observing sociocultural activity on three planes: Participatory appropriation, guided participation, apprenticeship. In: Wertsch JW, Alvarez A, del Rio P, eds. *Sociocultural studies of mind*. Cambridge: Cambridge University Press; 1995: 139–164.
28. Jordan B. The Double Helix of Learning: Knowledge transfer in traditional and techno-centric communities. Unpublished transcript. Palo Alto Research Center; 2011.
29. Billett S. *Mimetic learning at work: Learning in the circumstances of practice*. Dordrecht: Springer; 2014.
30. Gherardi S. Community of pratice or practices of a community? In: Armstrong S, Fukami CV, eds. *The Sage handbook of management learning, education, and development*. London: Sage; 2009: 514–530.
31. Brown AL, Palinscar AM. Guided, cooperative learning and individual knowledge acquisition. In: Resnick LB, ed. *Knowing, learning and instruction, essays in honour of Robert Glaser*. Hillsdale, NJ: Erlbaum & Associates; 1989: 393–451.
32. Marchand TH. *The pursuit of pleasurable work: Craftwork in twenty-first century England*. London: Berghahn Books; 2022.
33. Sticht TJ. *Functional context education*. San Diego, CA: Applied Cognitive and Behavioural Science; 1987.
34. Lave J. The practice of learning. In: Chaiklin S, Lave J, eds. *Understanding practice: Perspectives on activity and context*. Cambridge: Cambridge University Press; 1993: 3–32.
35. Gott S. Apprenticeship instruction for real-world tasks: The co-ordination of procedures, mental models, and strategies. *Review of Research in Education*. 1989;15:97–169.
36. Dore RP, Sako M. *How the Japanese learn to work*. London: Routledge; 1989.
37. Billett S, Olesen HS, Filliettaz L. *Sustaining employability through work-life learning: Practices and policies*. Vol 35: Dordrecht: Springer; 2023.
38. Makovichy N. 'Something to talk about': Notation and knowledge-making among Central Slovak lace-makers. *Journal of the Royal Anthropological Institute (NS)*. 2010;16(Supplement S1):80–99.
39. Gonon P. A short history of German Vocational pedagogy: From idealistic classics to 'Realistic' research. In: Mjelde L, Daly R, eds. *Working knowledge in a globalizing world*. Bern: Peter Lang; 2006: 197–212.

40. Greinert WD. *Vocational education and training in Europe: Classical models of the 19th-century and training in England, France and Germany during the first half of the 20th.* Luxembourg: Office for Official Publications of the European European Communities; 2005.
41. Troger V. Vocational training in French schools: The fragile State-employer alliance. Paper presented at: Towards a history of vocational education and training (VET) in Europe in a comparative perspective, 2002; Florence.
42. Billett S. *Vocational education: Purposes, traditions and prospects.* Dordrecht, The Netherlands: Springer; 2011.
43. Kirschner PA. Cognitive load theory: Implications of cognitive load theory on the design of learning. *Learning and Instruction.* 2002;12:1–10.
44. Billett S, Noble C. Utilizing pedagogically rich work activities to promote professional learning. *Éducation & Didactique.* 2020;14(3):137–150.
45. Sturman N, Tan Z, Turner J. "A steep learning curve": Junior doctor perspectives on the transition from medical student to the health-care workplace. BMC Medical Education. 2017;17(1):1–7.
46. Brown J, Wearne S. Supervision in general practice settings. In Nestel D, Reedy G, McKenna L, Gough S, eds. *Clinical education for the health professions: theory and practice.* Singapore: Springer; 2020:1–26.
47. Billett S. Conceptualizing learning experiences: Contributions and mediations of the social, personal and brute. *Mind, Culture and Activity.* 2009;16(1):32–47.
48. Billett S, Sweet L. Understanding and appraising healthcare students' learning through workplace experiences: Participatory practices at work. In: Cleland J, Durning S, eds. *Researching medical education.* Oxford: Wiley; 2015:117–127.

7 Practice pedagogies

Work, pedagogic practices and learning

Across human history, most of the learning for advancing occupational practice has occurred through the circumstances in which that practice is enacted (i.e., work settings), much of it through individuals' engagement in everyday work tasks,[1] that is, through individuals' learning as they participate in work activities and interactions, much of it premised upon mimetic processes such as observation, imitation and practice. Yet, it is also possible to identify a range of practices that have been adopted through which that learning has been guided and supported. These might be described as practice pedagogies. They comprise particular kinds of activities or interactions that augment or enrich learning experiences, often enacted by more experienced workers, but they include engaging in particular work activities and with artefacts.[1] Yet, not many of those practices resemble much of what would be classified as teaching of the kind that is practised in educational institutions. Instead, these practices are used in conjunction with the enactment of work activities and emphasise pressing novices or newcomers into initiating and taking responsibility for their learning. Almost universally, it seems that these practices have arisen because discovery efforts of individuals learning mimetically were insufficient to develop the required understandings or occupational processes necessary to learn the capacities required to perform work activities. This was particularly the case when the knowledge had to be made accessible to the learners and focused on their learning to construct it.

This chapter seeks to describe what constitutes the kinds and characteristics of these practice pedagogies. Examples of these practices are used to illuminate and elaborate these practices and to discuss their potential for supporting learning and development in and through workplace activities and interactions. So, beyond the organisation of access to and structuring of experiences in work settings (i.e., practice curriculum – see Chapter 6) are these practices that can be used to inform, support, augment or direct individuals' learning of the kinds of capacities required for workplace performance. As noted, much, and perhaps most, of the learning occurring in and through work activities and interactions arises through workers' active engagement with what they are afforded in work settings. Yet, there are limits to the degree by which their learning through discovery efforts alone can be sufficient. Because the knowledge to be learnt arises from and through history, culture and situation (i.e., the social world), it is necessary for individuals to be able to access, experience and construct that knowledge. This is referred to as inter-psychological or inter-mental processes, meaning the need to engage with the sources of knowledge beyond the person because that is where it is sourced and can be made accessible. Hence, assistance is required for individuals to engage with and mediate (i.e., make meaning of) that knowledge. This may require being guided and supported by experienced or expert co-workers who possess that knowledge and/or the artefacts that provide access to it. However, and importantly, these pedagogical practices are not restricted to interventions by other and more experienced practitioners, such as close guidance, modelling, coaching and mentoring. Instead, there is a wider range of means by which that knowledge can be mediated. This includes engagement with texts, artefacts and particular kinds of activities that provide access to the articulation, consideration and deliberations about knowledge they need to access and with which they need to engage. For instance, flotsam and jetsam can be used on beaches to assist fishers to remember the star patterns at night by which they will need to navigate.[2] Consequently, these practices comprise a far broader range of educative experiences than those associated with direct interpersonal interactions, such as through what is referred to as proximal or close interpersonal guidance (e.g., guidance, teaching, instruction, scaffolding). They can also include, for instance, the ability to utilise observation of half-completed jobs, engagement with artefacts, the use of mnemonics (i.e., aids to memory) and engagement in particular kinds of work activities. For instance, some work activities comprise activities in which problems or cases are presented and discussed, evaluations made and recommendations advanced that represent potentially powerful learning situations. These are referred to here as pedagogically rich work activities.[3] Key qualities of such activities are that they usually occur as part of ordinary day-to-day work activities and are embedded within those activities, strengthening their effectiveness as they are directly related to the kinds of knowledge that need to be learnt, thereby enhancing their applicability. Also, because they are enacted in the physical and social environment that provides cues and clues for their recall, this also enhances the cognition that is essential for the organisation and recall of knowledge that individuals learn. Indeed, it is these kinds of activities that are held to promote access to, construction of and indexation of the kinds of knowledge that are learnt and can be recalled through these experiences.

This chapter identifies and discusses a range of practice pedagogies and indicates the kinds of knowledge that they are likely to develop and the means by which they can be enacted. It does this by emphasising the importance of some kinds of learning needing to be mediated by others, by artefacts or by specific activities. Building upon that premise, the following sections introduce and discuss a range of such practices. The qualities of these pedagogic practices and their applicability to work settings are then discussed, including considerations of the kinds of knowledge of which they are likely to be generative. Finally, some conclusions about the importance of the worth and qualities of these practices are stated.

Mediating learning within work practice

Beyond identifying the organisation and sequencing of experiences within work settings that can assist the development of workers' capacities, as in the practice curriculum, it is also necessary to identify ways that can enrich those experiences, that is, identifying a set of pedagogic practices suited to work settings. Importantly, whenever possible, those practices must be relevant to, able to be applied to and germane to work settings and the productive tasks being completed. This is because of the importance of embedding them within authentic work activities and the social and physical settings that comprise the circumstances of the practice. It is these qualities that are important for cognition, as foreshadowed above. Also, in practical terms, these settings are likely to be the sites that are most accessible and scalable for developing further the capacities of workforces. That is, given the scale and task of developing, reinvigorating and maintaining the currency of the occupational competence of entire workforces, this is unlikely to be realised through participation in tertiary education institutions alone.[4] Not least here is that many capacities are unlikely to be effectively learnt elsewhere, because the kinds of experiences able to be provided in and through those work settings are not able to be reproduced elsewhere. For instance, traditional teaching methods will have limited efficacy for developing manufacturing employees' competencies.[5] Yet, given all of this, there is a need to ensure that those experiences can be as rich and effective in realising the kinds of knowledge that need to be learnt. So, there are both pedagogic and practical reasons why the development of workers' occupational competence and workplace requirements may well be most likely developed within work settings.[6] Hence, it is important to make explicit and to find ways of supporting workers' learning in those settings. This includes embedding or aligning them within work practice. As stated in earlier chapters, there are specific cognitive legacies arising from the kinds of work activities and interactions in which individuals engage – 'activities structure cognition.'[7] The indexical properties of work practices and work activities[8,9] and the physical and social contributions of workplace settings support both the processes of cognition (i.e., recognition, recall) and the organisation and recall of knowledge[10,11] that assist in easing the demands of activities requiring higher cognitive functions.[12,13] So, rather than being neutral, the social and physical environments where activities and interactions occur, such as workplace settings, are deeply informative and can support access to, ordering of, and engagement with what has been experienced.[14,15] There are also kinds of knowledge that may need to be mediated because they are difficult to observe, engage with or otherwise access. This is why interventions are required to achieve specific learning goals.

Consequently, those activities are shaped by particular social circumstances and interactions that are aligned with what will be needed for their performance. So, there may well be different and potentially inferior outcomes than when those experiences occur within a physical and social circumstance remote from the circumstances in which what is learnt needs to be applied. Part of those circumstances are the mediational means by which that knowledge can be made accessible and comprehensible or applicable. In the contemporary era, whilst this kind of mediation is often viewed as being best developed in hybrid learning spaces (i.e., classrooms) and by the actions and mediation of teachers,[16,17] this may not be the case with the kinds of knowledge required for work practice. Indeed, much evidence suggests that learning in school-like settings does not readily transfer to other settings.[18] Even in the circumstances of practice, there is often a need to use explicit examples or analogies to make accessible knowledge that cannot be experienced directly.

To identify the most effective mediational means for learning in and through work, it is necessary to go beyond the orthodoxies of 'classroom' activities and practices enacted in educational settings. This is because they are configured in different ways than the circumstances of practice, which often leads to failure to translate or transfer what has been learnt in those settings to other social and physical circumstances.[19,20] How they are experienced and constructed in these hybrid settings does not necessarily prompt recall or applicability to other kinds of settings where that knowledge needs to be applied.[21,22] This is referred to as the transfer problem.[20,23] But this problem is far more fundamental than the transference of knowledge from one situation to another (e.g., school to workplace).[24] That is, individuals' recall or recognition of that knowledge and its applicability can be hampered by differences in physical and social settings.[25] Having learned experiences in the kinds of settings and embedding them in work activities and interactions in which that knowledge will be deployed stands to minimise issues associated with learning transfer.[18] When the processes of knowledge construal and construction occur in physical and social settings distinct from those in which the knowledge needs to be applied, that learning may not be readily applicable to the requirements of other circumstances. This lack of adaptability is premised on how learners have construed and constructed the knowledge in those circumstances, making it less readily able to be recalled, applied and used effectively in other circumstances. The important point here is that the circumstances in which individuals engage in thinking and acting (i.e., cognition) are central to how that knowledge is structured, indexed cognitively and organised and associated. This influences how it is recognised, recalled and applied. To use another terminology, experiences that are authentic and guidance that is pertinent to the practices to be enacted are more likely to make the task of recalling and application 'near' rather than 'far' transfer.[22] All of this suggests that mediational means in the form of pedagogic practices for work settings often remain necessary to assist in the development of the knowledge required for occupational competence and workplace performance.

Towards pedagogies of and for practice

There is a need for pedagogies that can assist in providing access to socially and culturally derived knowledge. Without them, that knowledge may not be able to be engaged with and constructed by individuals; therefore, there is a need for strategies to assist in accessing what learners will find difficult to be learnt through discovery alone. So, interventions such as direct explanations, analogies, the use of artefacts and visual representations of concepts and procedures may be required to make that knowledge accessible and engaged with by workers.[26] One way of providing access to this knowledge is through the support and guidance of more experienced and informed interlocutors (e.g., co-workers). Across human history, there have been instances where interventions by more experienced practitioners have been necessary when the knowledge is hard to learn. Examples include the use of flotsam and jetsam on beaches to indicate positions of stars in the night sky as a means for assisting Micronesian fishermen learning to navigate at night,[2] birth attendants in Yucatán learning through stories and narratives from more experienced attendants, experienced potters placing their hands over those of novices to assist them in getting the feel for shaping pots on the wheel,[27,28] and experienced lace makers assisting novices in learning how to hold multiple needles when producing complicated lace patterns.[29] In all these instances, there is a combination of active engagement by the learners supported by insights, artefacts or direct support by a more knowledgeable interlocutor. However, as indicated, there are also various other pedagogic practices that are not shaped by dyadic and direct interpersonal interactions between the novice and the more experienced individual.

Whilst efforts to replicate workplace activities and interactions in education institutions are welcome and sometimes effective for initial occupational preparation, they may still lack the authenticity of the social and physical environments of workplaces and authentic bases for engaging and learning through work activities. For instance, an experienced nurse once critiqued the mock hospital wards that are used in universities' nurse education courses. Whilst conceding they had some contributions, she also stated in her interview informing this study:

> Do those substitute wards have nurses who are quarrelling and competing, doctors who have been awake for over 24 hours, patients who paint poo on the wall in the middle of the night?[30]

The point being made here is that many of the facets of actual work performance cannot be reproduced in these kinds of settings. While initiatives such as hybrid learning experiences in Dutch tertiary education institutions[31] are as helpful means of providing initial occupational preparation as are those enacted earlier through what were referred to as learning factories,[5] these kinds of experiences are incomplete as they may not provide access to learning through authentic work-related activities. It is not a question of either formal instruction or learning through practice, but a combination of these mediational means.[2] For the learning of work capacities across working life, this combination of contributions most likely needs to be accessed through work activities and interactions.

So, pedagogic practices aligned with, and which can be enacted through everyday work activities and interactions are those proposed in many but not all situations, likely to be helpful to secure access to knowledge such as kinds of conceptual and procedural work requirements that are difficult to access or discover alone. This means that orthodox instructional processes offered through educational institutions and programmes may not be optimal due to the specific requirements for accessing and mediating knowledge across working life. Consequently, workplaces or work practices are likely to be the circumstances for much of this development, and the pedagogic practices supporting it will likely be quite particular to the specific work practices.

Practice pedagogies

Practice pedagogies refer to activities or interactions that can augment or enrich the learning that can arise through everyday work activities and interactions. They can be enacted either directly or indirectly by more experienced workers or co-workers and include work activities and engagements with artefacts to promote specific kinds of learning in and through practice in work settings. Pedagogic practices are also what teachers utilise in classrooms to promote student learning in educational settings. However, here the focus is on pedagogies that are aligned to and occur within circumstances of actual practice (i.e., practice pedagogies), rather than those occurring in hybrid institutions whose focus is on education per se (e.g., teacherly practices and strategies). Most pedagogies identified in anthropological, historical or sociocultural literatures are those that either arise in or can be enacted through activities and interactions associated with the conduct of culturally derived practices such as occupations, as these practices are inherent and often essential to the communities in which they are enacted in their continuity. This circumstance perhaps explains why so many studies have referred to processes associated with this learning in the circumstances in which they are enacted (i.e., practice and practice settings). The key point here is that as these practices are essential to the communities where they are enacted, efforts associated with their remaking and reproduction are often quite explicit and observable.

Like those used in educational institutions, some of these pedagogies are associated with direct guidance for novices or newcomers provided by more experienced workers. However, many are associated with activities that are inherently supportive of learning, but in ways that are quite distinct from those that occur in educational institutions. Instead, they are shaped by the requirements of the circumstances of practice. So, it is important to move

Table 7.1 Workplace pedagogic practices – activities and interactions enhancing learning

Practice	Description	Purposes	Knowledge
Storytelling	Telling stories about work events and incidents	Illustrating or capturing concepts or hypothetical formulations to assist in decision-making; legitimate practitioner as expert	DC; PS/H; CS/D
Verbalisation	Talking aloud whilst performing a work task as a form of direct guidance; can be linked to 'hands on' engagement[27]	Explaining the thinking and acting being used whilst performing work tasks	DC/DP; CS/D; PH
Pedagogically rich activities	Workplace activities that are inherently pedagogically rich, e.g., handovers[33] or mortality and morbidity meetings	Developing conceptual and specific and strategic procedural capacities	DP/C; PS/H; CS/D
Guided learning (proximal guidance)	Direct interaction between more and less experienced co-workers to promote learning in work settings. Use of modelling, demonstrating, guided practice, monitoring progress and gradual withdrawal of direct guidance,[32,34,35] master placing hands on novices to assist getting the 'feel' of pottery,[27] guided discovery – placing novices in situations where they can practise, hone skills and gain experience independently, yet still have direct guidance[36]	Extending what individuals can learn through discovery alone, by modelling of activities to be learnt, guidance to assist in achieving modelled performance and providing opportunities to refine and hone	DP/C; PS/H; CS/D

(Continued)

Table 7.1 (Continued)

Practice	Description	Purposes	Knowledge
Partially worked example/direct instruction and hands-on	Combination of guidance and using a worked example, e.g., experienced lace-maker producing a small piece of simple lace, showing novice how bobbins are held, and placing hands on novices to assist in learning hand movements to use the bobbins. Also asking novice which bobbin they should use for the next stitch before novice makes movement, leading to confidence in action. Questioning gradually ceased as competence demonstrated[29]	Provision of models for performance, ability to engage in sub-skills associated with that performance and build understanding about procedural capacities	PS/H
Heuristics	Tricks of the trade (i.e., procedures that will give you certainty)[37]		PS/H
Mnemonics	Developing and using mnemonics (doctors' use of 5 Fs, DANISH to remember about cerebellar lesions) and actual patients (remember Mr Leeming and you will remember about duodenal ulcers, Freddie Mercury and missed seroconversion)[38] for procedural efficiency[39,40]	A means to remember and recall propositions and secure procedural efficacy	PS/H; CS
Artefacts	Artefact or notation system that assists by embedding the knowledge required in a localised context and assists skills and proficiency[29]	Providing clues and cues on how to proceed	PS/H; CS

Note. Factual conceptual knowledge (CS); deep or interlinked conceptual knowledge (CD); specific procedural knowledge (PS); strategic or higher order (PH); personal dispositions (DP); cultural norms, societal values or sentiments (DC).

away from the idea that practice pedagogies are analogies of teaching, but implemented in work settings: instead, a far broader range of pedagogic practices need to be considered and many of them predate and continue to be effective in the era of schooled societies, such as our own.

Table 7.1 provides a summary of examples of different kinds of practice pedagogies and their purposes and contributions to developing specific kinds of knowledge. This listing arose from a literature search for these kinds of practices and, whilst not comprehensive, it provides examples of the kinds and scope of such practices. In this table, the pedagogic practices are presented in the left-hand column, a brief description and source(s) presented in the column to its right, then the potential purposes of these practices for learning, and then in the right-hand column are indications of the kinds of knowledge that can be generated through these practices, as described and discussed in Chapter 4. A consideration of the particular kinds of mediation enacted by this selection of pedagogic practices is proposed here as being likely to be generative of these particular forms of knowledge, based upon earlier and highly detailed analyses of how activities and interactions in work settings led to specific kinds of outcomes.[32]

In all, practice pedagogies are those that can promote learning in and through workplace activities and interactions such as storytelling, verbalisation,[27] pedagogically rich activities,[41] guided learning/proximal guidance,[35,42] direct instruction and 'hands-on' guidance,[27-29] indirect/distal guidance,[27,28,32] heuristics[37] and mnemonics[38,40] and partially worked examples.[29] Also, there are pedagogic practices associated with the development of particular kinds of knowledge. Procedural development can be promoted through modelling, coaching and scaffolding.[34] Conceptual development can be promoted through questioning, diagrams and explanations.[32] Importantly, these learning opportunities arise through everyday work activities. Each of these practices is now briefly described and discussed in turn.

Storytelling

Storytelling provides narratives that can be used to illustrate concepts and inform about procedures that are used to secure outcomes. Narratives are particularly instrumental for assisting human cognition: they assist in organisation and recall of memory. That is, people can remember them, because they are memorable – they can be recalled because their indexicality (i.e., how they are organised and recalled) is strong. How knowledge is organised in memory is linked to rich associations that permit recall and utilisation. Hence, they are potent bases for individuals to remember and recall. Storytelling used by Mexican birth attendants occurs in walking round the village with novices and indicating houses where different kinds of births have occurred and what kinds of procedures were used and why, assisting novices to understand the community, the birthing process and the circumstances that have transpired. This assists the novices to remember through aids to memory acting as mnemonics;

that is, having the ability to observe the places where these births occurred aids processes of recall. However, storytelling also assists in illustrating procedures: that is, cases are mentioned and how the midwives responded, and the outcomes, become linked to these settings via storytelling, which makes them easy to remember and recall. Hence, these narratives provide ways of assisting the organisation and recall of facts, concepts or propositional links and procedures (i.e., means of achieving goals) through the stories acting as mnemonics (i.e., devices to remember and recall knowledge).

Verbalisation

Verbalisation or thinking aloud by more experienced or expert practitioners as they engage in tasks provides a way of articulating and understanding their thinking processes in ways that make those processes accessible to novices. This is particularly important in providing access to the kinds of knowledge that are otherwise difficult to access because the understandings are opaque or hidden. For instance, deliberate verbalisation during work-related tasks was observed to be used in assisting novices to learn how to undertake pottery tasks that they might not otherwise have learnt. This is because verbalisations can refer to a series of contingencies that novices may not be aware of or have not even considered.[27] Similarly, verbalisation by medical practitioners (e.g., surgeons) can also be helpful to assist others when the view of the task being performed (i.e., an operation) is restricted. So, even in such circumstances, the verbalisation of processes assists the novices to understand the approach being taken and the techniques used. Sometimes, this verbalisation occurs as part of the process of work activities: for instance, it is quite likely that a team of medical specialists in an operating theatre would talk aloud about the processes they are using to communicate with other team members. This includes informing others about those procedures and the next steps to be undertaken and providing cues for others to act. In this way, it assists with coordinating the activities of the team and their learning as cognition[43] and the performance in such circumstances is often distributed across teams.[44] Providing access to this knowledge is necessary because many of the aspects of the work or the sequences of activities can only be understood through more experienced or expert practitioners' accounts of experts' thinking as they enact work tasks. In this way, verbalisation can be central to effective and adaptable learning.

Pedagogically rich activities

Not all pedagogic practices are provided and enacted by more experienced workers. The physical and social environment of workplaces also supports learning pedagogically. Importantly, some work activities and interactions are inherently pedagogically rich; that is, they have qualities lending themselves to the promotion of learning. For instance, nurses' handovers have been identified as potentially rich learning activities:[33] when shifts of incoming nurses are briefed by the nurses finishing their shifts about patients on the hospital ward, it provides opportunities for developing rich understandings about nursing work. The handover process engages nurses in verbalising their understandings about (i) the patients, (ii) their condition(s), (iii) the treatment(s) they are receiving, (iv) how they are responding to those treatments and (v) what the prognosis is for their progression. This activity then provides the opportunity to develop understandings, linkages, modelling of processes and an increasingly wider set of understandings and linkages between patients' conditions, treatments and outcomes. Moreover, these kinds of work activities can be engaged with by individuals with different levels of knowledge and expertise as they can provide rich learning experiences of different kinds. For instance, novice student nurses can come to relate the language, concepts and use of terminology that they have experienced in the educational setting to what they are encountering in the hospital setting. More experienced students will be able to make links between the patient's condition and the treatments they are having and become aware of the links and associations amongst conditions and variable factors that need to be accommodated, such as co-morbidities (i.e., other and related health issues). Final-year student nurses or experienced nurses will likely engage in the discussion that includes weighing up different approaches to patient care and deliberating upon how the patient is responding to their treatment or care, and what the likely outcome is for them.

Opportunities to discuss and debate the merits of different approaches and the likely outcome with more experienced nurses clearly stand as an active and engaged learning process that is mediated by the access to other nurses and experts' knowledge and experience. These activities can position the participants actively in processes of comparing and contrasting, monitoring and projecting, analysing and arriving at conclusions about the patient's progress and the merits of different approaches. These qualities make handovers particularly rich learning experiences, something that has long been recognised by nurses. Therefore, it is often standard practice that students and junior nurses participate in these handovers as they comprise potentially rich learning experiences. This is more likely to be the case if learners are actively engaged and participating in the process of considering and making decisions across the five key focuses of the handovers. There are other examples of opportunities to engage in rich learning experiences, such as the hospital ward rounds and when events occur in hospital wards (e.g., cardiac arrests). When these events occur, there is an opportunity to engage workers in discussions about these events, as in debriefs, so that the goals for care and processes they might have observed can be understood. These instances can provide opportunities for rich learning (i.e., accessing and understanding the complex of factors that contributed to the structure, options that arose, decisions made and consequences of these decisions).

Other kinds of activities that can be pedagogically rich include planning processes such as teachers discussing plans, a process of instruction or the organisation of a unit of coursework. Here, again, options will be discussed and justifications made for favouring some activities over others, all of which may provide important insights for or considerations by novices. In addition, some workplaces make specific efforts to involve novices or even experienced workers in processes they have not had the opportunity to engage in previously to extend the scope of the competence through learning about that process. Indeed, this process is apparently a key feature of learning through workplaces in large Japanese corporations.[45] Consequently, these teachable moments need to be identified and utilised in assisting learners to develop the kinds of knowledge they need for effective practice. Part of this utilisation is preparing learners to identify and engage in such experiences to learn effectively. The educational worth of these experiences may not always be explicit or easy to understand (e.g., that the handover is more than merely a meeting of nurses). Therefore, preparing learners to engage in and utilise those experiences is at least as important as providing those experiences. Given their learning potential, arrangements should be made for identifying these experiences and permitting access for novices or learners.

Guided learning

Guided learning is premised on more experienced workers having the capacity to assist novices' learning through providing guidance and support, but in ways that press novices into engaging in the thinking and acting. This kind of support is referred to as close or proximal guidance[35,46] by a more expert other. It is usually undertaken face-to-face and with close physical contact, which has many analogies to teaching. An example of the provision of guidance is in reference to scaffolding[47] that assists and provides access to knowledge, including modelling, but not directly intervening as in instruction (although that can occur if necessary). The analogy is that scaffolding does not hold up the building, but it allows workers to gain access to and work on the building. There are also well-acknowledged approaches to skill development, such as those advanced by Fitts.[48] They progress from a high level of direct engagement to progressively withdrawing support as learners engage in practice and refine tasks that they had seen modelled, and then reproduce them. These practices exemplify a learning process with guidance by more expert partners who can assist the development of less experienced individuals through specific pedagogic practices such as (i) modelling at normal pace, (ii) breaking the task down into smaller sub-skills, and then (iii) demonstrating them slowly, before (iv) providing practice to workers to complete those tasks in even more precise and quicker ways. This approach has been popularised[2] in accounts of 'cognitive apprenticeships'[34] and reciprocal teaching and learning within educational settings[49] in which performances are modelled by the teacher and then students engage in the modelled processes, for instance in reading. Guided learning, in and through work, attempts to encourage learning in the workplace to be supported through processes in which the learner does the thinking and acting. So, rather than direct teaching, strategies such as the use of questioning, modelling and opportunities to practise are exercised in work settings that indirectly press the novices into engaging in thinking and acting from which learning arises.[42] Again, the concept of guided learning comprises an approach that both complements and supplements the contributions to learning through everyday activities in the workplace. The use of strategies within a guided learning model can support and monitor the development of workplace learners' knowledge by making accessible and guiding the development of the kinds of conceptual knowledge that would otherwise remain hidden yet are salient for effective work practice.

Whilst the processes of guided learning at work offer great potential, much of their realisation depends on the understandings and practices of those who are guiding the learning and the learners.[42] That is, these practices are dependent on both occupational learning and development of expertise in the workplace. Essentially, these individuals may not have the capacities to optimise guided learning approaches:[42,50] often they are too time constrained or lack understanding about guidance in workplaces and may just simply tell, rather than guide. Where the guided learning approach has been shown to be successful in healthcare settings is when doctors and other healthcare professionals have themselves been the subject of well-modelled practices. There are also many instances of work that do not occur in the settings. So, the principal concern is that these processes of guidance are likely to be important for developing understanding (i.e., conceptual knowledge) and securing this often requires using questioning – asking novices questions and assisting them in constructing responses. Yet, these more experienced workers and supervisors may well struggle to use questioning in this way. On the other hand, opportunities for guidance are probably where these co-workers are most effectively utilised because they can guide the development of the capacities they deploy. The strategies below are examples of how guided learning in work settings can draw upon a range of pedagogic practices, some of which are using expertise as much as pedagogic strategies.

Mnemonics

Mnemonics are means by which knowledge can be remembered and recalled.[39] Musicians might use them to remember guitar tunings – Eddie Ate Dynamite, Good Bye Eddie (E-A-D-G-B-E). Medical doctors use mnemonics to remember and recall conditions in patients; for instance, FAST – face, arms, speech, time – is used to assess for strokes. Also, conditions that were reported in celebrities can be remembered and recalled, because they are memorable and provide prompts and reminders of particular healthcare consequences and problems. Junior doctors are advised to recall symptoms comprising particular medical conditions mnemonically by reference to the first patient in whom they encountered those conditions, rather than abstracted sets of conditions.[38] So, rather than relying on knowledge learnt by rote, these mnemonics serve as an effective means of stimulating recall and utilisation. Much of that learning is about propositions, concepts and causal associations amongst concepts, such as occurs when engaging in problem-solving activities, as in clinical reasoning. Some of these mnemonics comprise a series of letters to remind doctors about a series of interrelated conditions.[38] This practice provides a reference point for recalling evidence of the disease later. So, whilst these pedagogic strategies are associated and embedded within instances of practice, they play important roles in supporting the kinds of learning required for that practice. Importantly, these are all aids to memory and recall which are necessary when dealing with complex and demanding work such as medicine, and they assist in managing the cognitive load, particularly when practitioners are engaged in demanding tasks.

Heuristics

There is also the sharing of 'tricks of the trade' or heuristics to assist novices to develop schemas or procedures (i.e., how things are done) for undertaking their tasks.[37] Heuristics comprise procedures that have been derived from practice and are likely to achieve specific outcomes. Problem-solving strategies are delineated between algorithms and heuristics. Algorithm provides certainty with solutions: for example, a calculation we know is that $2 + 6 = 8$. However, not all problem-solving occurs in circumstances of certainty. Heuristics offer procedures that are likely to be helpful in addressing problems, but without the guaranteed success. To take an example, early in my work life when I used to measure men for suits, it was important to get them to relax and breathe so that you are measuring them in their normal posture. The heuristic here was to get them to talk and, in responding to your questions, they exhale, and their body relaxes. Then, there are the almost instantaneous applications of problem-solving procedures (i.e., spontaneous heuristics) that are likely to secure effective outcomes.[51] This knowledge, which is described as intuition to be a component of expertise, is developed over time by experience and eventually by engagement within a professional domain of occupational activities.[51] A well-known example refers to chicken sexers who work at chicken farms and distinguish male and female chickens at the age of just a few days, on a basis in which rational descriptions seem to fail. This profession was imported from Japan, where chicken sexing has a long tradition and an apprenticeship that focuses on a long process of implicit learning by doing and enculturation and refers to the Far East Zen philosophy.[52]

However, not all instances of effective intuitive performance are aligned to this kind of capacity (i.e., practiced and proceduralised capacities). For instance, neither the emergency surgery workers nor the pilot Sullenberger who landed a plane in the Hudson River had been exposed to multiple instances of the experiences for which they intuitively developed effective responses. So, it is necessary to go beyond accounts of highly practised procedures that can be applied almost automatically (i.e., through automaticity[8]) to

Practice pedagogies 133

understand and develop what constitutes intuition. That is, the development of intuitive expertise requires going beyond accounts of rehearsal and practice, as in proceduralisation,[53] to engage a broader set of perspectives and accounts that can be used in circumstances which are not rehearsed. Sullenberger knew he needed to land the plane into the Hudson River when it lost forward propulsion; the fact that landing on water is something that is mentioned by flight crew on every flight indicates that it was a possibility in this field. When faced with the available options, it was the most likely survivable option. It was then that other skills associated with landing a plane in restricted circumstances came into play, which included hitting the water in a way that knocked off the plane's engines that otherwise would have led the plane to sink.

All of this emphasises that heuristics are important as a means of securing procedural intuitive expertise that is likely to be associated with the development of domains of knowledge, yet also having capacities and facilities that permit openness and flexibility in their execution. In many ways, when dealing with intuitive expertise within professional roles, having knowledge of the scope of possibilities is at least as important as routinised and rehearsed procedures.

Examples and partially worked jobs

Other forms of indirect guidance include being able to see examples of completed tasks to provide models for what novices must achieve, or partially worked examples so they can understand how work or occupational processes progress. Again, these practices provide guidance in their efforts to replicate those tasks through processes of discovery. Similarly, half-completed jobs provide instances that model and guide their discovery learning processes. Having access to partially worked examples, such as half-completed jobs, can provide models that are helpful for informing and modelling what novices need to achieve, for instance, in the production of lace. Such examples are helpful and indicate to novices what they must produce as well as the required standard of work.

Hands-on – direct guidance

Direct guidance in the form of instruction or hands-on interventions is enacted when the goals, understandings and procedures may not be easily learnt through other means. So, if explanation is required to assist understanding or justifying what is to be learnt, the more experienced practitioners might use examples, statements or stories to develop those understandings. These strategies can be helpful when what needs to be learnt cannot be experienced directly by learners because the processes are hidden (e.g., within machines or equipment) or rendered abstract, such as with symbolic knowledge that underpins electronically mediated work processes. In these circumstances, direct guidance is welcomed. So, in learning how to make lace, the positioning and holding of multiple needles can be directly modelled by an experienced lace-maker.[29] Also, when procedural capacities are difficult to articulate, then hands-on approaches might be required. Thus, experienced potters may place their hands on those of novices to assist them in gaining the feel or haptic qualities required to shape the clay as it turns on the potter's wheel.[28] So, these forms of direct guidance are helpful for those specific kinds of learning.

Artefacts

A review of anthropological studies of learning in non-schooled societies and situations[2] identified instances where artefacts and direct instruction assisted practitioners' learning. This direct interaction extends to more experienced co-workers placing their hands on those of novices to assist the development of haptic capacities that are difficult to articulate.[27,29] This kind of support for learning through apprehending is referred to as guided discovery:[36] how more experienced workers guide apprentices' thinking and acting. For instance, as noted, shells and other beach debris were used to assist Micronesian fishermen learn the patterns of stars by which they navigate at night. It was necessary to provide artefacts to assist this learning that might not otherwise easily occur (i.e., in a tiny boat at sea, in the dark at night). This guidance can also include the use of artefacts such as notation systems used for making lace as a basis through which novices can learn lace-making relatively independently.[29] For novice lace makers, the notation system became a form of distal guidance and scaffolding. Yet, in reviewing this literature, very few instances were identified in which direct interpersonal engagement and guidance by experts or co-workers occurred. Where they were identified, they comprised experts assisting novice to do something they might find difficult to learn independently. This form of guidance is perhaps best exemplified in instances of more expert partners engaging in hands-on interactions with novices, for instance, to assist them in getting the feel for correctly shaping pottery.

Pedagogic practice considerations

From the sections above, it can be seen that there are sets of distinctly pedagogic activities, often organised or enacted and used by more experienced partners, including modelling processes, providing close guidance to develop capacities, coaching individuals and progressive withdrawal of support, referred to as scaffolding,[34] that can extend to the use of artefacts to make accessible what cannot be directly experienced.[2] Each of these pedagogic practices can be directed towards learning particular kinds of knowledge. Some establish goals for learning; others discuss prompt recall and augment linkages and associations that aid conceptual and procedural development and promote work-related dispositions. Importantly, all these practices are usually enacted as part of everyday work activities and make particular contributions to apprehending the knowledge to be learnt. Yet, the efficacy of these pedagogic practices is largely mediated by individuals' engagement with them. This reminds us that the augmentation provided by these pedagogic practices is shaped by learners' engagement with and apprehension of what they have experienced. Hence, central here is how learners apprehend and mediate that learning, which is premised on their personal epistemological practices (*see* Chapter 8).

References

1. Billett S. *Mimetic learning at work: Learning in the circumstances of practice.* Dordrecht, The Netherlands: Springer; 2014.
2. Pelissier C. The anthropology of teaching and learning. *Annual Review of Anthropology.* 1991;20:75–95.
3. Billett S, Noble C. Utilizing pedagogically rich work activities to promote professional learning. *Éducation & Didactique.* 2020;14(3):137–150.
4. Billett S. Relevance of workplace learning in enterprise transformation: The prospects for Singapore. *Singapore Labour Journal.* 2023;2(01):6–21.
5. Hämäläinen R, Lanz M, Koskinen KT. Collaborative systems and environments for future working life: Towards the integration of workers, systems and manufacturing environments. In Harteis C, eds. *The impact of digitalization in the workplace.* Dordrecht: Springer; 2018: 25–38.
6. Harteis C. Supporting learning at work in an era of digitalization of work. In: Bahl A, Dietzen A, eds. *Work-based learning as a pathway to competence-based education.* Opladen: Barbara Budrich; 2018: 85–97.
7. Rogoff B, Lave J, eds. *Everyday cognition: Its development in social context.* Cambridge, MA: Harvard University Press; 1984.
8. Anderson JR. Acquisition of cognitive skill. *Psychological Review.* 1982;89(4):369–406.
9. Ericsson KA, Simon HA. *Protocol analysis – verbal reports as data.* Cambridge, MA: MIT Press; 1984.
10. Lave J. The culture of acquisition and the practice of understanding. In: Stigler JW, Shweder RA, Herdt G, eds. *Cultural psychology.* Cambridge: Cambridge University Press; 1990: 259–286.
11. Lave J, Murtaugh M, de la Roche O. The dialectic of arithmetic in grocery shopping. In: Rogoff B, Lave J, eds. *Everyday cognition: Its development in social context.* Cambridge, MA: Harvard University Press; 1984: 76–94.
12. Glaser R. Education and thinking – the role of knowledge. *American Psychologist.* 1984;39(2):93–104.
13. Glaser R, Bassok M. Learning theory and the study of instruction. *Annual Review of Psychology.* 1989;40(1):631–666.
14. Barsalou LW. Situated simulation in the human conceptual system. *Language and Cognitive Processes.* 2003;18(5/6):513–562.
15. Goodyear P. Navigating difficult waters in a digital era: Technology, uncertainty and the objects of informal lifelong learning. *British Journal of Educational Technology.* 2021;52(4):1594–1611.
16. Diakidoy I-AN, Kendeou P. Facilitating conceptual change in astronomy: A comparison of the effectiveness of two instructional approaches. *Learning and Instruction.* 2001;11:1–20.
17. Limon M. On the cognitive conflict as an instructional strategy for conceptual change: A critical apraisal. *Learning and Instruction.* 2001;11:357–380.

18. Lobato J. Alternative perspectives on the transfer of learning: History, issues, and challenges for future research. *The Journal of the Learning Sciences.* 2006; 15(4):431–449.
19. Beach K. Chapter 4: Consequential transitions: A sociocultural expedition beyond transfer in education. *Review of Research in Education.* 1999;24(1):101–139.
20. Pea RD. Socializing the knowledge transfer problem. *International Journal of Educational Research.* 1987;11(6):639–663.
21. Hatano G, Greeno JG. Commentary: Alternative perspectives on transfer on transfer studies. *International Journal of Educational Research.* 1999;31(7):645–654.
22. Royer J. Theories of the transfer of learning. *Educational Psychologist.* 1979; 14:53–69.
23. Royer JM, Mestre JP, Dufresne RJ. Introduction: Framing the transfer problem. In: Mestre JP, ed. *Transfer of learning from a modern multi-disciplinary perspective.* Washington, DC: Information Age Publishing; 2005: vii–xiv.
24. Raizen SA. *Learning and work: The research base. Vocational education and training for youth: Towards coherent policy and practice.* Paris: OECD; 1991.
25. Lobato J, Rhodehamel B, Hohensee C. "Noticing" as an alternative transfer of learning process. *Journal of the Learning Sciences.* 2012;21(3):1–50.
26. Ley T. Knowledge structures for integrating working and learning: A reflection on a decade of learning technology research for workplace learning. *British Journal of Educational Technology.* 2020;51(2):331–346.
27. Gowlland G. Learning craft skills in China: Apprenticeship and social capital in an artisan community of practice. *Anthropology and Education Quarterly.* 2012;43(4):358–371.
28. Singleton J. The Japanese folkcraft pottery apprenticeship: Cultural patterns of an educational institution. In: Coy MW, ed. *Apprenticeship: From theory to method and back again.* New York: SUNY; 1989: 13–30.
29. Makovichy N. 'Something to talk about': Notation and knowldge-making among Central Slovak lace-makers. *Journal of the Royal Anthropological Institute (NS).* 2010;16(Supplement S1):80–99.
30. Billett S. Constructing Knowledge in the workplace: Potential and pitfalls. *Adult and continuing education under conditions of free market economy, Russian Academy of Education, Moscow, Russia.* 1994:7–10.
31. Zitter I, Hoeve A, de Bruijn E. A design perspective on the school-work boundary: A hybrid curriculum model. *Vocations and Learning.* 2017;9(1):111–131.
32. Billett S. *Learning in the workplace: Strategies for effective practice.* Sydney: Allen and Unwin; 2001.
33. Billett S. The practices of learning through occupations. In: S.Billett, ed. *Learning through practice: Models, traditions, orientations and approaches.* Vol 1. Dodrecht: Springer; 2010: 59–81.
34. Collins A, Brown JS, Newman SE. Cognitive apprenticeship: Teaching the crafts of reading, writing and mathematics. In: Resnick LB, ed. *Knowing, learning and instruction: Essays in honour of Robert Glaser.* Hillsdale, NJ: Erlbaum & Associates; 1989: 453–494.
35. Rogoff B. Observing sociocultural activity on three planes: Participatory appropriation, guided participation, apprenticeship. In: Wertsch JW, Alvarez A, del Rio P, eds. *Sociocultural studies of mind.* Cambridge: Cambridge University Press; 1995: 139–164.
36. Ingold T. *The perception of the environment: Essays on livelihod, dwelling and skill.* London: Routledge; 2000.

37. Billett S. Experts' ways of knowing. Paper presented at: 5th Annual International Conference on Post-compulsory Education and Training, Learning and Work: The Challenges; 26–28 November 1997; Surfers Paradise Travelodge, Gold Coast, Queensland, Australia.
38. Sinclair S. *Making doctors: An institutional apprenticeship*. Oxford: Berg; 1997.
39. Rice T. Beautiful murmurs: Stescopic listening and acoustic objectification. *The Senses and Society*. 2008;3(3):293–306.
40. Rice T. Learning to listen: Auscultation and the transmission of auditory knowledge. Journal of the Royal Anthropological Institute (NS). 2010;16:S41–S61.
41. Billett S, Sweet L, Glover P. The curriculum and pedagogic properties of practice-based experiences: The case of midwifery students. *Vocations and Learning: Studies in Professional and Vocational Education*. 2013;6(2):237–258.
42. Billett S. Guided learning at work. *Journal of Workplace Learning*. 2000;12(7):272–285.
43. Salomon G. *Distributed cognitions: Psychological and educational considerations*. Cambridge: Cambridge University Press; 1997.
44. Boyle JG, Walters MR, Jamieson S, Durning SJ. Distributed cognition: Theoretical insights and practical applications to health professions education: AMEE Guide No. 159. *Medical Teacher*. 2023;45(12):1323–1333.
45. Dore RP, Sako M. *How the Japanese learn to work*. London: Routledge; 1989.
46. Rogoff B. *Apprenticeship in thinking – Cognitive development in social context*. New York: Oxford University Press; 1990.
47. Kosslyn SM. *Image and mind*. Cambridge, MA: Harvard University Press; 1980.
48. Fitts PM. Perceptual-motorskill learning. In: Melton AW, ed. *Categories of human learning*. New York: Academic Press; 1964.
49. Palinscar AS, Brown AL. Reciprocal teaching of comprehension-fostering and comprehension-monitoring activities. *Cognition and Instruction*. 1984;1(2):117–175.
50. Billett S, Boud D. Participation in and guided engagement at work: Workplace pedagogic practices. Paper presented at: 2nd International Conference on Learning and Work; 26–28th July 2001; Calgary.
51. Harteis C, Billett S. Intuitive expertise: Theories and empirical evidence. *Educational Research Review*. 2013;9:145–157.
52. Lunn JH. Chick sexing. *American Scientist*. 1948;36(2):280–287.
53. Anderson JR. Problem solving and learning. *American Psychologist*. 1993;48(1):35–44.

8 Personal (epistemological) practices at work

Personal epistemological practices

When reviewing literature on how individuals learn occupational capacities through practice, one factor becomes very apparent. Overwhelmingly, it presents as being largely a learning process, not one relying on individuals being taught.[1-6] The centrality of personal practices or epistemological acts is quite apparent in this literature. This is exemplified by, and perhaps most principally through, the processes of mimesis (i.e., observing, imitation and practice), listening and actively engaging in work tasks and interactions.[7] In anthropological accounts, repeatedly, it was emphasised that novices had the responsibility to learn, rather than others being required to teach them.[4,8,9] This responsibility commences by them putting themselves forward as wanting to learn the occupation,[6,10] then learning to engage in ways that permit them to acquire knowledge through observation and imitation[3] and then actively promoting their learning through work.[6] Therefore, it is necessary to acknowledge, describe and elaborate the central role of personal practices and epistemologies in explaining the processes of learning through work.[3,6,11] This includes how individuals mediate what is afforded to them in workplace settings through the structuring of experiences (i.e., practice curriculum) and how others, artefacts and opportunities are directed to assist their learning (i.e., practice pedagogies).

These personal epistemologies are bases by which individuals engage in construing and constructing knowledge from what they experience when engaged in activities such as work.[7] These are more than beliefs (i.e., personal values and intentions); they also include individuals' capacities to achieve outcomes and their ways of knowing and engaging in the learning process to construct the capacities required for occupational competence and workplace performance. These capacities include the procedural, conceptual and dispositional qualities underpinning that competence and performance, extending to what constitutes and directs individuals' capacities and embodied knowledge, their sense of self (i.e., subjectivity) and gaze (i.e., how they view the world and how they believe the world is viewing them).[12] The salience of personal agency and intentionality is essential to individuals' engagement in effortful processes of learning, such as their taking responsibility for it.

DOI: 10.4324/9781003519416-11

This responsibility extends to individuals learning to know how to act in workplaces in terms of the kinds of activities and interactions in which they engage, how they should do so and with whom.[6,13] They have to learn how to participate in these work settings and also how to learn effectively through and from them, including how they build relationships with those from whom they need to secure access to opportunities for practice, new opportunities and support for their learning. This positioning extends to having to act agentically in the absence of such direct support. For instance, apprentice minaret builders needed to 'steal' the knowledge required for this occupation as taught.[3] These apprentices had the responsibility to position themselves in ways permitting access to the required knowledge.[3] There was a physical as well as a social dimension to this positioning: it required apprentices to become competent to work with the minaret builders where the stones were being placed on the outside of the minaret. This necessarily included building a production relationship with the masons through bringing them cement and stones. Unless they demonstrated the capacity to work alongside expert builders, they would not be able to access (i.e., observe and practice) the understandings and procedures needed to perform this crucial task.

Similarly, here, as elsewhere, was the need for apprentices to engage in the effortful and deliberate practice[14–16] required for effective performance, whether referring to haptic or other sensory forms of knowing; that is, to engage in practice to develop the skill and required understanding to perform tasks. Through such activities arises the important embodied knowledge.[1,17,18] For example, these include the capacities of midwives in diagnosing the health of a foetus's heart by hearing and appraising its sound or the skilled artisan judging the line, organisation or flow of some process, all essential elements for effective occupational practice.[19]

Consequently, individuals' personal epistemological practices are central to understanding how learning in, through and for work practice progresses and how it can be enhanced by these practices. A range of these practices are summarised in Table 8.1 and described and discussed below. As foreshadowed, perhaps the most central of these processes is mimesis (i.e., observation and imitation)[1,3,15,20,21] or mimetic learning.[22] As Jordan reminds us

> Apprenticeship learning is based on imitation and behavioural matching. It is ancient for the human species and is rooted in our evolutionary history. Learning through observation and imitation, rather than following genetically programmed action sequences, is important in all higher social animals, but it is humans who have developed this propensity into the primary modality for the acquisition of skills.[1]
>
> (p.931)

Despite its centrality to human progress and individuals' development over time, mimesis is seemingly routinely misunderstood and even maligned in schooled societies,[23] often being associated with mimicking (i.e., mindless copying).[21,24] This misunderstanding persists despite strong and growing evidence that it comprises processes that are fundamental to human cognition[24,25] and both requires and is generative of higher order cognitive capacities.[26] More than mimicry, mimesis comprises appraising a circumstance, deciding the most appropriate pathway of action, taking action and monitoring that action to see whether what is intended is achieved.[27] Engagement in observations has specific purposes, such as understanding goal states (i.e., what needs to be achieved), and is central to the process of monitoring progress and evaluating the effectiveness of what is being enacted. Observations can also be generative of cognitive representations and their deployment. These representations are increasingly held to be multimodal and sensory,[28,29] and observations provide a key form of sensory representation in their organisation and structuring.

Also identified in the literature are other epistemological processes founded in personal practices central to learning through practice. These include processes of learning how to negotiate with others about working together and securing knowledge from them, referred to as ontogenetic ritualisation,[21] that is, the process of building productive relationships with the person from whom you work to engage with and learn. However, fundamentally across this literature is the emphasis on individuals' active engagement and construction of knowledge, which is identified widely.[3,6,9] It is also suggested that the word 'apprenticeship' has its origins in the requirement for learners to *apprehend* or to seize knowledge, because it is not taught.[30] Yet, these processes of learning are unlikely to be effective unless individuals engage effortfully in them. This includes novices having to volunteer and express their interest in learning a particular occupation. Just being in the community, even within family, was not always sufficient to be invited to learn that occupation.[6,31] Instead, learners had to volunteer and indicate their interest and willingness to engage in the effortful process of learning this knowledge. As Mishler notes, individuals have to assent to engage and learn in the occupational practice.[32]

Individuals' engagement, agency and subjectivity

While contributions of workplaces in the forms of activities and interactions they afford are important for learning through work and can be gauged in terms of their invitational qualities, individuals' agency is also an important basis for engagement with and learning through work.[33,34] In particular, the exercise of their personal agency, and their subjectivity or sense of self that drives the kinds, direction and focus of their intentionality, does much to shape their learning.[35] Importantly, that learning is not a process of socialisation or enculturation determined by historical, cultural and situational factors, because it is individuals who actively interpret and construct knowledge from what they experience. They decide if they appropriate what they experience or more cautiously question its veracity. Thus, they mediate the construction of that knowledge. Therefore, despite the important contributions arising from participation in workplaces, including those that can be exercised quite forcefully and with great social press, individuals make meaning and personally mediate the deployment and construction of their knowledge.[36,37] Individuals' agency also determines how they engage in work practice, which then has consequences for how and what they learn.

There are many dimensions to this engagement and subsequent learning. As noted, one is the interest, effort or intentionality that individuals exercise. Effortful engagement is certainly required for learning knowledge that is complex and demanding to learn, yet the learning is directed and sustained by individuals' interests or intentionality.[35] Superficial engagement in workplace activities likely leads to shallow or less rich learning outcomes. There are also more foundational issues, such as basic cognition. Not all individuals comprehend and understand in the same way, and nor should they. Hence, the kind of discourses of which individuals have knowledge and to which they have access, and their knowledge of a particular domain of occupational activities, shape how they construe and construct what they experience. This refers to their readiness. Readiness is the level and kinds of knowledge that individuals process, shaping what and how they can subsequently learn, for instance in work settings,[38] that is, the degree by which what they know, can do and value allows them to engage productively with what they experience, or that potentially can lead to confusion and dissonance if they are not ready to engage constructively.

These bases for individuals' engagement in social practices are likely to be differentiated and overlapping, and in person-particular ways. First, individuals participate simultaneously in a number of social practices.[39] However, the quality of their engagement in these practices is unlikely to be uniform. Individuals' interests and priorities temper participation.[40] Full-bodied participation in one social practice (e.g., a workplace) may be mirrored by reluctance in another (e.g., a school tuck shop roster), and at particular points in time. Second, individuals' engagement with what is to be learnt is likely influenced by their values and beliefs. This is evidenced by workers of South Vietnamese heritage rejecting teamwork in an American manufacturing plant, as they believed this kind of work organisation reflected communistic values and practices from which they had fled in their country of birth.[41] Similarly, coal miners and aged-care workers engaged in practices in ways that reflect a gendered subjectivity.[42] This identity permitted them to accept workplace injuries and accidents as inevitable consequences of their participation in their work. So, individuals' engagement at work is premised on and can be understood and engaged with as a product of their personal histories or ontogenies.[43] This can lead to person-particular ways of understanding and engaging with the social world[44] and is shaped by their subjectivities – their sense of identity and purpose – that arise through social experience.[42] It follows that individuals' subjectivities (i.e., their sense of self) shape what they perceive to be invitational, rather than merely accepting what is afforded them. For example, Hodges[45] rejected the approach to teaching children that she encountered in a university teacher education course, believing that children should not be treated in the ways proposed in this educational programme and rejecting the community of practice in which she was participating. So more than her values being subject to the social practice, her agency and subjectivity served to reject what was being afforded.

In sum, individuals use their subjectivities to make sense of what they encounter, and not some objective view of what is afforded them, to decide what is desirable invitation, and subjectivities shape how and what they learn through their engagement in workplace activities and interactions. These subjectivities are often social in origin. They arise through personal histories from societally derived experiences, such as conceptions of masculinity or femininity and the standing of occupational practices. Yet, they are constructed as personally unique outcomes through individuals' process of experiencing.[44]

Personal and social experiences

The construction of this knowledge – learning – arises as we engage in different and overlapping ways in social practices throughout our lives. Hence, dualities between the personal and the social experience should not be taken as making distinctions between the individual and the social. Instead, the individual here is seen as being a social product that arises through a socially derived personal history (i.e., ontogeny) that is shaped in personally particular ways across a life history (i.e., ontogenetic development). Harré[46] proposes that an individual is born a potential person and the personal is generated through their interactions with the social world. So, individuals and their subjectivities and sense of engaging with the world and so on represent personal and possibly unique sets of social legacies (i.e., social origins). It is the uniquely social person who encounters, makes sense of, responds to and enacts their occupational practice in particular circumstances and at that moment in time. It is individuals' agency that arises through these subjectivities that shape how they work and learn microgenetically (i.e., moment by moment), through the duality of social affordances and personal engagements.

Duality of affordances and engagements

Regarding the process and outcomes of learning through experiences in work settings, the duality comprising a negotiated and relational reciprocity between social practice and individuals' agency is held to be a central explanatory concept. The interpsychological processes (i.e., between/among social partners, artefacts, symbols and the physical environment) are reciprocal, with individuals making judgements about, and potentially transforming their perceptions of and engagement with, what is suggested to them by the social world. Valsiner[47] describes this process as the co-construction of knowledge – the reciprocal act of construction through which both the object and the subject are remade and transformed. That is, learning is not the mere acceptance of knowledge from an external source: instead, individuals are active and discerning in how they engage with what is suggested to them. This includes the relations between experience and processes, making judgements about what they encounter and how they respond to what they experience. Analogously, individuals' development through work is also held to be reciprocal and interdependent between how the work settings afford participation and how individuals elect to engage in and learn from the work practice. Therefore, engagement in work is relationally constituted between the affordance of the setting's practice and how individuals elect to engage with what is afforded them.

In describing the relationship between the social and cognitive experience, Valsiner[47] refers to the degree of 'relatedness' between the individuals' values and the norms of the social practice as a consideration of the kinds of interactions, and the learning that will likely arise, through these interactions. When considering the qualities of learning as products of these reciprocal interpsychological processes, Wertsch[48] proposes distinguishing between the intrapsychological attributes described as 'mastery' – that is, knowledge constructed without commitment or enthusiasm, and 'appropriation' – in which the learner constructs knowledge, 'taking it as their own' as Luria[49] proposes. Hence, there can be no situationally determined or uniform outcome to interpsychological processes or intrapsychological attributes. These are negotiated reciprocally between individuals' personal epistemologies and the suggestions from social practices in which they participate, as a socio-personal process.

This dualistic and relational basis for learning underscores the point that what a social practice and setting (e.g., educational institution or workplace) affords individuals can only ever be an intention or invitation to engage and change (i.e., to learn). It is ultimately individuals who shape how and what they construct from what they experience, based on what they know, can do and value (i.e., the conceptual, procedural and dispositional knowledge that comprises their cognitive experiencing). Consequently, the degree by which what is afforded is viewed as being positively invitational is not a given. Instead, individuals will construe and construct it through an interaction between their cognitive experiencing and what is projected by the social experiences.[50] Figure 8.1 depicts these dualistic participatory practices. On the left-hand side is the evolving social practice of the work setting; on the right, the evolving personal history of individuals, that is, their ontogenies. The intersections that constitute the interactions in workplaces are those encountered through participation in work. Changes in occupational practice are brought about by historical factors (e.g., changes in tools and technologies), cultural factors (e.g., needs for goods and services) and situational factors (e.g., the goals, practices, and participants in the workplace).

The duality discussed here as participatory practices and as relational interdependence between the personal and social[51] is conceptually significant.[52] It can be seen as illuminating relations between the social world and

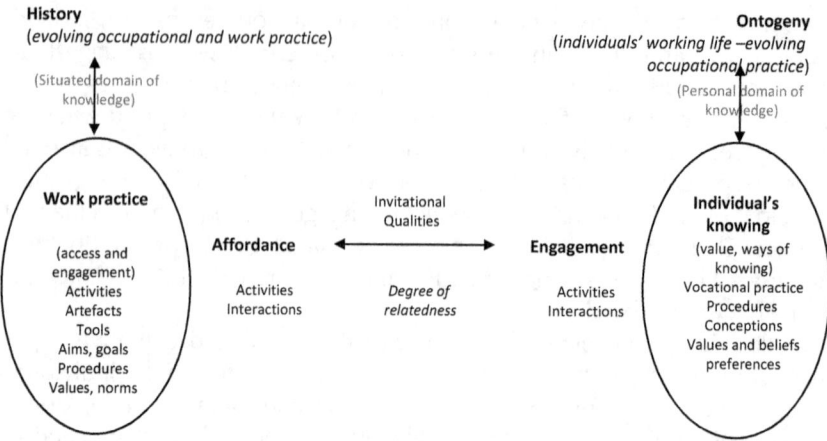

Figure 8.1 Affordances and engagement in learning through work.

individuals' minds at intersections of transforming social practice comprising the work, how it is undertaken, and individuals' evolving ontogenetic development, including their subjectivities as they engage in work activities. This duality also implies that individuals' thinking and acting require delineating and identifying the invitational qualities of the work setting, from both a social practice and also personal perspectives, and then how individuals elect to engage in social practice.

These conceptual and methodological interpretations are aligned with current understandings about human cognition. Having proposed that there are relations between the mind and society,[48,53] it is important to elaborate and understand further these relationships, including their contributions to both personal (i.e., learning) and social (i.e., norms, forms and practices) changes. Central to these relations are the origin and sourcing of knowledge, such as that required for occupations that have historical and cultural geneses. Yet, that knowledge is required to be taken up by each generation and to be purposeful for the social and cultural purposes for which it is being enacted.[43,54] Another issue that needs to be understood is the degree of social embeddedness of knowledge.[55-57] This embeddedness has three elements: (i) the degree to which learning is embedded in its source, (ii) the relationship between individuals' thinking and social practice[58] and (iii) the consequences of those relations.[51] Therefore, understanding (a) the affordance of social practice such as work, and (b) how individuals' engagement influences knowing associated with that social practice, and the negotiated and dualistic interdependence between (a) and (b), can make useful contributions to understanding the relations between social practice and individuals' knowing (i.e., their thinking, acting, and learning). Hence, the kinds of learning or intrapsychological outcomes that arise through participation in social practices and socially derived activities, such as those in workplaces, are assisting with this elaboration.

Personal practices at work 145

Illustrating the kind of contributions that might arise, the next section briefly discusses how these relationships inform conceptions of shared understanding (i.e., intersubjectivity) and the kinds of learning that occur through participation in occupational practice.

Intersubjectivity, appropriation and extending knowledge

Within sociocultural constructivism, a key goal for learning in social practices is intersubjectivity – shared understanding between those who are learning and the more experienced partners. The concern here is that the historically derived, culturally purposeful and situationally pertinent knowledge needs to be learnt by those who are to practise that knowledge. Shared understanding is seen as a basis for having a common focus of attention and some shared presuppositions that form the ground for communication and working towards shared goals.[5] As humans construct meaning in personally particular ways, the key purpose of communication is to develop shared understanding.[59] Newman, Griffin and Cole[59] note that if humans developed understandings in uniform ways, there would be no need to communicate. However, as we do not, there is a need to work towards achieving intersubjectivity or shared understanding because it is quite central to the conduct of everyday human activities and human interactions in processes such as living and working. In terms of learning an occupational practice that is historically and culturally constituted, intersubjectivity is seen as a means of achieving shared understanding and as a capacity to perform those practices through interactions with co-workers. This is a purposeful goal for learning in workplaces and for the development of much of the vocational competence and expertise required for work performance in novel circumstances. That subjectivity is essential for work that is conducted through teams or across shifts of workers, for instance, because common goals and processes are necessary for effective work performance. Yet, given the discussions above, it would clearly be wrong to consider that intersubjectivity will necessarily arise from individuals' construction of knowledge in a socially rich milieu. There is a need, however, to identify the kinds of personal epistemological practices that can realise these kinds of outcomes in and through work and workplace settings.

Epistemological practices at work

In preview, from a review of a range of sources and disciplines, the epistemological practices that individuals adopt and use to learn effectively through their work include those identified as imitation,[1,15] processes of observation,[6] mimetic learning,[27] ontogenetic ritualisation,[21] active engagement with and apprehending knowledge (the knowledge to be learnt),[3,9] learner readiness[6,31] and assent[60] and critical engagement.[61] In Table 8.1 are set out a range of these personal epistemological practices, with a description provided and

Table 8.1 Personal epistemological practices for learning through work

Practice	Description	Purposes	Knowledge
Mimetic learning	Ability to imitate and interest to do so at work.[27] A fundamental process of human learning,[1] by imitating implicitly or explicitly what they do,[3] including asking questions or listening to more knowledgeable individuals,[15] is a higher order activity	Process through which goals, procedures (both specific and strategic), propositional links and associations can be learnt through personal engagement	DP/C; PS/H; CS/D
Ontogenetic ritualisation	A system of communication and engagement between social partners negotiated through repeated social interactions[21] supports close guidance and reciprocal interactions in workplaces permitting co-workers to engage in learning reciprocally	Basis from which to engage with others from whom guidance is derived	PS/H; CD
Embodied knowledge	Ability to do rather than talk about it arising through practice;[1] renders unconscious much of what is required for performance (claims over 90% rendered non-declarative)[17,18]	Procedural learning derived through practice and rehearsal that becomes able to be applied without conscious recall	DP; CS; PS/H
Deliberate practice	Practising skills and monitoring its improvement[15] as the means by which agency, focussed intentionality and the act of rehearsal come together to secure effective performance[63]	Process of rehearsal, refinement, monitoring of personal performance and conscious efforts to improve the performance	DP; CS; PS
Guided re-discover	Novices engaging in situations where they can practise, hone skills, and gain experience by themselves, yet can still access direct guidance[64,65]	Process of remaking knowledge through opportunities for observation, listening and other forms of social engagement and practice	DC; PS/H; CS/D

(Continued)

Table 1.2 (Continued)

Practice	Description	Purposes	Knowledge
Active engagement and construction	Importance of active engagement (i.e., observation, listening and mimesis). Apprenticeship means apprehender (i.e., to seize, lay hold of, apprehend, and appraise with the mind; to inform, give form: to shape[9])	Through participating in goal-directed activities, learning arises through seeking out, actively constructing and appropriating the knowledge able to be accessed	DC; PS/H; CS/D
Observation	Japanese word for apprentice is 'minarai' – one who learns by observation – also unobtrusive observation 'minarai kyouiku' – serious learning progresses without didactic instruction[6]	Provides access to goals, models for procedures and bases for developing procedural capacities	DP/C; PS/H; CS/D
Readiness	The level and qualities of what individuals know, can do and value	Mediates the capacities for learning as a result of earlier experiences (and learning)	
Assent	Individuals' willingness to assent to effortful learning[60]	Mediates how individuals engage with external suggestions, supports	DP/C

Note Factual conceptual knowledge (CS); deep or interlinked conceptual knowledge (CD); specific procedural knowledge (PS); strategic or higher order (PH); personal dispositions (DP); cultural norms, societal values or sentiments (DC).

those purposes associated with learning in and through work, and the kinds of knowledge likely to be developed through their exercise. In the left column are the practices, and in the columns to its right a description of each of these practices, their purposes and the kinds of knowledge likely to be developed through them, as described in Chapter 4. A consideration of the particular kinds of mediations enacted by this selection of personal practices are proposed here as likely to be generative of these particular forms of knowledge, based upon earlier and highly detailed analyses of how activities and interactions in work settings led to specific kinds of outcomes.[62]

As presented and previewed in Table 8.1, the literature identifies a range of ways through which these epistemological practices support learning through work, and these are briefly elaborated in the following sections.

Mimetic learning

The process referred to as mimesis or mimetic learning comprises observation, imitation and practice.[66] As noted, this is a fundamental process by which individuals' learning and development have occurred across human history and continues today. Prior to our present 'schooled societies' in which teachers, instruction and structured educational experiences have become the norm, across human history occupational capacities were largely learnt in and through work and in work settings; they were not taught.[27] There are only few instances in which education provisions have been enacted across human history and these are often associated with key professions such as medicine, philosophy and architecture. Even then, earlier models of medical education were premised upon novices' learning in circumstances of practice, as described in Chapter 2. Instead, the common and orthodox approach to learning occupational practices was largely based upon individuals' processes of meaning making, understanding[67] and including personal processes of engagement in increasingly mature approximations of the tasks to be learnt.[68] Indeed, the evidence suggests that mimesis or mimetic learning was the common and orthodox means by which occupational practices have been learnt across human history, and this likely continues today. Individuals observe what others are doing and then attempt to reproduce those modelled tasks through conscious processes of replication and rehearsal. Rather than viewing these processes as mindless copying, these comprise highly constructive and engaged activities and demand conscious engagement and effort through practice. These processes are used regularly not only for learning occupational skills, but also for a range of other human purposes such as communicating with others.

Ontogenetic ritualisation

The process of ontogenetic ritualisation is one that has been identified in how primates come to engage with each other and negotiate and secure outcomes.[21] The classic examples are the baby orangutan seeking to build a relationship with its mother that will secure milk from her teat. In the human context and when considered in terms of learning about and through work, it is often the relationship built between novices and experts that are helpful for sharing of knowledge and joint problem-solving. This can be more than merely developing an amicable working relationship, such as is captured in the phrase 'making nice,' but extending to a form of reciprocal engagement in and for work. For instance, as noted in Marchand's study of minaret building, the apprentice masons were given access to learning the process of placing stones and constructing the minaret through the process of providing stones and mortar to the masons in ways and at the time that they needed it.[3] So, through building reciprocal working relationships, benefits accrue to both parties. For novices, this is about gaining access to the knowledge they require to practise the occupation. Often, the goal here is to achieve a level of intersubjectivity or shared understanding that will allow the work tasks to proceed.

Embodied knowledge

Embodied knowledge refers to the outcome of procedural learning derived through repeated practice that leads to it being enacted without apparent conscious engagement. Although this term has been advanced by anthropologists, it has meaning in other disciplines. The learning of procedural capacities (e.g., skilfulness) is understood to arise through processes of automatisation and compilation. Automatisation refers to the process through which, when specific procedures (e.g., tying shoelaces or ties) become learnt through practice, each sub-task does not require conscious thought[69] because through rehearsal these tasks are freed from requiring conscious engagement, except perhaps monitoring.[63] Compilation is when a number of specific procedures are compiled into a single procedure, which would occur in these processes and then can be enacted without requiring conscious thought.[63] The principle here is that it is a human process of managing cognitive load.[70] That is, we can hold only certain amounts of information in our short-term memories.

Hence, through rehearsal, a series of specific procedural tasks are reduced to single compiled processes. These are what we use to engage in activities such as walking, driving cars, tying shoelaces and ties and performing a whole range of specific procedures. Compiling automatised procedures reduces the demand upon working memory and allows other tasks to be conducted simultaneously as those that have become compiled.[70] That leads to individuals being able to perform these tasks seemingly without access to conscious thought; hence, they are referred to as embodied knowledge, and in other instances, intuition.[71] However, the core quality is that they are procedures that have arisen through extensive rehearsal (i.e., practice). One of the issues associated with embodied knowledge is that it can become quite difficult to change. Hence, how we speak, our dialects, through to which side of the road we drive on, can all become problematic when we wish to change them. That is when intentional processes are used to bring about that change. Deliberate practice is one of these.

Deliberate practice

Deliberate practice, as the term suggests, refers to the process of intentionally and in a focused way rehearsing tasks to improve performance with them, honing and refining them to achieve a high level of precision and performance. This is a process that would be common to the daily routines of sports persons, musicians and others engaged in high-performance activities that are reliant on precision and effective performance. This process is underpinned by individuals' intentionalities and agency as they alone can initiate and engage effortfully and critically in improving their practice. An example here would be the medical student who intentionally engaged in learning how to take bloods from different kinds of patients through working alongside nurses who perform those tasks well. Through that practice, they will likely be able to perform that task across a range of different situations (in this case, patients).

Guided rediscovery

Guided rediscovery refers to the process through which novices engage in situations where they can practise, hone skills and gain experience by themselves, albeit guided by interactions with a more experienced interlocutor (e.g., more experience worker, expert and teacher). Consequently, whilst they engage with tasks in a self-directed and relatively independent way, they can still access direct guidance from others who are more experienced and knowledgeable in the field in which they are learning.[64,65] So, whilst this process is premised upon the agency and initiative of the learner, it is one that is encompassed within the environment of potential support. In this way, individuals are able to engage in a personal process of discovering knowledge that is already known about but, in doing so, developing their own personal domain of occupational knowledge through that discovery process. The principal is that it is the students or novices who need to initiate the engagement with more experienced interlocutors, rather than being closely monitored and directed by them. For instance, a more experienced practitioner might provide an activity that will lead to that outcome. Curiously, this was the process that was used in earlier models of education. The mode of education in Madras, in what is now referred to as Central Asia, was for the students to study independently. Only when they encountered a problem that they could not address independently would they seek the guidance of the teacher. This, in many ways, is the model that is useful for the supervision of research higher degree students within universities. The point here is that the locus of learning resides with the learners.

Observation

As indicated within the process of mimetic learning, observation can be deployed to secure access to the goals to which their efforts are being directed, models for how to undertake tasks or achieve those goals, and how to develop the capacities to achieve them. Observation and observational learning is a skill that has been used intentionally in the processes of learning across human history and cultures.[27] It is particularly salient to processes of learning that sit outside of didactic teaching efforts that have come to dominate the processes of and discourse about learning and education. For instance, the Japanese word for apprentice is 'minarai' – one who learns by observation. In this model of apprenticeship, it is expected that the important aspects of learning an occupation will progress without didactic instruction.[6] Observation is a key means by which novices come to understand what they need to learn, how they need to learn it and at what point they will have learnt it. There is also a term about how this observation is conducted in an unobtrusive way – 'minarai kyooiku.'[6] So this process emphasises the personal practice of active observation to understand the performance being enacted and the bases of that performance and to identify and enact ways of developing what has been observed.

Readiness

The concept of readiness, as noted, refers to the degree by which what individuals know, can do and value permits them to progress to learn further on those bases. One of the first uses of this term was with Piagetian accounts of children's development related to their biological maturation and degree to which that biological maturation permitted them to move to the next level of cognitive functioning. However, in the context of adults' learning and development, it refers to the capacities that individuals possess that allow them to engage in productive learning experiences, that is, to engage, extend further and adapt what they already know, can do and value. For instance, if individuals have no knowledge of the field of occupational practice, nor know how to undertake procedures required for the kind of norms and practices required for it, they may struggle to learn effectively. If the gap between the current knowledge and what they are required to learn is so great from what their experiencing, dissonance is likely to be an outcome. For example, if individuals have no knowledge of a particular language or its grammatical structure, then merely being immersed in a situation where that language is being used may not be a productive learning experience, because they are not ready to engage effectively.

An important aspect of readiness is not just individuals' conceptual and procedural development, but also their dispositions: that is, their interest in engaging and learning through work. Without interest, they may not be willing to exercise the kinds of effort required to learn and effectively organise a personal domain of occupational knowledge. Consequently, when considering the organisation of learning experiences and expectations of what individuals might learn through work activities and interactions, it is helpful to assess their readiness to participate in those activities. For instance, in one workplace – an emergency department – the lead clinician would ask medical interns when they arrived in the department what they had previously undertaken and what they hoped to learn from their engagement in the clinical work. Based upon their responses she would then allocate roles for them to perform.

Assent

Assent refers to individuals' willingness to assent to participate in activities associated with learning, which includes whether they believe they are engaged in merely performing an occupation or that that occupation comprises their vocation. It is also central to what constitutes the requirements for effortful learning.[60] That is, if individuals do not value the experiences nor the goals to which their activities are being directed, they may well engage in mastery rather than appropriation, to use Wertsch's terms; thereby their learning is likely to be superficial, focused on compliance, rather than being richly constructed and organised in ways that are valued and warranted by the individual.[48] Of course, as with the divide between appropriation and mastery, there are situations in which individuals will actively decide not to appropriate something if they believe that it is inappropriate, not in their interests or against their beliefs. So, assent is something which is personally constructed and enacted and likely arises from individuals' earlier experiences, shaping what constitutes their personal pedagogies.

In all, the kinds of personal practices described and discussed in this chapter emphasise the importance of individuals mediating what they experience, how they construe and construct knowledge from it and how they come to value and organise that knowledge. It emphasises the importance of intentional and focused engagement by individuals to learn, hone and further develop their capacities. Such activities are most likely to occur when individuals conclude that these activities are helpful for themselves and for those with whom they associate.

Personal practices: participation and learning

In sum, individuals' epistemological practices are central to learning through work and comprise essential attributes for rich learning from work-based experiences. Overall, these attributes include:

- an active interest in and engagement in work-related activities and, therefore, learning;
- the level of readiness in terms of interest and knowing, which positions individuals to be effective learners;
- working to know how to engage and learn independently in practice settings and through activities and interactions;
- developing capacities to effectively come to know, including haptic, auditory, sensory and procedural capacities;
- engaging with others and artefacts to actively access understandings, values and procedures; and
- developing and engaging interdependently.

A consideration of epistemological practices assists in explaining the processes of learning through work and informs how they might be effectively enacted. Central here is the need to elaborate further the nature and consequences of relations between individuals and the work setting in which they engage. It has been proposed that these relations are structured by individual participatory practices that comprise, on the one hand, the affordances of the practice setting, and on the other hand, how individuals elect to engage with what is afforded them.[52] It is through these dualistic, but negotiated, processes that individuals construe and make judgements about the invitational qualities of what they experience and, hence, how they participate in and learn from these experiences. The outcomes of learning, as much as the processes themselves, are socially shaped. This is not a negotiation between the individual and social, but between individuals who have construed and constructed knowledge in personal ways throughout their life histories participating in a further negotiation of that knowledge while they engage in work. This learning can be seen as being directed towards promoting intersubjectivity within the knowledge required for workplace tasks and interactions. However, central to these explanations is the significance of the relationship between the social practice and the socially derived person. Whether referring to the construal of affordances (i.e., the setting's invitational qualities), the kinds of interactions that occur, or the learning processes and outcomes in the forms of specific types of knowledge that arise, the dual, interdependent, yet negotiated relations between individuals as workers and the social practice that comprises that work setting remain a predominate consideration. Understanding these relations in terms of reciprocal participatory practices is central to elaborating learning through work, also extending to learning more generally.

References

1. Jordan B. Cosmopolitical obstetrics: Some insights from the training of traditional midwives. *Social Science and Medicine.* 1989;28(9):925–944.
2. Jordan B. The Double Helix of learning: Knowledge transfer in traditional and techno-centric communities. Unpublished transcript. Palo Alto Research Center; 2011.
3. Marchand THJ. Muscles, morals and mind: Craft apprenticeship and the formation of person. *British Journal of Education Studies.* 2008;56(3):245–271.
4. Pelissier C. The anthropology of teaching and learning. *Annual Review of Anthropology.* 1991;20:75–95.
5. Rogoff B. *Apprenticeship in thinking – cognitive development in social context.* New York: Oxford University Press; 1990.
6. Singleton J. The Japanese folkcraft pottery apprenticeship: Cultural patterns of an educational institution. In: Coy MW, ed. *Apprenticeship: From theory to method and back again.* New York: SUNY; 1989: 13–30.
7. Billett S. Personal epistemologies, work and learning. *Educational Research Review.* 2009;4(3):210–219.

8. Lave J. Situating learning in communities of practice. In: Resnick LB, Levine JM, Teasley S, eds. *Perspectives on socially shared cognition*. Washington, DC: American Psychological Association; 1991: 63–82.
9. Webb E. Making meaning: Language for learning. In: Ainely P, Rainbird H, eds. *Apprenticeship: Towards a new paradigm of learning*. London: Kogan Page; 1999: 100–110.
10. Marchand TH. *The pursuit of pleasurable work: Craftwork in twenty-first century England*. London: Berghahn Books; 2022.
11. Billett S, Choy S, Le AH. Worklife learning: Personal, educational, and community contributions. In: Evans K, Lee WO, Markowitsch J, Zukas M, eds. *Third international handbook of lifelong learning*. Cham: Springer International Publishing; 2022: 1–21.
12. Davies B. *A body of writing 1990–1999*. New York: Altamira Press; 2000.
13. Gowlland G. Learning craft skills in China: Apprenticeship and social capital in an artisan community of practice. *Anthropology and Education Quarterly*. 2012;43(4):358–371.
14. Ericsson KA. The influence of experience and deliberate practice on the development of superior expert performance. In: Ericsson KA, Charness N, Feltowich PJ, Hoffmann RR, eds. *The Cambridge handbook of expertise and expert performance*. Cambridge: Cambridge University Press; 2006: 685–705.
15. Gardner H. What we do & don't know about learning. *Daedalus*. 2004;133(1):5–12.
16. Sinclair S. *Making doctors: An institutional apprenticeship*. Oxford: Berg; 1997.
17. Lakoff G, Johnson M. *Philosophy in the flesh: The embodied mind and its challenge to western thought*. New York: Basic Books; 1999.
18. Reber AS. An evolutionary context for the cognitive unconscious. *Philosophical Psychology*. 1992;5(1):33–51.
19. Billett S. Experts' ways of knowing. *Australian Vocational Education Review*. 1999;6(2):25–36.
20. Marchand THJ. Embodied cognition and communication: Studies with British fine woodworkers. *Journal of the Royal Anthropological Institute (NS)*. 2010;16(Supplement S1):S100–S120.
21. Tomasello M. Learning through others. *Daedalus*. 2004;133(1):51–58.
22. Billett S. Mimetic learning in the circumstances of professional practice. In Littlejohn A, Margaryan A, eds. *Technology-enhanced professional learning*. New York: Routledge; 2013: 85–96.
23. Downey G. Practice without theory: A neuroanthropological perspective on embodied learning. *Journal of the Royal Anthropological Institute (NS)*. 2010(Supplement 1):S22–S40.
24. Meltzoff AN, Decety J. What imitation tells us about social cognition: A rapprochement between developmental psychology and cognitive neuroscience. *Philosophical Transactions of the Royal Society* B29. 2003;358:491–500.
25. Iacoboni M, Woods RP, Brass M, Bekkering H, Mazziotta JC, Rizzolatti G. Cortical mechanisms of human imitation. *Science*. 1999;286:2526–2528.
26. Byrne RW, Russon A. Learning by imitation: A hierarchical approach. *Behavioral and Brain Science*. 1998;21(5):667–721.
27. Billett S. *Mimetic learning at work: Learning in the circumstances of practice*. Dordrecht: Springer; 2014.
28. Barsalou LW. Grounded cognition. *Annual Review of Psychology*. 2008;59:617–645.
29. Glenberg AM, Schroeder JL, Robertson DA. Averting the gaze disengages the environment and facilitates remebering. *Memory and Cognition*. 1998;26(4):651–658.

30. Bourdieu P. *Outline of a theory of practice*. New York: Cambridge University Press; 1977.
31. Bunn S. The nomad's apprentice: Different kinds of apprenticeship among Kyrgyz nomads in Central Asia. In: Ainely P, Rainbird H, eds. *Apprenticeship: Towards a new paradigm of learning*. London: Kogan Page; 1999: 74–85.
32. Kosslyn SM, Thompson WL, Ganis G. *The case for mental imagery*. Oxford: Oxford University Press; 2006.
33. Smith E. Vocational education and training in schools in Australia: What are the consequences of moving from margins to mainstream? *Journal of Vocational Education and Training*. 2004;56(4):559–578.
34. Taylor C. *Human agency and language: Philosophical papers 1*. Cambridge: Cambridge University Press; 1985.
35. Malle BF, Moses LJ, Baldwin DA. Introduction: The significance of intentionality. In: Malle BF, Moses LJ, Baldwin DA, eds. *Intentions and intentionality: Foundations of social cognition*. Cambridge, MA: The MIT Press; 2001: 1–26.
36. Billett S. Sociogeneses, Activity and ontogeny. *Culture and Psychology*. 2003; 9(2):133–169.
37. Valsiner J. *Culture and human development*. London: Sage Publications; 2000.
38. Billett S. Readiness and learning in healthcare education. Clinical Teacher. 2015; 12:1–6.
39. Lave J, Wenger E. *Situated learning – legitimate peripheral participation*. Cambridge: Cambridge University Press; 1991.
40. Glassman M. Dewey and Vygotsky: Society, experience, and inquiry in educational practice. *Educational Researcher*. 2001;30(4):3–14.
41. Darrah CN. *Learning and work: An exploration in industrial ethnography*. New York: Garland Publishing; 1996.
42. Somerville M, Bernoth M. Safe bodies: Solving a dilemma in workplace. Paper presented at: Knowledge Demands for the New Economy. 9th Annual International Conference on Post-compulsory Education and Training, 2001; Gold Coast, Queensland.
43. Scribner S. Vygostky's use of history. In: Wertsch JV, ed. *Culture, communication and cognition: Vygotskian perspectives*. Cambridge: Cambridge University Press; 1985: 119–145.
44. Billett S. Ontogeny and participation in communities of practice: A socio-cognitive view of adult development. *Studies in the Education of Adults*. 1998;30(1):21–34.
45. Hodges DC. Participation as dis-identification with/in a community of practice. Mind, Culture and Activity. 1998;5(4):272–290.
46. Harre R. The necessity of personhood as embedded being. *Theory and Psychology*. 1995;5:369–373.
47. Valsiner J. Bi-directional cultural transmission and constructive sociogenesis. In: de Graaf W, Maier R, eds. Sociogenesis re-examined. New York: Springer; 1994: 101–134.
48. Wertsch JV. *Mind as action*. New York: Oxford University Press; 1998.
49. Luria AR. *Cognitive development: Its cultural and social foundations*. Cambridge, MA: Harvard University Press; 1976.
50. Valsiner J, van der Veer R. *The social mind: The construction of an idea*. Cambridge: Cambridge University Press; 2000.
51. Billett S. Relational interdependence between social and individual agency in work and working life. *Mind, Culture and Activity*. 2006;13(1):53–69.

52. Billett S. Learning through work: Workplace affordances and individual engagement. *Journal of Workplace Learning.* 2001;13(5):209–214.
53. Cole M. Interacting minds in a life-span perspective: A cultural-historical approach to culture and cognitive development. In Baltes PB, Staudinger UM, eds. *Interactive minds: Life-span perspectives on the social foundation of cognition.* New York: Cambridge University Press;1996:59–87.
54. Rogoff B. *The cultural nature of human development.* Oxford: Oxford University Press; 2003.
55. Hutchins E. The social organization of distributed cognition. In: Resnick LB, Levine JM, Teasley SD, eds. Perspectives on socially shared cognition. Washington, DC: American Psychological Association; 1991: 283–307.
56. Pea RD. Learning scientific concepts through material and social activities: Conversational analysis meets conceptual change. *Educational Psychologist.* 1993; 28(3):265–277.
57. Resnick LB, Pontecorvo C, Säljö R, Burge B. Introduction. In: Resnick LB, Pontecorvo C, Säljö R, Burge B, eds. *Discourse, tools and reasoning: Essays on situated cognition.* Berlin: Springer; 1997: 1–20.
58. Cole M. Can cultural psychology help us think about diversity? *Mind, Culture and Activity.* 1998;5(4):291–304.
59. Newman D, Griffin P, Cole M. *The construction zone: Working for cognitive change in schools.* Cambridge: Cambridge University Press; 1989.
60. Mishler EG. *Storylines: Craftartists' narratives of identity.* Cambridge, MA: Harvard University Press; 2004.
61. Dewey J. *How we think.* Mineola: Dover Publications; 1977.
62. Billett S. *Learning in the workplace: Strategies for effective practice.* Sydney: Allen and Unwin; 2001.
63. Anderson JR. Acquisition of cognitive skill. *Psychological Review.* 1982; 89(4):369–406.
64. Makovichy N. 'Something to talk about': Notation and knowldge-making among Central Slovak lace-makers. *Journal of the Royal Anthropological Institute (NS).* 2010;16(Supplement S1):80–99.
65. Ingold T. *The perception of the environment: Essays on livelihod, dwelling and skill.* London: Routledge; 2000.
66. Billett S. Mimesis: Learning through everyday activities and interactions at work. *Human Resource Development Review.* 2014;13(4):462–482.
67. Coy MW, ed. *Apprenticeship: From theory to method and back again.* New York: SUNY; 1989.
68. Gott S. Apprenticeship instruction for real-world tasks: The co-ordination of procedures, mental models, and strategies. *Review of Research in Education.* 1989;15:97–169.
69. Dreyfus HL, Dreyfus SE. *Mind over machine: The power of human intuition and expertise in the age of the computer.* Oxford: Basil Blackwell; 1986.
70. Kirschner PA. Cognitive load theory: Implications of cognitive load theory on the design of learning. *Learning and Instruction.* 2002;12:1–10.
71. Harteis C, Billett S. Intuitive expertise: Theories and empirical evidence. *Educational Research Review.* 2013;9:145–157.

9 Prospects for learning through work

Emerging purposes, processes and outcomes for learning through work

Occupations as cultural practices and workplace requirements are all subject to change given their need to respond to changing circumstances and imperatives,[1] and the provision of workplace practices, bases for learning and means of supporting that learning are no exceptions.[2] In particular, as new requirements and needs of nation states, their communities and the individuals who live within them arise and evolve, what are needed for and what constitutes occupational practices and the capacities to perform them in a particular workplace or work setting change. This change is also shaped by the adoption of new technologies and ways of working and other institutional factors associated with the organisation and enactment of paid employment, including factors that are shaped by local as well as global imperatives.[3] As community, technological and societal imperatives evolve, and goals of nation states are transformed, these warrant changes in societal, community and individual priorities, all of which influence the manifestation of paid employment, workplace practices and individuals' participation in those work settings. Consequently, what constitutes purposes, processes and outcomes for learning through work and across working life will inevitably change.[4,5] That inevitability points to the need for intentional efforts to secure the kinds of outcomes that national governments, communities, workplaces and individuals favour.[6]

It follows that this final chapter sets out what might comprise some of these changes in the purposes of, processes for and outcomes associated with learning through work activities and interactions in the near future. Rather than engaging in potentially far-fetched and speculative accounts of what may occur in the future, the focus here is on emergent issues that are and are likely to become more central to considerations of learning in, through and for work before too long. For instance, the purposes might include a greater role in assisting younger[7,8] and not so young people[9] to identify the occupations to which they are suited through experiences in workplaces and engaging in placements in which they encounter their potential occupation or come to witness a range of occupations in practice.[10,11] Then, in terms of occupational preparation, albeit in the transition to working life for young people[2,12] or transitions of adults later in and across their working lives,[13] there is likely to be a growth and continuing interest in providing vocational and higher education students with experiences in work settings aligned with the educational programmes in which they are enrolled.[14,15] While this alignment and integration currently occur in some occupations, the need for students to be more ready to move directly into the workforce and to engage in their occupations upon graduation is a growing focus across the entire range of fields within tertiary education.[8] That educational activity often focuses on providing and then integrating experiences from practice settings within the programmes of study.[16] Then, given the ongoing change in the capacities needed for occupational practice and workplace performance, it would seem that an increasing and inevitable role in the provision of continuing education and training or professional development will be necessary for all kinds and classifications of workers.[17] As work settings are highly accessible and can provide authentic learning experiences of the kind needed to sustain workers' employability and to meet the imperatives that workplaces are facing, there are potentially crucial and necessary sites for ongoing learning within a discipline or field of employment.[18]

Yet, there are limits associated with being able to provide the scale and scope of workplace provisions, given the demands and requirements made upon both private and public sector enterprises from schooling, tertiary and continuing education. Part of this quantum of demand arises from requirements within tertiary education and professional body requirements for practicum experiences for initial occupational preparation and registration, and then for maintaining their employability through meeting either desirable or mandatory professional development requirements. Therefore, the scale of access to learning experiences will need to be managed in ways that are viable for the hosting public and private sector enterprises and, wherever possible, may need to be augmented by experiences elsewhere to ease the scale of demand. All of this demand is also accentuated by the need for all kinds and classifications of workers to engage in ongoing learning across their working lives to sustain their employability and contribute to their enterprises' viability.

Moreover, and in part because of these changes, the processes of learning through and for work are likely to be increasingly mediated by digital or electronic means to provide the kinds and quantum of experiences that will be necessary for that employability.[4] More than that, as work itself becomes increasingly engaged with and mediated by new technologies, the equipment that uses such processes will also necessarily become part of the learning experiences,[19] just as manual tools have always been.[20] Hence, there is likely to be a shift from developing dexterity with manual tools to different kinds of electronically mediated and mechanically operated tools. This will occur albeit in construction sites, offices, healthcare facilities or manufacturing plants. These new kinds of electronic and mechanical tools need to be engaged with to learn about, develop capacities to use effectively and innovate in practice with them.[21] Then, there are changing ways of working, and for forms of work that go beyond the competence of individuals to require the contributions and attributes of teams of workers,[22] either intraprofessional or interprofessional or some combination of both, to achieve work and occupational outcomes.[23,24] So, rather than the focus for learning being on individuals, there is a shift to ways of working and learning that are shared and collective within and across occupational groupings. Concepts such as intersubjectivity (i.e., shared understanding about concepts, procedures and values)[25,26] are likely to become not only the focus of performance outcomes but also the kinds of processes used in work settings for their development. Consequently, there is likely a shift from possessing only individual competence, to capacities to work and learn in collective and/or shared ways for work performance, much of which is already occurring in sectors such as healthcare.[23] The selection of purposes and practices discussed below is indicative of likely future directions and challenges.

Purposes of workplace learning

Essentially, the purposes of learning experiences in work settings are likely to become wider rather than the initial occupational preparation that dominates many current considerations, including those that have been advanced in this volume. Three such purposes are suggested here: (i) assisting individuals to identify occupations to which they are suited, (ii) integrating work experiences within tertiary education provisions and (iii) ensuring provision of continuing education and learning across working lives.

Assisting identifying occupations to which individuals are suited

A key educational concern is how both young[27] and older[28] individuals can become informed and make informed choices about their preferred occupations, and the development of capacities to practise them. Individuals' choice of a preferred occupation is consequential as it leads to significant personal and societal investment as they pursue access to and are prepared for those occupations. However, the concern in many countries is that those decisions are not always fully informed, nor do they lead to suitable choices.[29] The strongest evidence here is in the high rate of attrition within apprenticeship programmes and also the low levels of retention in some occupations, either during or shortly after the completion of tertiary education provisions.[30] This leads to problems including long and circuitous journeys undertaken by young people which increasingly accrue significant cost and do not always lead to their engagement in occupations they find fulfilling (i.e., become their vocations).[31] In many countries, the high attrition rate in a range of occupations, such as in apprentice trades and nursing, has led to significant skill shortages in crucial areas of the economic and social economy.[32,33] This results in significant cost to nation states and individual workplaces who have invested in occupational preparation, usually for young people.[33] Often, the reasons given for young people leaving occupations are that it is not how and what they envisaged when making occupational choices, and also their treatment within work settings, which they often claim is unsatisfactory and unhelpful.[10] It seems that the current generation of young people not only have high aspirations, which is understandable and worthy of merit, but also are not willing to put up with poor behaviour in workplaces that an earlier generation might have tolerated.

Consequently, there is a need for informing young people and their parents about what constitutes their preferred occupation in actual practice to assist them to make informed choices.[34,35] Also, once those choices have been made, workplace experiences are either a part of their preparation or something occurring beyond the practices that form their preferences, and the experiences they have when engaging in and learning about working life. There are two roles here that workplace experiences can provide. First, providing access to workplaces for young people so that they can observe the kind of occupations that have formed their initial preferences may be helpful in refining or changing their choices. Often those decisions are made without any real knowledge of how the occupation is being practised, rather from perceived ideals about that practice. For instance, sports-orientated young people might be attracted to physiotherapy work because they associate it with caring for athletes, when much of that work is about clinical support in hospitals for recovering patients and fragile elderly people. Similarly, it seems many young women are drawn to nursing or hairdressing because they are seen as feminine occupations, and they make that choice at the time they are forming a gendered identity.[36] The same is likely to be true for young men who make the choice about occupations based upon them being associated with masculine work at a time when forming their gendered identity. Yet, the high levels of attrition in apprenticeships and courses preparing young people for those occupations indicate that these are idealised, and often uninformed, preferences that do not meet their expectations or ideals about that work.[37] Consequently, the opportunities for young people to experience – either directly or indirectly – the occupations they are considering may help them to make more informed choices.

However, engagements in workplaces to provide these insights will need to be well managed to achieve the kind of outcome being desired. For instance, in a recent project that was trying to align young Indigenous people with work in healthcare systems, the local hospital had an open day in which the community was invited into the hospital to understand the range of activities and occupations being enacted there. In another instance, young people were provided with a 'walk-through' of the hospital so that they could come to understand the range of occupations that were being enacted beyond those that they might have experienced through attending emergency departments, appointments with doctors or visiting relatives in hospitals (e.g., nurses and doctors).[38] Instead, through structured experiences such as a walk-through, they learn about a range of occupations that support healthcare work and the functioning of the hospital.

Certainly, the key concerns for these young people in the circumstances can be about the quality of work, their engagement and the prospects for fulfilling working lives. Of course, such requirements make demands upon enterprises which some are unwilling to make. However, when dealing with skill shortages and lack of interest by young people in those forms of work and occupations, this may well be a good investment by enterprises to secure continuity of their workforce and to identify and support potential employees. Certainly, local social partnerships can play an important role in engaging local workplaces with educational institutions and in providing these kinds of opportunities for young people.[39]

This then leads to how trainees, apprentices and students are treated in the workplace during their placements and subsequent employment. The time has long passed when young employees are subjected to bastardisation and/or humiliation as part of their initiation into workplaces. Instead, workplaces have incentives and need to positively engage young people in a sequence of experiences that develop their capacities, allow them to contribute to the workplace and generate their beliefs about the work and workplace contributions. This has been seen as a process in which individuals proceed through 'being an employee,' to the sense that they 'belong to the workplace' and then they 'become' occupational practitioners.[40] In her study of young people who never intended to become bakers, Chan[40] found that a skilled worker shortage prompted bakeries to approach and encourage young people who were seen to be punctual and diligent. Subsequently, despite the antisocial hours that bakers work, many of these young people referred to the worth they found in contributing to the bakery that employed them and the products they made and then, over time, began to view themselves as a baker and then went on to practising baking as their selected occupation and vocation. Evident here are the enactments of the practice curriculum (see Chapter 6) in which these young people were guided through the processes of baking and making baked products, engaging in and being guided in the process of making more sophisticated baking products including artisan work and sometimes specialising in particular kinds of baked products.[40] Throughout, they were supported and guided by other bakers. This kind of engagement seems imperative for securing young people to engage in an occupation that otherwise they would not have considered and seems to be effective when the young people were able to enjoy success with their work and came to take pride in their baked products. So, there is a key role here in workplaces informing young people about potential preferred occupations by exposing them to these and then providing supportive experiences that allow them to come to view themselves as being an occupational practitioner.

Work-integrated education and learning

There has been a growing realisation that experiences in tertiary education institutions (e.g., vocational schools, colleges and universities) are insufficient to adequately prepare students to move into their preferred occupations upon graduation.[15] Instead, there is a requirement for students from the entire range of occupational fields to have access to and experiences in work settings so that they can come to augment and extend the knowledge that they have acquired within education programmes through those experiences.[41] Moreover, workplaces can provide experiences that are simply unavailable in educational settings. Consequently, to assist students to be more adequately prepared to engage in employment and their occupation after graduation, there is a growing need for students in all kinds of programmes to have access to workplace experiences[16] or, failing that access, simulations may provide access to the experience that they need to generate so that they engage productively in employment after graduation.[42] Beyond those programmes that have traditionally provided such experiences in the form of supervised placements (i.e., medicine, nursing, social work, education), there is a need to find ways of providing these kinds of experiences for other students. However, such a quest is complicated and complex. There is no one simple mechanism; and the supervised placements that are a feature of the occupations referred to above will not be possible in a whole range of other occupational fields.[43,44] Therefore, other models of providing work experiences will be necessary. These can include periods of observation, students working in pairs, projects being undertaken in association with workplaces, and also providing vicarious experiences for students who are unable to access either work settings or quality experiences in workplaces.[44]

The provision of these workplace experiences alone is insufficient, however. What is also required is the integration of the experiences and learning arising from students' such placements and intentional efforts with what is afforded by the tertiary education institution. On their own, whilst helpful and potentially informative, work placements are often inadequate or not fully optimised without the intentional experiences to integrate those learnings. It is suggested that intentional action needs to occur prior to, during and after the students have engaged in their workplace experiences.[41] For instance, when observing the proceedings of a handover session in an Australian hospital, it was noticed that two student nurses were present but were not optimising their experience. In these handovers, there is a process of considering i) the patient, ii) their condition(s), iii) their treatment(s), iv) their progress and then v) a prognosis about how the patient is expected to be progressing at the end of the shift or the following day. Yet, these two student nurses seemed unprepared to follow the conversations or to use such a set of considerations for enriching their learning. As stated elsewhere, it would also have been highly useful for those students to have had a task, such as to virtually or actually be subsequently caring for one of those patients. That would have engaged them more fully in that learning experience.

Consequently, augmenting those experiences and relating them to the content of courses and the experiences provided within tertiary education institutions stands to enhance the educational worth of optimising both the learning from them and those within educational settings. Again, there will be no single model of how those experiences might progress. Examples from practical investigations indicate that the use of student-run forums,[45] teacher-led activities,[46,47] presentations to peers,[48] meetings in which students discuss their experiences in structured ways[49–51] and activities that deliberately intend to replicate tasks the students will need to perform in work settings after graduation.[52] Thus, beyond providing placements and opportunities to observe, engage and participate in work activities, there will be an important role to be played by educators and tertiary educational institutions in the active and intentional integration of the two sets of experiences, so students are able to reconcile the two sets of experiences and generate their own personal domain of occupational knowledge. However, work experiences are not restricted to initial occupational preparation.

Ongoing learning and development across working life

As noted throughout and above, the ongoing change in the capacities needed for occupational practice and workplace performance requires working-age adults to continually engage in learning and development.[53,54] Therefore, there is an increasing and inevitable role for all kinds and classifications of workers to engage in provision of continuing education and training, albeit labelled professional development, continuing professional development or learning across working life.[55] It is not feasible to rely upon their participation in structured programmes within tertiary education, as having entire workforces continually rotating through such institutions is not feasible because of its scale, nor is it probably desirable.[18] That is because there is often a lack of adoption of what is learnt in such programmes into individuals' work practices.[56] Work settings are often widely accessible to working age people and have the ability to provide educative experiences aligned with the kinds of knowledge they need to learn to both sustain their employability and meet the kinds of imperatives that workplaces are facing.[18] Moreover, as noted, there is much evidence to indicate that professional development programmes of the kind that comprise taught experiences in tertiary education institutions and removed from the circumstances of practice are relatively ineffective model of ongoing learning and development.[56,57] There are, of course, the inevitable exceptions. One of these is if individuals decide to change their occupations; then, most likely, they will need to participate in a structured programme to achieve that goal and these are often best found within tertiary education institutions. Not least here is that the kinds of experiences they need and the knowledge to be learnt will not be found or made accessible in their existing workplaces.[58] But even these kinds of educative provisions will require access to workplace experiences to assist in the development, augmentation and utility of what is being learnt in those programmes.[59]

Educative access and reach: A caveat

There is an important caveat that needs to nuance the discussion here. As foreshadowed, there are clear limits to the extent and kinds of experiences that can be provided through work settings because of issues of access and availability of those experiences. For instance, much earlier, the limited opportunity of access to the potter's wheel[60] is just one example of where the imperatives of production and the need to optimise time, artefacts and resources within work settings will restrict opportunities for developing occupational capacities. Then, there are experiences and kinds of access that cannot be found in work settings because they do not exist. These are some of the reasons for establishing hybrid educational institutions and experiences for developing occupational capacities with the formation of modern nation states.[61–63] A key concern is that these experiences could not be provided, and in the scale required for developing occupational skills needed for national workforces. Certainly, there are elements and aspects of the requirements for many contemporary occupations that are unlikely to be learnt through learners' lived experiences in those workplaces alone.

Consequently, either some structured experiences within the workplace or provisions outside of them may be required, and increasingly. The growing requirement for accessing and comprehending the kinds of symbolic and conceptual knowledge required for contemporary working life represents such a challenge. The fact that much of this knowledge is relatively opaque (i.e., hard to access in work situations) suggests a growing need for both the structuring of work experiences and also efforts to make accessible this knowledge that might otherwise remain inaccessible to learners (i.e., students or workers).[6] These requirements need to be addressed through engagement in specific educative experiences, yet also linked back to circumstances where those occupations are practised. So, in other areas of education, there is a growing focus on work-integrated education that seeks to integrate the two sets of experiences (i.e., those in the education setting and in the workplace). This then makes experiences in the work setting an integral part of not only the tertiary education programme, but also the experiences of young and not so young students in those programmes. In these ways, there are at least three emerging educational issues that can, in part, be addressed through engaging in experiences in educational settings.

Future directions of work and working life

As is now commonly understood, the demand for occupations and the capacities needed for their effective enactment are constantly changing, as are the requirements for performance in specific work settings. These changes play out across nation states in different ways. In many Western countries with modern industrial economies, there has been a significant decline in numbers of people employed in manual work, manufacturing, retail work and also service-related work such as clerical activities.[1] Part of the reason for this decline is the use of electronic technologies including information processing ones that have rendered many jobs either obsolete or requiring fewer skills and fewer workers. Often, these changes have both positive and negative qualities. For instance, the work of language translators using digital technologies has actually increased the complexity of the capacities required to conduct that work, which includes using that technology. However, there are now far fewer translators requiring to be employed.[1] Also, many aspects of manual work on construction sites, for instance, have been replaced by machines, tools and devices that have removed elements of work that otherwise would have been conducted using physical strength and now require different kinds of dexterity. Yet, operating this equipment also demands heightened skills and the kind of dexterity allowing a huge mechanical machine to lift small objects and place them gently and exactly where they need to go, for instance. This situation, of course, likely reduces health-related risks associated with participating in potentially injurious physical work. One outcome here is that such equipment means that these kinds of workers can now have longer working lives, because by reducing the amount of manual work it is more age tolerant.

What is also evident is that the increase in employment opportunities (i.e., the demand for occupations) is found within two different classifications of work in many Western countries. On the one hand, there is the low discretion and low skill service work such as in aged care, which is increasingly commensurate with the demographics of ageing populations. On the other, there is the growth of professional roles that require lengthy tertiary education and extensive experience. Moreover, these kinds of jobs are seemingly expanding the range of tasks for which competence is required. This is often in contrast to occupations that are in decline which can be characterised by a reduced range of work tasks. So, in addition to the decline of some occupations and the rise of others, the scope of tasks within those jobs is also changing. Those occupations with declining levels of skill requirements potentially need lower levels of preparation and are subject to declines in wages, conditions and the standing of that work. A key issue arising here is that some classifications of workers, such as those in manufacturing, manual work, sales and retail, are being displaced in perhaps far larger numbers than new jobs are being created, jobs for which these individuals are likely to be unsuited.

This kind of change leads to disharmony within communities and resentments of the kinds often witnessed in volatile political movements that pander to individuals who are disenchanted by such changes and displacements. The consequence here for individuals and nation states is how such a situation can be effectively managed. It is possible to suggest that the large number of males and females who have been displaced by the decline of the occupations mentioned above has added to the erosion of social harmony, the decline of communities and employment crises for large elements of the working-age adult population.

Consequences for learning in and through work

There are at least three consequences arising from these changes for considerations of learning in and through work. The first is that many of the 'in-demand' professional occupations require specialised knowledge associated with that occupation and its application that comprises a specialisation or subfield of that occupation. That is, specialised and sometimes even enterprise-specific capacities are required to perform the work. Most likely, the key source of developing, honing and maintaining currency with such specific occupational capacities will be through experiences in the circumstances in which they are practised and engaged.

The second is that the development of many emerging requirements for work is associated with vendor-specific software, equipment and processes that are particular to the kind of work being undertaken within the workplace. Consequently, there is likely to be a need for engagement with these vendors rather than with tertiary education institutions and attempts for fitting these kinds of vendor-specific applications within the workplace. So, there are a range of skills that likely need to be developed which are associated with specific technologies, software and equipment that will not necessarily be transferred to other applications or processes. This can lead to a narrowing of the set of occupational competencies within work settings and to making enterprises in some ways far more beholden to the companies that provide these technologies. This, in turn, narrows either the skills of the existing workforce or what can be provided through the tertiary education system. In this way, there is a risk that such processes challenge the autonomy of enterprises and the options available to them.

Thirdly, the processes of career transitions from those working-age adults displaced by economic and structural changes will likely not be realised through tertiary education provisions alone. As indicated above, it is essential for these individuals to have experiences in the circumstances in which these new occupational capacities are practised. This is because they require authentic or simulated experiences of the kinds that are generative of the knowledge needed to perform those occupations, but in the particular ways required by the enterprise that employs them. Consequently, there is a significant role to be played by workplace experiences in assisting working-age adults, including displaced workers, to develop the capacities for becoming proficient in a new occupation. Working-age adults may well be more suited to learning through the kind of experiences they have in work settings than those that might be provided wholly through tertiary educational provisions, with their requirements for assessment through tasks with which these adults may be unfamiliar (i.e., written assignments, exams).

So, workplace experiences or simulated versions of them are likely to be needed to assist these workers to develop and accommodate the kinds of capacities that they will require for their employability (i.e., to be employed and to secure advancement). Again, positive and supportive experiences in work settings are likely to be important for working-age adults as the loss of sense of self associated with occupational displacement is likely to have a negative impact.

Kinds of knowledge to be learnt

Discussions about the changing competencies needed for occupational practice and workplace requirements can emphasise enterprise-specific ways of working, technologies and goals. This suggests that the kinds of knowledge to be learnt are potentially becoming more specific to these enterprises and more difficult to access and construct. As demonstrated in the classical studies of the transformation from manually operated lathes to those which are controlled by computers,[64] there are significant differences in the form of knowledge required to perform these tasks. This case exemplified the decline of tactile and haptic knowing (e.g., the manual controlling of dials that determined how the metal was shaped). These forms of symbolic knowledge were required for a computer to perform tasks unaided by human interventions once the procedure commenced. The operation of lathes had shifted from being progressively controlled by operators' hands to the lathe being operated through a series of predetermined electronic commands. Whilst the former forms of knowledge required years of practice to perfect, the latter is of a totally different order, requiring different types of understandings and procedures. Much of these symbolic forms of knowledge are difficult to access, monitor and perfect and have displaced manual skills that have been used over millennia. Therefore, they often require interventions to be made accessible and learnt.[65] This situation leads to questions about how best these skills can be developed in ways that are not limited to controlling the lathe but involve an understanding of and ability to set up and change procedures driving the machines, that is, going beyond being just operators to programming machines. The same can be suggested for optimising productive processes in the workplace, whether manufacturing plants, legal offices, hospital wards, accounting systems and so on. So, rather than reducing the skilful knowledge of operators, there is potential to extend those capacities. But more than the technical aspects are the social ones.

Team and interconnected work

There is a growing emphasis on work tasks being distributed across workers who are working as teams, either directly interpersonally or through electronically mediated interactions. Sometimes, these teams can be within the same occupation, referred to as intraprofessional working, but they can also be across disciplines or occupations and are referred to as interprofessional ways of working and learning.[66] Much of this trend has arisen because of the demands of contemporary working life and the need to engage a range of expertise when addressing complex challenges in the provision of goods or services.

Healthcare is an exemplar of this kind of work. Nurses caring for patients across shifts need to work intraprofessionally so that patient safety is supported through a continuous care model based upon the team of carers who are finishing their shift briefing those who are commencing theirs, as discussed above.[67] So, this intraprofessional mode of working requires engagement with and communication across individuals acting in the same occupational practice, drawing upon the richness and diversity of their experiences but also having the means to provide a form of collective care, even when not physically proximal.[67] Through these processes, these workers' learning and development by the processes of engagement, deliberation and monitoring performance in and through work events. In this case, it comprises how patients are responding. There is also interprofessional working and learning that comprises workers from a range of disciplines collaborating to achieve outcomes.[25] This is again exemplified by what occurs within healthcare institutions and settings. Teams of healthcare workers from different specialities and disciplines are required to inform and coordinate patient care. For instance, in what is referred to as allied health handovers, a range of healthcare practitioners participate in these meetings to discuss patients, their conditions, treatments and anticipated progress. The practitioners usually include doctors, specialists, nurses, physiotherapists and social workers. As the cases are being discussed, the contribution of each of the participants is encouraged and welcomed as each potentially has a role in patients' healthcare.[67]

The key point here is that, given its complexity, work performance is increasingly being premised on the collective contributions of team members of different kinds, not just on the capacities of one individual alone.[68] This collective contribution has arisen elsewhere with the concept of expert performance of medical practitioners being premised upon a collective concept, and wisdom in practice being premised upon an openness to engage with others. So, this collective consideration of working and learning emphasises the importance of both the exercise and the development of professional competence and workplace performance in circumstances in which individuals come to think and act together, to engage in shared activities and interactions and valuing of the contributions of other practitioners from the same discipline and those provided across disciplines in addressing demanding work challenges.

Emerging prospects for and requirements of learning through work

In sum, there is a set of ways in which learning experiences in work settings can assist educationally in the process of individuals identifying what occupations suit them and warrant their commitment and being prepared for them, which includes a significant personal and institutional investment. The same can be said for the growing importance of providing and integrating work experiences as part of tertiary education programmes to assist students to become more job-ready on graduation. The concern here is that experiences in educational institutions alone are insufficient to develop the kinds of capacities they will need to be able to practise their preferred occupations. Hence, whilst the provision of workplace experiences is important, integrating them within tertiary education programmes becomes paramount. Then, there is the inevitable need for ongoing learning and accessing educative experiences across lengthening working lives with the prospect that much but not all those experiences can be found within work settings, including those in which working-age adults are currently employed.

Also, as the requirements for occupational competence and workplace performance continually evolve and are transformed over time, there are other implications for learning in and through work. These include, but are not restricted to, finding ways to develop the specialised knowledge required for occupations that are experiencing growth in demand yet are often characterised by having quite specialised forms of occupational competence (i.e., subfields). Much of the learning of these capacities is likely required to be generated through circumstances of practice in which those forms of occupational practice are being enacted, including the vendor-specific applications being employed in specific enterprises. Unlike many earlier forms of knowledge that could be easily observed, imitated and practised through traditional models of mimetic learning, some of the new kinds of knowledge require means by which they can be made accessible to be engaged with and learnt. Sometimes, it requires engagement with the artefacts, equipment or electronic interface. Again, this emphasises that even though this knowledge is conceptual and symbolic, its learning likely requires it being indexed to instances of practice. Finally, the complexity of many occupational and work tasks is such that they require the contributions of either teams of the same occupation or those from across a number of occupations. Consequently, the processes for learning in and through work need to include access to and engagement in how teams or groups of workers come to work and learn collaboratively. In this way, the shift is from an individualised project to an individual engaging with others in processes of work and learning.

References

1. Autor D, Chin C, Salomons A, Seegmiller B. New frontiers: The origins and content of new work, 1940–2018. *The Quarterly Journal of Economics*. 2024;139(3):qjae008.
2. Billett S. Learning through work: Augmenting vocational educational experiences to meet 21st-century work requirements. In: Tierney RJ, Rizvi F, Ercikan K, eds. *International encyclopedia of education*. 4th ed. Oxford: Elsevier; 2023: 452–461.
3. Billett S. Building VET systems to advance communities: Beyond responsiveness. Ammattikasvatuksen aikakauskirja. 2024;26(1):98–104.
4. Harteis C. Machines, change, work: An educational view on the digitalization of work. In: Harteis C, ed. *The impact of digitalization in the workplace: an educational view.* Cham: Springer; 2018: 1–10.

5. Frey CB, Osborne MA. The future of employment: How susceptible are jobs to computerisation? *Technological Forecasting and Social Change*. 2017;114:254–280.
6. Billett S. *Work, Change and workers*. Dordrecht: Springer; 2006.
7. Ågren S. Shaping worker-citizenship: Young vocational education graduates' labour market positionings within new adulthood. *Journal of Youth Studies*. 2023:1–16.
8. Tan N, Shien C, Ong C, Billett S. Promoting student readiness for work-life through internships: Challenges and support. *Australian Journal of Adult Learning*. 2023;63(3):343–367.
9. Billett S, Le AH, Choy S, Smith R. The imperatives of and for worklife learning: A review. In: Billett S, Salling Olesen H, Filliettaz L, eds. *Sustaining employability through work-life learning: Practices and policies*. Singapore: Springer Nature Singapore; 2023: 55–82.
10. Laugaland KA, Thorsen Gonzalez M, McCormack B, Skovdahl K, Åshild, S, Billett S, Akerjordet, K. Improving quality in clinical placement studies in nursing homes (QUALinCLINstud): The study protocol of a participatory mixed-methods multiple case study design. BMJ Open. 2020;10(10):e040491.
11. Jackson D. Students' and their supervisors' evaluations on professional identity in work placements. *Vocations and Learning*. 2019;12(2):245–266.
12. Molloy L, Keating J. Targeted preparation for clinical practice. In: Billett S, Henderson A, eds. *Developing learning professionals: Integrating experiences in university and practice settings*. Dordrecht: Springer; 2011: 59–82.
13. Choy S, Billett S, Dymock D. Continuing education and training: Needs, models and approaches. In: Billett S, Dymock D, Choy S, eds. *Supporting learning across working life: Models, processes and practices*. Dordrecht: Springer; 2016.
14. Orrell J. *Good practice report: Work integrated learning*. Sydney: Australian Learning and Teaching Council; 2011.
15. Cooper L, Orrel J, Bowden M. *Work integrated learning: A guide to effective practice*. London: Routledge; 2010.
16. Billett S. Promoting graduate employability: Key goals, and curriculum and pedagogic practices for higher education. In: Ng B, ed. *Graduate employability and workplace-based learning development: Insights from sociocultural perspectives*. Singapore: Springer Nature Singapore; 2022: 11–29.
17. Billett S, Leow A, Le AH. *Continuing education and training: Purposes, practices and futures*. Dordrecht: Springer; 2024.
18. Billett S. Relevance of workplace learning in enterprise transformation: The prospects for Singapore. *Singapore Labour Journal*. 2023;2(01):6–21.
19. Billett S. Mediating worklife learning and the digitalization of work. *British Journal of Educational Technology*. 2021;52:1580–1593.
20. Harteis C, ed. *The impact of digitalization in the workplace*. Vol 21. Dordrecht: Springer; 2018.
21. Harteis C. Supporting learning at work in an era of digitalization of work. In: Bahl A, Dietzen A, eds. *Work-based learning as a pathway to competence-based education*. Opladen: Barbara Budrich; 2018: 85–97.
22. Molyneux J. Interprofessional teamworking: What makes teams work well? *Journal of Interprofessional Care*. 2001;15(1):29–35.
23. Reeves S, Hearn S. Why we need theory to help us better understand the nature of interprofessional education, practice and care. *Journal of Interprofessional Care*. 2013;27:1–3.

24. Thistlethwaite JE, Forman D, Matthews LR, Rogers GD, Steketee C, Yassine T. Competencies and frameworks in interprofessional education: A comparative analysis. *Academic Medicine.* 2014;89(6):869–875.
25. Billett S. Securing intersubjectivity through interprofessional workplace learning experiences. *Journal of Interprofessional Care.* 2014;28(3):206–211.
26. Cronick K. Community, subjectivity and intersubjectivity. *American Journal of Community Psychology.* 2002;30(14):529–547.
27. Billett S, Thomas S, Sim C, Johnson G, Hay S, Ryan J. Constructing productive post-school transitions: An analysis of Australian schooling policies. *Journal of Education and Work.* 2010;23(5):471–489.
28. Leow A, Billett S, Le AH. Towards a continuing education and training eco system: A case study of Singapore. *International Journal of Training Research.* 2023: 21(3):226–242.
29. Clement U. *Improving the image of technical and vocational education and training.* Bonn, Germany: GIZ; 2014.
30. Keane S, Lincoln M, Smith T. Retention of allied health professionals in rural New South Wales: A thematic analysis of focus group discussions. *BMC Health Services Research.* 2012;12:1–11.
31. Billett S, Choy S, Le AH, Hodge S. Vocational education teachers: Perspectives on the standing of their educational sector and how it might be improved. *International Journal of Training Research.* 2023;21(1):1–17.
32. Martin CA, Medisauskaite A, Gogoi M, Teece L, Nazareth J, Pan D, Carr S, Khunti K, Nellums LB, Woolf, K. Discrimination, feeling undervalued, and health-care workforce attrition: An analysis from the UK-REACH study. *The Lancet.* 2023;402(10405):845–848.
33. Wolf A. *Review of vocational education: The Wolf report 2011.* London: DfE. 2011.
34. Taggart B, Sammons P, Siraj I, Sylva K, Melhuish EC, Toth K, Smees R, Hollingworth K, Welcomme W. Effective pre-school, primary and secondary education (EPPSE 3–16+) project: Post age 16 destinations. Project report. London: Institute of Education. 2014.
35. Billett S, Choy S, Hodge S. Enhancing the standing of vocational education and the occupations it serves: Australia. *Journal of Vocational Education and Training.* 2020;72(2):270–296.
36. Newton J, Kelly C, Kremser A, Jolly B, Billett S. The motivations to nurse: An exploration of factors amongst undergraduate students, registered nurses and nurse managers. *Journal of Nursing Management.* 2009; 17(3): 392–400.
37. Wolf A. *Remaking tertiary education: Can we create a system that is fair and fit for purpose.* London: Education Policy Institute, Kings College London; 2016.
38. Billett S, Le AH. Engaging young people in occupations served by vocational education: Case study from healthcare. *International Journal for Research in Vocational Education and Training (IJRVET).* 2024;11(2):200–222.
39. Billett S, Choy S, Gibbs K, Le AH, McKay L, Hay S. Initiating, enacting and sustaining partnerships to inform post-school pathways. *Journal of Education and Work.* 2024;37(1–4):149–164.
40. Chan S. Learning through apprenticeship: Belonging to a workplace, becoming and being. *Vocations and Learning.* 2013;6(3):367–383.
41. Billett S. Realising the educational worth of integrating work experiences in higher education. *Studies in Higher Education.* 2009;34(7):827–843.

42. Billett S, Choy S. Intergrating professional learning experiences across university and settings. In: Billet S, Harteis C, Gruber H, eds. *International handbook of research in professional and practice-based learning*. Vol 1. Dordecht: Springer; 2014: 485–512.
43. Billett S, Newton JM, Rogers GD, Noble C, eds. *Augmenting health and social care students' clinical learning experiences: Outcomes and processes*. Dordrecht: Springer; 2019.
44. Billett S, Orrell J, Jackson D, Valencia-Forrester F, eds. *Enriching higher education students' learning through post-work placement interventions*. Dordrecht: Springer; 2020.
45. Newton J. Reflective learning groups for studnets nurses. In: Billett S, Henderson A, eds. *Developing learning professionals: Integrating experiences in university and practice settings*. Dordrecht: Springer; 2011: 119–130.
46. Antwertinger Y, Larkin I, Lau E, O'Connor E, Santos M. Transition to a successful career: Pharmacy, psychology and business students reflecting on practicum feedback. In: S. Billett, J. Orrell, Jackson D, Valencia-Forrester F, eds. *Enriching higher education students' learning through post-work placement interventions*. Dordrecht: Springer; 2020:47–67.
47. Clanchy K, Sabapathy S, Reddan G, Reeves N, Bialocerkowski A. Integrating a career development learning framework into work-integrated learning practicum debrief sessions. In: Billett S, Newton JM, Rogers GD, Noble C, eds. *Augmenting health and social care students' clinical learning experiences: Outcomes and processes*. Dordrecht: Springer; 2019: 307–330.
48. Steketee C, Keane N, Gardiner K. Consolidating clinical learning through post-rotation small group activities. In: Billett S, Newton JM, Rogers GD, Noble C, eds. *Augmenting health and social care students' clinical learning experiences: Outcomes and processes*. Dordrecht: Springer; 2019: 185–207.
49. Cardell E, Bialocerkowski A. Bouncing forward: A post-practicum workshop to promote professional identity, self-efficacy, and resilience in Master of Speech Pathology students. In: Billett S, Newton JM, Rogers GD, Noble C, eds. *Augmenting health and social care students' clinical learning experiences: Outcomes and processes*. Dordrecht: Springer; 2019: 211–234.
50. Williams LM, Ross L, Mitchell L, Markwell K. The reflective debrief: Using students' placement experiences to enrich understandings of distinct kinds of nutrition and dietetics practice. In: Billett S, Newton JM, Rogers GD, Noble C, eds. *Augmenting health and social care students' clinical learning experiences: Outcomes and processes*. Dordrecht: Springer; 2019: 259–281.
51. Harrison J, Molloy E, Bearman M, Ting CY, Leech M. Clinician Peer Exchange Groups (C-PEGs): Augmenting medical students' learning on clinical placement. In: Billett S, Newton JM, Rogers GD, Noble C, eds. *Augmenting health and social care students' clinical learning experiences: Outcomes and processes*. Dordrecht: Springer; 2019: 95–120.
52. Levett-Jones T, Courtney-Pratt H, Govind N. Implementation and evaluation of the post-practicum clinical reasoning exam. In: Billett S, Newton JM, Rogers GD, Noble C, eds. *Augmenting health and social care students' clinical learning experiences: Outcomes and processes*. Dordrecht: Springer; 2019: 57–72.
53. Organisation of Economic and Cultural Development (OECD). *Lifelong learning for all*. Paris: OECD; 1996.

54. Organisation of Economic Cooperation and Development. *Economics and finance of lifelong learning*. Paris: OECD; 2000.
55. Billett S, Choy S, Dymock D, Smith R, Henderson A, Tyler M, Kelly A. *Towards more effective continuing education and training for Australian workers*. Adelaide: National Centre for Research in Vocational Education; 2014.
56. Noble C, Billett S. Sustaining and transforming the practice of communities: Developing professionals' working practices. In: Billett S, Dymock D, Choy S, eds. *Supporting learning across working life: Models, processes and practices*. Dordrecht: Springer; 2016: 147–167.
57. Eppich W, Rethans JJ, Tueunissen PW, Dornan T. Learning to work together through talk: Continuing professional development in medicine. In: Billett S, Dymock D, Choy S, eds. *Supporting learning across working life: Models, processes and practices*. Dordrecht: Springer; 2016: 47–73.
58. Billett S, Choy S, Tyler M, Smith R, Dymock D, Kelly A, Henderson A, Lewis J, Beven F. *Refining models and approaches in continuing education and training*. Adelaide: National Centre for Vocational Education Research; 2013.
59. Billett S, Choy S, Tyler M, Smith R, Dymock D, Kelly A, Henderson A, Lewis J, Beven F. *Refining models and approaches in continuing education and training*. Adelaide: National Centre for Vocational Education Research; 2014.
60. Singleton J. The Japanese folkcraft pottery apprenticeship: Cultural patterns of an educational institution. In: Coy MW, ed. *Apprenticeship: From theory to method and back again*. New York: SUNY; 1989: 13–30.
61. Gonon P. A short history of German Vocational pedagogy: From idealistic classics to 'Realistic' research. In: Mjelde L, Daly R, eds. *Working knowledge in a globalizing world*. Bern: Peter Lang; 2006: 197–212.
62. Greinert WD. *Vocational education and training in Europe: Classical models of the 19th-century and training in England, France and Germany during the first half of the 20th*. Luxembourg: Office for Official Publications of the European European Communities; 2005.
63. Troger V. Vocational training in French schools: The fragile State-employer alliance. Paper presented at: Towards a history of vocational education and training (VET) in Europe in a comparative perspective, 2002; Florence.
64. Martin LMW, Scribner S. Laboratory for cognitive studies of work: A case study of the intellectual implications of a new technology. *Teachers College Record*. 1991;92(4):582–602.
65. Billett S. Accessing and securing conceptual and symbolic knowledge required for digital era work In: Harteis C, ed. *The impact of digitization in the workplace – An educational view*. Dordrecht: Springer; 2018: 197–212.
66. Reeves S, Perrier L, Goldman J, Freeth D, Zwarenstein M. Interprofessional education: Effects on professional practice and healthcare outcomes (update) (Review). *The Cochrane Collaboration*. 2013;3:1–47.
67. Billett S, Noble C, Sweet L. Pedagogically-rich activities in hospital work: Handovers, ward rounds and team meetings. In: Delany C, Molloy L, eds. *A practical guide for learning and teaching in a clinical context*. Melbourne: Elsevier; 2017:207–220.
68. Noble C, Brazil V, Teasdale T, Forbes M, Billett S. Developing junior doctors' prescribing practices through collaborative practice: Sustaining and transforming the practice of communities. *Journal of Interprofessional Care*. 2017;31(2):263–272.

Index

active engagement and construction 140, 147
agency 44, 50, 52–53
Anderson JR. 72
artefacts 119, 126, 134
assent 147, 152

Bauman Z. 68
Blyton P. 69
Bobbitt F. 103
brute fact 55, 57; brute factors 52, 55
Bunn S. 104, 106, 108

canonical occupational knowledge 61–62
Chan S. 161
Cole M. 145
communities 7, 16–17
conceptual knowledge 71–73
continuing education 158, 163
co-occurrence of innovations and learning 79, 81, 83, 85; reciprocity between innovations and learning 84
co-participation 49
Coy MW. 107

deliberate practice 146, 149–150
Dewey J. 9, 52, 68, 103
dispositional knowledge 71–73
domains of knowledge 62, 70–73
duality between affordances and engagements 111

Early Imperial China 26
educative experiences 25, 31, 35
embodied knowledge 146, 148–149
employability 4
employee-driven innovations 80–83
enterprise viability 79

epistemological practices 145–148
experiences and experiencing 92

Fitts PM. 130

Glaser R. 72
goal-directed activities 31, 45, 83, 91
Gott S. 106
Griffin P. 145
guided learning 125, 127, 130–131
guided re-discovery 146, 150
guilds 26

Harré R. 52, 142
heuristics 126, 132–133
Hodges DC. 141
human history 25–26, 34, 36

individual engagement 33
individuals 6–12
initial occupational preparation 123, 158
innovation 84–85
institutional fact 52
intentionality 47, 50, 52–53
intentional structuring of experiences 108–110
intersubjectivity 145, 149, 153, 159
intraprofessional 159, 167–168

Jordan B. 104, 113, 139

Lave J. 26, 45, 56, 103, 105, 113
learning through work: historicity 26; imperatives 24; legacies 31; origins 24
Leontyev AN. 53
lived experience of communities 104–108
Luria AR. 143

Index

Marchand TH. 11, 107, 109, 148
mediation 50, 54, 57, 122, 127, 147
Menon J. 106
Mezirow J. 72
microgenesis 54; microgenetic 54, 56, 92, 142
mimesis 138–140, 148
mimetic learning 146, 148
Mishler EG. 140
mnemonics 126, 131–132
models of practice curriculum 111–113, 115

national governments and supranational agencies 7, 17–18
Newman D. 145
Noon M. 69

observation 147, 150–151
occupational competence 70–71; occupational expertise 70
occupational knowledge 61–63; occupational capacities 69, 71
occupational practice 61–63
ongoing learning and development 163
ontogenetic ritualization 146, 148–149
ontogeny 142, 144; ontogenetic 51, 52, 54, 57, 142, 144, 148
outcomes 157–159

participatory practices 49
pathways 102–106
pedagogically rich activities 125, 128–130
pedagogic practice 121–124, 134–135
Perkins D. 72
personal curriculum 54
personal epistemologies 138, 143
personal fact 52, 55–56; personal factors 44, 49
personal legacies 51–54
personal practices 152–153
personal processes 44, 49, 51
practice curriculum 101–104
practice pedagogies 124–127
procedural knowledge 71–73

processes 157–159
purposes of workplace learning 159–164
Pusey M. 69

readiness 147, 151
relational interdependence 50
Rogoff B. 45, 71, 102, 105
Ryle G. 72

Scribner S. 70
Searle JR. 52
Singleton J. 105, 107, 109
situational performance 107; situated performance 62
skilfulness 149
social contributions 44, 49
social legacies 51, 54–56
social suggestions 53
societal needs 26
storytelling 125, 127–128
subjectivity 52, 71, 140–142
Sun R. 72

tertiary education institutions 7, 14–16
Tulviste P. 57
Tyler RW. 103

Valsiner J. 52, 53, 142, 143
Varma S. 106
verbalisation 125, 128
Vygotsky LS. 48, 53

Wertsch JV. 11, 46, 51, 57, 92, 143, 152
work-integrated education 111, 162–163
work-integrated learning 162–163
workplace activities and interactions 102, 127
workplace affordances 33, 46
workplace curriculum practices 114
workplace learning 91, 159
workplaces 7, 12–14
Wright Mills C. 68

zones of development 80–81, 93